Can Science Come Back to Islam?

K. Razi Naqvi

ISBN: 978-82-999923-0-5

Zakia Begum (d. 2014)

David Wright (1937–2002)

I dedicate this book to the memory of my mother and my friend David. For different reasons, both had to enter practical life without much formal education, but their innate abilities and zest for learning enabled them to pick up all the knowledge they were capable of acquiring and cared for, an experience that made them more learned than the average university graduate. They also understood that learning is not confined to classrooms (which often interrupt or even impede it), and that only those deserve to be called educated who think of education as a life-long process. I regret that they did not live to read this book and to debate some of its points with me. As people with independent minds, they may not have agreed with all my conclusions, but they would have both been delighted that I asked the question raised in the title and tried to answer it honestly.

Contents

Notes on Transliteration

Stephen Hawking, perchance the most photographed scientist in history, owes his iconic recognisability to his best-selling book *A Brief History of Time*[1] (hereafter abbreviated as *ABHT*). A worldly-wise editor, who knew that nothing is more disagreeable to the happy-go-lucky reader than eyeing an equation, warned Hawking [2, p. 223]: "Look at it this way, Steve—every equation will halve your sales." I have also read a version of this warning in which *readership* replaces *sales*. Hawking, keen to publish a marketable book, heeded the caution and opted for a book containing only a single equation. Did you buy the book? Did you read it from cover to cover? If your answers are *Yes* and *No*, respectively, you will be happy to know that *ABHT* has been called, according to Ellenberg [3], "the most unread book of all time".

You will find no equations in this book, but diacritical marks are as indispensable for my purpose as symbols (and equations containing symbols) are to the author of a book dealing with a scientific topic. I have no idea how many diacritical marks per page would halve the readership of this book, and I have no intention of finding out by publishing two versions, one with and another without the dreaded diacritics, which rile many readers and are reviled by not a few authors, including two of my favourites, Richard F. Burton and H. W. Fowler. Burton thought that these "devices perplex the simple and teach nothing to the

---

[1] I have omitted basic bibliographic information (publisher, date and place of publication) because Hawking [1] himself has compared his book to the Bible and Shakespeare, not only as regards sales figures but also because, according to his own admission, many buyers of his book do not bother to read it.

learned" [4, p. xviii]. A little disagreement prevents a friendship from degrading into a cold acquaintanceship, and I suspect that neither Burton nor Fowler would be critical in the afterlife of my preference for diacritical marks in this life.

Table 1: Notation for long and short vowels

ā	long	as in	b*a*r, c*a*r
ī	long	as in	mach*i*ne
ū	long	as in	J*u*ne, r*u*le
a	short	as in	ov*a*l, dism*a*l
i	short	as in	f*i*t
u	short	as in	p*u*t

These notes are aimed at the "novice" (those whom Burton called the "simple"). Table 1, which I will call an *extentionary*, since it merely extends the existing English alphabets, explains the devices used for discriminating between short and long vowels. The extentionary will not help you tell *Qatar* from *Katar*, and it is more likely than not that you will pronounce both like the English word *catarrh* (kəˈtar). This pronunciation neglects the equivalence of the two a's, which is its most serious fault, but also the easiest to correct, if you are prepared to use the extentionary. The fact that the letters "k" and "q" stand for two different Arabic letters need not be a source of concern to you. When you see any other diacritical marks, as in *Muḥammad* or *ʿUmar* or *Qurʾān*, you should ignore them and pronounce these words as you would *Muhammad* or *Umar* or *Qurān*. Strictly speaking, the second syllable of *Islam* and *Baghdad* should have a macron (¯), but I have omitted diacritical marks in words that have become part of standard English vocabulary.

Most of the "learned" will be able to deduce the the system of transliteration used here, but Appendix A has been included in the belief that leaving no stone unturned is the only safe remedy against ambiguity.

Prologue

'A good book needs no preface; a bad book deserves none.' That is no doubt true. But ...

PREFACE to John Ray's biography by Charles E. Raven [5, p. xi]

But an old friend assures me, that to publish a book without a preface is like entering a drawing-room without making a bow.

PREFACE by Thomas Love Peacock to a collection of novels published previously without prefaces [6, Vol. 1, p. v]

To write a preface or to dispense with it, that was not the question that tormented me. The idea of sidestepping the *but*-trap (see above if you skipped the two quotations in your keenness to read *my* words) was not foremost in my mind when I chose the word *Prologue* as an alternative heading for these pages, which should be likened, not to making one's bow on entering a drawing-room, but to some promotional words spoken by an honest vendor to prospective customers. It is the only opportunity for me to be personal, to label my merchandise—to ticket it, so to speak, with that professional hallmark without which the displayed article would be difficult to authenticate.

The Muslim world is caught in the throes of ideological tumult, sectarian slaughter, abject anarchy, debilitating anomie. The causes are clear to all. Muslim societies are crippled by the ills of illiteracy, ignorance, and intolerance; held in bondage to superstitions and pernicious traditions; beholden to saints (mostly dead) and their scions (still living), pīrs and faqīrs, mystics, magicians, forgers of talismans, soothsayers, exorcists, and all manner of other mountebanks and madcaps for whom I cannot find appropriate words. The Muslim intelligentsia, a typical member of which is expected, or at least fervently hoped, to be among my readers, knows the paramount importance of scientific knowledge and is searching for the route to an affirmative answer to the question raised in the title of this book, but it seems to shy away from asking the closely related questions "At whose behest were the seeds of science planted in the House of Wisdom?" and "Under whose leadership was science banished from the House of Islam?". There is a need for a book that seeks to answer all three questions. Such a book should have an author whose scientific credentials are beyond doubt; who has an intimate knowledge of the religious literature; who can trace the changes that have occurred, over the millennia, in the vocabulary and conceptual framework of science; who is prepared to use this knowledge to try to bring contemporary Muslims around to abandon antiquated and anti-scientific interpretations of their scriptures, to warn them that, unless they back away from their dogma peddlers, they will continue to live and die in cauldrons of communal strife, in wastelands of unfulfilled lives, in countries where the scientific enterprise cannot flourish, from where a creative individual will be desperate to flee, to which no serious scientist plying his vocation elsewhere would voluntarily relocate.

mountebank: hawker of quack medicines; flambuoyant charlatan

The present contents have been brewing in my head for more than two decades, and I had decided to assemble them in the form of a book [7] soon after I published a short letter in the correspondence columns of the scientific periodical *Nature* [8]. My main aim there was to suggest that, if science is to take root in an Islamic state, a revolution is indispensable, and that the necessary upheaval need not be a bloody affair, and regardless of whether it is violent or peaceful, it must involve the transition from a closed to an open society. In other words, a popular revolution alone cannot lead to conditions conducive to intellectual autonomy and scientific progress. A commitment at the very least to introduce scientific literacy into the curriculum (whether or not it includes a programme for producing scientific workers) is absolutely vital. Since the same issue of *Nature* happened to contain a news feature on Portugal, I ended the letter with the remark, 'In Portugal, democracy needed to mature after the bloodless carnation revolution in the 1970s ended a long spell of dictatorship'.

It took me more than five years to finish the present little book. The necessity of earning a livelihood (by performing my duties as a full-time academic) while the book was being written was not the only cause of this slow progress. I chose, for reasons that need not be spelled out here, to write what I would call *My Other Book* (hereafter abbreviated as *MoB*), for which purpose I had had to read thousands of pages written by authors whom I had previously found, after only a cursory reading of their works during my youth, to be uninspiring and disappointing, irrelevant and regressive, obstinately opposed to a scientific frame of mind. Since a careful re-reading, during the last few years, of the major works of these authors did not induce me to change my mind, I have been driven to the conclusion that the mass appeal of these giants of the past can be understood only by supposing that their admirers have not really read their works, or that their acolytes lack the mental equipment, critical attitude and background knowledge without which reading inevitably degenerates into a mindless muttering and a pathetic display of awe-inspired hagiolatry.

hagiolatry: worship of saints; veneration of famous persons

Only a concrete example can illustrate the intellectual nullity and mental degeneration that blocks all progress; to this end, I reproduce below (with all the typographic aberrations intact) a comment, posted on the Internet [9] by an ardent Muslim:

> The eBook of Ihya Uloom ad-din (The Masterpiece of Al Ghazali) is in the eBook Section. Kindly take time to read it. I have been so amazed by the extraordinary Ilm of Imam Ghazali. Even if i tend to read one page everyday, i learn so much and often it becomes difficult even to memorize what one learns !

Let me repeat: *it becomes difficult even to memorize what one learns!* How comforting it would have been to suppose that the writer of these words—who was evidently unable to differentiate between reading, memorizing and learning—was a half-witted, untutored and incorrigible ignoramus. But this explanation does not hold water, or anything else. The following pages will show that such intellectual servility afflicts even those who might be deemed highly educated on the basis of their formal qualifications. For all I know, the above message might have been composed and typeset by a "highly educated" and successful professional—a lawyer or a doctor or an accountant or an engineer or (perish the thought!) a teacher.

Science came to Islam after the decimation of the Umayyad dynasty (661–750), which had directed the affairs of the Muslim community following the assassination of ʿAlī ibn Abū Ṭālib, the fourth Caliph. The overturn, which placed the ʿAbbāsids at the helm of the Caliphate, was not the result of some petty palace intrigue, unpremeditated murder or sudden death of the last member of the incumbent Umayyad dynasty, but of a revolution that is as significant in the history of Islam as the French revolution is in the annals of the West [10, 11]. The founding of the city of Baghdad marks a true turning point because the "Caliphs of Baghdad", many of whom turned out to be great patrons of the fine arts and secular sciences, had a different world view from that of the "Caliphs of Damascus", who had no interest whatsoever in secular scholarship. By opening its gates to foreign books and their tireless translators, the founder of Baghdad became the first Muslim patron of science.

Specifying the decades during which the decay of Islamic science became manifestly irreversible, or identifying all the major causes which eroded the glorious scientific edifice whose foundations were laid in eighth century Baghdad is a little harder than naming the principals who led the struggle against the spirit of inquiry, one of whom was Ghazālī, the person extolled in the fatuous eulogy quoted above. "Kindly take time to read it", is what the Ghazālī fan has asked others to do, and I could not escape the conclusion, after reading Ghazālī's magnum opus and a few other of his major works, that with such paragons, Islam really needs no ill-wishers.

I find it baffling that the stranglehold of revered theologians asphyxiates even those Muslims who live in the West, and that intelligent and certificated persons, diploma and degree holders, are willing to surrender their decision-making to those whose learning is supposed to entitle them to make up a list of dos and don'ts for the faithfuls, those who still approach the task of interpreting their guidebooks, just as their forebears have been doing, through an uncritical acceptance of the reported words and views of the holy men of the past, of dogma, of unverified speculation. T. S. Eliot could not have been thinking of these theologians when he wrote *East Coker*, but their legacy cannot be described better if I use my own words:

And the wisdom of age? Had they deceived us,
Or deceived themselves, the quiet-voiced elders,
Bequeathing us merely a receipt for deceit?
The serenity only a deliberate hebetude,
The wisdom only the knowledge of dead secrets
Useless in the darkness into which they peered
Or from which they turned their eyes. There is, it seems to us,
At best, only a limited value
In the knowledge derived from experience.

hebetude: dullness

The House of Islam needs a new brand of theologians, persons who will feel at home in a contemporary House of Wisdom, but they in turn would need, if they are to exert some influence, a new brand of faithfuls, persons who really respect human rights and the Qur'ānic words "There is no compulsion in religion" (2:256).

There are indications that a handful of the younger Muslims are turning to the rational attitude of using fact as the touchstone, but most are still unwilling to acknowledge that the gap between fact and dogma cannot be papered over, that progress will be possible, and that science will come back to Islam, only when a clean break is made from those whose preaching has created the current malaise.

In my beginning is my end. My prologue is also my epilogue.

1 Who Brought Science to Islam?

I have yet to come across some evidence showing that a caliph of the Umayyad lineage embarked on a sustained project for translating the books of the conquered people into Arabic, or on some other plan for promoting profane scholarship. To be sure, Khālid bin Yazīd bin Muʿāwiyah,[1] the prince who indulged in alchemy, has been mentioned as someone who commissioned translations of alien scientific works into Arabic [12, pp. 242, 354], but his kith and kin must have realized that plunder was an easier—and fail-safe—way to obtain gold. I will assume that the absence of evidence is, indeed, evidence of absence, and continue to think of the Umayyad reign as a barren period for secular thought. Scholars, who flourish only where they find patronage, had to wait until the emergence of the ʿAbbāsid dynasty and the founding of its new capital, the Round City of Manṣūr [13], to sense a definite change in the rulers' attitude to learning. They found the place to be a veritable sanctuary, and it would not surprise most readers if I assert that one (or some) of them decided to call it *Madīnat al-Salām* (meaning *City of Peace*), but the truth is that this name was chosen by the founder himself, and Baghdad was the Persian name of the town then standing on the site selected for the new capital [14, 15].

[1]For some background information on the Umayyad dynasty (661–750) and the early caliphs of the next dynasty, see Appendix E. Muʿāwiyah, the founder of the Umayyad dynasty, was succeeded by his son Yazīd.

Scientists swear by Occam's (or Ockham's) razor, which is a principle of parsimony, stated nowadays as follows: *entities must not be multiplied beyond necessity.*[2] In this chapter, I will drop nonessential details by following my own maxim of minimalism: names are not to be mentioned beyond necessity. The caliphs belonging to the ʿAbbāsid dynasty will be called ʿAbbāsī I, ʿAbbāsī II (and so on), and I will mention only three of them by name. Each caliph in this dynasty had his own name, but he also took a "royal name", a grandiloquent title which implied Divine approval of his incumbency. With one exception, the royal name alone is used for identifying an ʿAbbāsid caliph. The exception is Hārūn (ʿAbbāsī V), whose royal name was al-Rashīd, pronounced ar-Rashīd (see p. 177). The royal names of ʿAbbāsī II and ʿAbbāsī VII were al-Manṣūr and al-Māʾmūn, respectively, and I will follow those who drop "al", the definite article in Arabic, when it occurs as a prefix to a proper noun.

evanesce: to fade; to go out of sight, memory or existence

In Nabia Abbott's opinion, "Manṣūr is rightly accounted as the greatest of the ʿAbbāsid caliphs" [18, p. 1], but in popular imagination, where fiction endures and fact evanesces, only the legendary Hārūn will live for ever, as will Māʾmūn in the annals of science. For us it is enough to know that Manṣūr, the founder of the new capital, was grandfather to both Hārūn and his wife Zubaidah, and that the only male issue of this marriage of two Arab royals became ʿAbbāsī VI, despite being slightly younger and markedly less gifted than his half-brother Māʾmūn, born of a Persian concubine.

The short and sad life of ʿAbbāsī VI, who reigned for only four years (809–813), was too turbulent to permit patronage of any

---

[2] As the principle is commonly used nowadays without any reference to the scholastic theory of entities or universals, the precise form in which William of Occam (d. 1347) phrased it is no longer relevant, nor, for that matter, even the fact that he was not the first to state it in a different but equivalent form [16]. Put simply and in a scientific context, the principle would not permit more elements in an explanation when fewer would suffice; a new ingredient should be added only when the existing recipe fails to provide a satisfactory account of the observations. Newton commenced Book III of his *Principia* by stating four *Rules of Reasoning in Philosophy*, the first of which is a statement of the "razor" in the following words [17, p. 398]: We are to admit no more causes of natural things than such as are both true and sufficient to explain their appearances.

activity unrelated to self-preservation. Whether Mā'mūn should be called the first non-Arab caliph or the first Persian caliph is completely equivalent to the question whether Barack Obama should be considered as America's first non-white president or first black president, and he has been called both [19–22].

Though most of the early 'Abbāsīs turned out to be ardent supporters of secular learning and the fine arts, it is Mā'mūn alone who deserves to be called the protagonist or the patron saint of the profane sciences. By all accounts, Mā'mūn (786–833) was a remarkable man, endowed with a stupendous store of talents, good education, and an insatiable appetite for combats, military as well as intellectual [23–27]. His aim was to rise above his predecessors and establish himself as the *Imām*, the supreme religious and political head of the Islamic empire. He spent the last two years of his life in leading a military campaign against the recalcitrant Byzantians, but felt secure enough to launch, just four months before his untimely and mysterious death, a second offensive against those he regarded as weeds and vermin in the unkempt garden of Islam. The outcome of this unwholesome chapter of Mā'mūn's life and its impact on Islamic history will be the subject of this chapter.

Who were Mā'mūn's opponents among fellow Muslims?

In order to address the above question satisfactorily but briefly, it is necessary to introduce some terminology.

All information whatsoever about matters historical, theological, social, ritual, legal, etc, was preserved and passed down through the first centuries of Islam in the form of oral "traditions" (sayings of the Prophet), each "tradition" (or *ḥadīth*, literally "talk") consisting of two parts: the pedigree (*sanad*) and the text (*matn*). The former gives the chain of reporters (see below), whereas the latter embodies the information thus preserved, usually in the form of a short paragraph, sometimes a single sentence.

A *muḥaddith* ("traditionist") is a scholar who collects *ḥadīthes*,[3]

[3]I will use *ḥadīthes* for the plural form, *ḥadīth* for the singular and collective forms. Guillaume adopted a different policy [28, p. 11]: "The word *ḥadīth*

and the plural form of the noun is *muḥaddithūn*. Those who assert that the Qur'ān and *ḥadīth* provide a sufficient basis for religious authority call themselves *ahl al-ḥadīth* (meaning *people of the ḥadīth*), a term aptly rendered by Hodgson as ḥadīth-folk [31, p. 386].

Some of the terms which recur in the statement of a *sanad* are: *ḥaddathana* (he narrated to us), *akhbārana* (he informed us), *sami'tu* (I heard), *'an* (on the authority of). If the *muḥaddith* (M) heard it from A to whom it was narrated by B who was informed by C who heard the Prophet (P) say something, we can represent the chain by $M \Leftarrow A \Leftarrow B \Leftarrow C \Leftarrow P$.

In this notation, *ḥadīth* 5782 in the Bukhārī collection may be stated as follows [32, p. 372, Vol. 7]:— Bukhārī $\Leftarrow A \Leftarrow B \Leftarrow C \Leftarrow D \Leftarrow E \Leftarrow F \Leftarrow P$:[4] *If a fly falls in the vessel of any of you, let him dip all of it (into the vessel) and then throw it away, for in one of its wings there is a disease and in the other there is healing (antidote for it) i.e. the treatment for that disease.*

You might think that no medically informed reader of the above *ḥadīth* will deny that it is a negation of our current knowledge concerning the infection of foods and drinks through flies, but the truth is otherwise, as you will find out after reading Appendix B, which is a mock letter written in response to an enquiry by a long-lost friend from my school days, who consulted me about the scientific soundness of the ḥadīth. Few contemporary Muslims appear to adopt the attitude taken by Kepler more than four hundred years ago (see p. 156) and to say, "In theology we balance authorities, in science, we weigh reasons. A holy man was Bukhārī, who compiled his collection in accordance with his faith and judgment, but more holy to me is scientific evidence; and hence I agree with bacteriologists and epidemiologists,—and this I do with no disrespect to the great *muḥaddith*.

The Muslims who stood in Mā'mūn's way were *muḥaddithūn*

---

throughout this book will be used both as a singular and a collective noun. *Ḥadiths* is scarcely possible in English, and the constant employment of the Arabic broken plural *aḥādīth* is hardly to be desired." Goldziher, writing in German, faced no such problem and used *Ḥadith* and *Ḥadīthen* [29, Ch. 1], but those who translated him into English used *Ḥadīths* for the plural form [30].

[4]Here A is Qutaybah, B is Ismā'īl bin Ja'far, C is Yaḥyā ibn Sa'īd al-Anṣārī, D is 'Atabah bin Muslim, Chief of banī Tamīm, E is 'Ubayd bin Ḥunayn, Chief of banī Zurayq, and F is Abū Hurayrah.

and their votaries, the ḥadīth-folk, who saw Aḥmad bin Ḥanbal (hereafter AbḤ) as their leader, the "Defender of the Faith". The *EoI*[5] article on AbḤ begins with the following words [33]:

votary: a devoted adherent or follower

> **AḤMAD b. ḤANBAL**, "the imām of Baghdād",[6] celebrated theologian, jurist and traditionist (164–241/780–855), and one of the most vigorous personalities of Islam, which he has profoundly influenced both in its historical development and its modern revival. Founder of one of the four major Sunnī schools, the Ḥanbalī, he was, through his disciple Ibn Taymiyya [*q.v.*], the distant progenitor of Wahhābism, and has inspired also in a certain degree the conservative reform movement of the Salafiyya.

The reader would be justified in concluding that, in the contest between Mā'mūn and the orthodox recusants led by AbḤ, the latter emerged victorious, for no one speaks today of *Imām* Mā'mūn even though 'Abbāsī VII coveted the title, but AbḤ, who had no intentions of founding a school of jurisprudence, became Imām Ḥanbal, the patron saint of conservatism and Wahhābism. Patton calls him a "great saint and defender of orthodoxy" and writes [34, p. 5]: "I do not believe that Aḥmed himself had the idea that such would occur. That a school was formed spontaneously is a testimony to the powerful impression of the man's personality upon his own age and that following". And a testimony (in my opinion) to the stagnation which has afflicted Islam.

recusant: someone who refuses to submit to authority

The conflict between Mā'mūn and AbḤ cannot be understood without examining the history of the birth of the Islamic empire and the forces which steered it during the first century and a half, and it is to this topic that we should now turn.

Arab conquests

Large-scale expansion of Islam began during the reign of 'Umar bin Khaṭṭāb, the successor to Abū Bakr, himself the first successor to the Prophet of Islam, who died in 632. History tells us that 'Umar had the genius to build, during the heady days of

[5] Abbreviation for *Encyclopaedia of Islam* (see p. 177 for more details).

[6] *EoI* uses 'Baghdād'. When the diacritical marks in a quoted text follow a different convention, they will be replaced by those used here.

conquest and capture of foreign riches, a political structure that could hold the rapidly expanding empire intact. What did this peerless administrator, who adopted the title *Amīr al-Mominīn* (Commander of the Faithful) know about the rest of the world? What was his attitude to the knowledge acquired by other nations? Did he approve of collecting *ḥadīthes*? Does the prevailing view among Muslims concerning the status of science differ substantially from that held in the first century of Islam?

To answer the first two questions we need not look beyond the *Muqaddimah* of Ibn Khaldūn [35–37]. Ibn Khaldūn (1332–1406), perhaps the last of the intellectual giants produced by the glorious Islamic civilization, has been called the father of many disciplines, among them sociology, economics, and philosophy of history [38, p. 206]; Toynbee, who did not hesitate to call the *Muqaddimah* the greatest work of its kind, has also discussed the limitated range of Ibn Khaldūn's historical vision [39, pp.84–7], especially as it relates to the latter's attempt to answer the question: "How comes it that empires suffer the decline and fall exemplified in the history of the Islamic Commonwealth?".

The second Caliph and the sea

The primary source here is Ṭabarī, who quotes several (similar) versions of ʿUmar's correspondence on naval operations. Muir has skillfully woven them into a single account [40, p. 205]:

> Muʿāwiyah had long keenly missed the support of a fleet, and in fact had sought permission from ʿOmar to embark his soldiery in ships. "The isles of the Levant," he wrote, "are close to the Syrian shore; you might almost hear the barking of the dogs and cackling of the hens; give me leave to attack them." But ʿOmar dreaded the sea, and wrote to consult ʿAmr, who answered thus:—"The sea is a boundless expanse, whereon great ships look tiny specks; nought but the heavens above and waters beneath; when calm, the sailor's heart is broken; when tempestuous, his senses reel. Trust it little, fear it much. Man at sea is an insect on a splinter, now engulfed, now scared to death." On receipt of this alarming account, ʿOmar forbade Muʿāwiyah to have anything to do with ships;—"The Syrian sea, they tell me, is longer and broader than the dry land, and is instant [old meaning: insistent] with the Lord, night and day,

reel: to sway, to whirl about

> seeking to swallow it up. How should I trust my people on its accursed bosom? Remember Al-ʿAlāʾ. Nay, my friend, the safety of my people is dearer to me than all the treasures of Greece.
>
> Nothing, therefore, was attempted by sea in the reign of ʿOmar. But on his death, Muʿāwiyah reiterated the petition, and ʿOthmān at last relaxed the ban ...[7]

Ṭabarī (839–923) has also added that ʿUmar justified his decision by saying that, since neither his predecessor nor the Prophet had undertaken a naval expedition, he was going to follow their example. It was not long before caution was thrown to the wind by Muʿāwiyah, whom Fahmy has rightly called the "Founder of [the] Muslim Navy" [42, p. 78]. There can be no doubt that the new empire would not have survived without a powerful navy [43, p. 55].

One can understand ʿUmar's trepidation of the unknown and his concern for the safety of his troops, but a sensible precaution of today can easily turn into a silly superstition of tomorrow. Nabia Abbott [44] has made the very interesting comment that though this episode has been too readily accepted as a manifestation of the Arab's general ignorance and fear of the sea, it could perhaps be understood in the light of the character and ambition of the three personalities involved. ʿAmr, the governor of Egypt, was perhaps not too eager for the Caliph to grant permission to Muʿāwiyah, then the governor of Syria, to travel by sea, which would have allowed him to approach the coastal waters of Egypt, ʿAmr's territory.

How the early Muslims did learn about maritime navigation and how quickly they mastered the seas has been described by Fahmy [42] and Hourani [43]. What would have happened if the ban on sea travel had not been abrogated is a what-might-have-

---

[7] Ibn Khaldūn states (presumably a memory lapse) that the ban on sea travel remained in force until Muʿāwiyah's reign, and it was Muʿāwiyah who "permitted the Muslims to go by sea and to wage the holy war in ships" [41, Vol. 2, p. 39]. For him, Muslims are under obligation to gain power over other nations [41, Vol. 1, p. 473]: "In the Muslim community, the holy war [*jihād*] is a religious duty, because of the universalism of the (Muslim) mission and (the obligation to) convert everybody to Islam either by persuasion or by force." He goes on to add: "The other religious groups did not have a universal mission, and the holy war was not a religious duty for them, save only for purposes of defense."

been that need not detain us here. Why Muslims have failed to realize that many other decisions taken by ʿUmar should also have been discarded in the interests of progress, is a question that is intimately linked to the title of this book.

ʿUmar's horror of ḥadīth

Someone who is not familiar with the background would be justified in thinking that most of the primary reporters of the sayings of the Prophet would be those of his contemporaries who were closest to him, and would expect to find that the largest contribution to the ḥadīth literature must have been made by Muḥammad's first four successors, the revered "Rightly Guided Caliphs". If one casts a glance at the list of those from whom the ḥadīthes have originated, one can hardly fail to notice that the cream among the Prophet's companions died within thirty years of his demise, namely, during the period of the wars, both foreign and civil, which completely fill Islamic history down to the establishment of the Umayyad dynasty. And it is precisely these who have passed down to us nothing, or next to nothing. Abbott has argued that it would be wrong to attribute the paucity of reports in the first few decades of the Caliphate to general illiteracy [45, p. 10]. She suggests that ʿUmar vehemently opposed the recording of traditions because he feared that a body of sacred literature might accumulate in Islam, just as extrascriptural sacred literature had grown in Judaism and Christianity, and might compete, merely by offering a greater variety, with the Qur'ān, even if it did not distort or challenge the message of the Qur'ān. Abbott has also cited Zuhrī [45, p. 7], who asserted, on the authority of Abū Hurayrah, that so long as ʿUmar was alive, no one dared say "The Apostle of Allāh said that" lest he be whipped or otherwise punished by ʿUmar.[8] Now, the prolific Abū Hurayrah, to whom thousands of traditions are ascribed, converted to Islam only four years before the Prophet's death, and was noted during his youth mostly for being a felophile;[9] his credibility as a ḥadīth reporter has been questioned by many, but his recollection of ʿUmar's at-

[8]Needless to say, the ḥadīth-folk dispute this.

[9]The nickname Abū Hurayrah means 'father (lover) of cats'.

titude may well be right, for he (and a handful of others like him) must have been itching to tell people that "The Apostle of Allāh said that ..."

The perceptive ʿUmar, whose whip was as famous among his subjects as Occam's razor is among scientists,[10] was not wrong, but he too had to leave this mortal world before he could turn the entire globe into an ideal Islamic state. He succeeded, while he was alive, in suppressing the manufacture of traditions, but whipping a man can terrify him into silence only when the whip-cracker is around. As soon as the hand that brandished the whip became still, people started recalling what they or someone else had heard from Allāh's Apostle. Shortly afterwards, a bitter civil war broke out (p. 103), as a result of which Muʿāwiyah came into power and turned the Caliphate into a hereditary monarchy, a drastic departure that created the need for legitimizing the new institution, and those who would be called spin doctors today obliged by churning out traditions implying the propriety of the process that put Muʿāwiyah and his progeny into power [30, Ch. 1].

An apposite ḥadīth became more valuable than a thousand arguments in *any* dispute, not just that concerning the selection of the supreme leader. One can easily imagine the zest and keenness with which one of the faithful would try to 'outḥadīth' another. The corpus of traditions swelled prodigiously in the course of a few centuries, running into hundreds of thousands and touching upon every conceivable topic, however substantial and however trivial. Even the number of traditions recorded in one of the six so-called *ṣaḥīḥ* (authentic or genuine) collections run into several thousands.

ʿUmar's horror of heathen literature

ʿUmar's sea-weariness was matched by his horror of heathen books. Ibn Khaldūn tells us that when the Muslims conquered Persia and came upon an indescribably large number of books and scientific papers, Saʿd bin Abī Waqqāṣ wrote to ʿUmar bin

---

[10] This may be judged from the saying "The whip of ʿUmar is more terrible than another's sword" [46, p. 142]

Khaṭṭāb, asking him for permission to take them and distribute them as booty among the Muslims.

> On that occasion, ʿUmar wrote him: "Throw them into the water. If what they contain is right guidance, God has given us better guidance. If it is error, God has protected us against it." Thus, the (Muslims) threw them into the water or into the fire, and the sciences of the Persians were lost and did not reach us [41, Vol. 3, p. 114].

A number of points arise here: What would an Arab soldier, more likely to be illiterate than not, have done with a Persian book after receiving his share? In fact, Rosenthal's translation deviates a little from the Arabic text [35, Vol. 3, p. 73], which merely speaks of Saʿd asking ʿUmar if the captured books and documents should be "transferred to Muslims". Why did the conquerors fling, in their zeal to destroy heathen learning, some books into fire and others into water, when the Caliph had chosen drowning as the means of liquidation? Such acts of cultural cleansing are usually performed as choreographed spectacles. Witness the destruction, at the hands of the *Ṭālibān*, of the Buddhas of Bamiyan, of video tapes, and of whatever else they considered to be impious and impermissible. The idea of preserving the books (for future generations of Muslims) did not cross ʿUmar's mind because, in his opinion, the Qur'ān contained all the guidance Muslims would ever need, and since it did not provide any instructions for traversing the oceans, there was no need to imitate insects creeping over a splinter.

For my part, I look upon the above anecdote (and its Alexandrian variant, discussed below) as a cock-and-bull story. Ibn Khaldūn, who needed the story for explaining the (supposed) total annihilation of Persia's intellectual legacy, did not think that it was his place to rationalize (see below), let alone criticize, the decision taken by the venerable ʿUmar.

A more widely advertised variant, involving the burning, after the capture of Egypt, of all the books in the well-stocked library at Alexandria seems to be apocryphal [47, Ch. 25], but this opinion is not shared by Joseph [48] or by Canfora [49]. Lewis, aware that myths survive because they serve a purpose, asks what purpose was served by this myth [50]. It would be absurd to suggest that the story was fabricated for bringing Islam into disrepute, because it originated from Muslim sources, and Lewis stresses that "not the creation, but the demolition of the myth was the achievement of European scholarship, which from the 18th century to the present day has rejected the story as false and absurd, and thus exonerated the Caliph ʻUmar and the early Muslims from this libel." Lewis offers an interesting explanation, but I will not reproduce it here. A fabrication or not, the Alexandrian version has been widely believed to be true by Muslims themselves, recorded by their own authors, recounted by the vast majority of Muslims with a satisfaction comparable to that of a miser counting his money over and over again, and by others with amusement and scorn.

exonerate: to clear (or free) from a blame (or a duty)

ʻUmar in hindsight

Kātib Chelebi (1609–57) was perhaps the first Turkish intellectual who clearly understood that the ignorance of the masses and the scientific illiteracy of the theologians were the principal factors behind the dwindling power of the Ottoman empire [51, p. 8]. However, he did not blame the founding architects of the House of Islam for the malaise. According to him, it was imperative, during the infancy of Islam, to focus on the Qur'ān and the sayings of the Prophet, and prohibit everything else [51, p. 24]:

> In the beginning of Islam, the Companions of the Prophet applied themselves to the Book and the Sunnah which they had received from him and handed on, and permitted no work on the sciences apart from a thorough grounding in the principles of the Faith. They showed the utmost rigour in prohibiting. ʻUmar even went so far as to have many thousands of Greek books burned, at the conquest of Cairo and Alexandria, lest the people should neglect for them the memorizing of the Book of God and the Sunnah of the Prophet of God, and the principles of the Faith be not so firmly rooted. Such was their view of the public interest, in the first generation. In the second and third generations, those who had known the Companions and were *mujtahid* codified the traditions they had handed down. They derived the Divine Ordinances, on the basis of the Roots and Branches, with legal proofs; they wrote

mujtahid: someone competent to practice *ijtihād* (making an independent judicial judgment).

> them down and formulated them. After the Islamic sciences had been codified, and protected and safeguarded against any possible corruption, the leaders of the Muslims realised that the first generation's prohibition had been for this very purpose. The danger once eliminated, this purpose was no longer valid. In the Umayyad and 'Abbāsid periods, the prevailing view was that it was important for Muslims to know the science of the truth of things. Hence they translated the books of the ancient peoples into Arabic.

In my opinion the inclusion of the Umayyads, none of whom is remembered as a patron of 'the science of the truth of things', is merely an instance of inventing a fact to support a thesis, and I will argue that, even during the 'Abbāsid period, the prevailing view among theologians (and therefore among plebeians) did not change from that held during the days of 'Umar. In fact, Kātib Chelebi himself goes on to complain about the persistence of the anti-science attitude of learned men in the Ottoman empire [51, p. 25]:

> But many unintelligent people, seeing that the transmission of these sciences had once been banned, remained as inert as rocks, frozen in blind imitation of the ancients. Without deliberation or consideration of the truth of the matter, they rejected and repudiated the new sciences. They passed for learned men, while all the time they were ignoramuses, fond of disparaging what they called 'the philosophical sciences', and knowing nothing of earth or sky. The admonition 'Have they not contemplated the Kingdom of Heaven and Earth?' [Qur'ān 7:184] made no impression on them: they thought 'contemplating' the world and the firmament meant staring at them like a cow.

The birth of modern science, an astonishing enterprise which took place at first in Europe, did much to loosen the stranglehold of the Church on society; it also liberated thinkers from the yoke of ancient authorities (like Aristotle and Ptolemy), and they even began to expound their ideas in the 'vernacular dialects' of Europe, instead of Latin or Greek, which had until then been considered as the only European languages fit for a solemn discourse. Curiously enough, many professional clergymen participated in this enterprise and became leading scientists themselves;[11] a common interest brought them into regular contact, professional as well as physical, with other, non-clerical scientific investigators, many of whom happened to be, or thought of themselves as, devout Christians. There has never been an Islamic counterpart of this phenomenon. It is true that formal priesthood has no place in orthodox Islam (see Appendix D), but the existence in the Muslim world of learned "divines" who needed no secular vocation for sustenance cannot be denied, and I am not aware of any such person's involvement in scientific investigations (properly so called).

The prevalent view

When I was in my teens, my friends and I spent countless hair-splitting hours on the conundrums that confront, at one time or another, everyone brought up to believe in a supreme deity that is omnipotent, omnipresent, omniscient, always watchful and never scrutable, remote yet involved with everything, invoked by both sides in a conflict. Does man have, we wanted to know, a free-will, or is he a slave to the Divine decree? And whatever the answer, does it not undermine belief in the above listed Divine attributes? Occasionally, I would consult a grown-up, hoping to benefit from the wisdom of age, but the quiet-voiced elder, instead of confessing that (s)he too was baffled by these questions, tried to disillusion me from philosophical speculations by remarking that ordinary folk cannot resolve such issues, and added for good measure that a predilection for these topics is likely to lead one to the flames of hell.

Ibn Khaldūn listed the foundations of Muslim faith by quoting the Prophet [52, p. 43, Vol. 3]: "(Faith is) the belief in God, His angels, His Scriptures, His messengers, the Last Day, and the belief in predestination, be it good or bad." The report from which these words have been excerpted is in the compilation

[11] I will mention only four members of this illustrious group: John Ray (1627–1705), Stephen Hales (1677–1761), Lazaaro Spallanzani (1729–99), and Gregor Mendel (1822–84). The first two are mentioned elsewhere in this book; Spallanzani is best known for his refutation of the theory of spontaneous generation of life and the first systematic investigation of how bats navigate, and the last named needs no introduction.

known as *Ṣaḥīḥ Muslim* [53, p. 94], one of the six canonical collections of ḥadīthes. Muslims who lived during the later years of the Prophet and immediately after his death believed in absolute predestination, and shrugged off the sporadic jabs of a few philosophically oriented individuals within Islam by calling them innovators. To portray the orthodox attitude towards the omniscience of Allāh, I quote the English rendering of a couplet by the Pashtūn poet Rahmān Bābā [54]:

> *All the pages not yet written, He has read,*
> *Perfect knowledge of all secrets has my Lord*

How this squares with the free will of the authors who are still to come is a conundrum that did not tease the mind of the poet.

To return to the early Muslims. It is reasonable to speculate that the thoughts which troubled my youthful mind stirred the curiosity of many of them as well, but, sensing that there is safety only in numbers or in silence, they kept their thoughts to themselves. The very existence of such terms as *ahl al-ahwā'* (libertines), *jabariyyah* (predestinarians) and *qadariyyah* (believers in free will) testifies to the presence of individuals who liked to excogitate, to think through an argument on their own, but the climate was not yet propitious for such individuals to form a proper sect. The replacement of the Arabocentric Damascene Caliphate with a system more in tune with with the ethnic and cultural diversity of the Islamic empire and more receptive to alien ideas blew away some theological taboos, and a group of heretical theologians, called *Mu'tazilah* (literally *the separatists*) by their adversaries, could now count on the new Caliphs for political and financial patronage and on Hellenic philosophy for intellectual support and inspiration.

I cannot devote much space to the Mu'tazilites, and indeed I should not, because I became acquainted with their tenets only by reading secondary sources. Ibn Khaldūn, an orthodox in theological matters, gives a bird's-eye view of the theological landscape that may suffice for most readers. An excellent survey of their beliefs and fluctuating fortunes may be found in the *EoI* article on "Mu'tazila[h]" [55]. It will be enough for my purpose to state that under this label I include the theologians whom many have credited, in the face of evidence to the contrary (see below), with a comparatively liberal outlook; that they were entirely indigenous to the House of Islam, but gained confidence and maturity by coming in contact with Greek philosophical works; that they accepted the broad outlines of Islamic dogma and were the first to discuss it in terms of Greek philosophical notions; that they focussed on the ethical aspects of the conception of God, which is why they designated themselves with the label *Ahl al-ʿAdl wa'l-Tawḥīd* (people of justice and oneness); that they interpreted good and evil in terms of human free will; that they strenuously denied, in order to oppose anthropomorphic conceptions of God, the independent existence of the divine attributes, including speech, as a corollary of which they held the Qur'ān to have been created and not uncreated (eternal).

Every Muslim believes that God, who created the entire universe, is uncreated, and the Qur'ān is His direct speech (in Arabic, *kalām Allāh* as distinct from *kalimat Allāh*, meaning 'words of God'). It appears that the question 'Is the Qur'ān created or uncreated?' was not hotly debated until almost a century after the Prophet's death. Now, why would anyone want to claim that not only God but the Qur'ān too is uncreated? It has been said that the eternality of the Qur'ān is 'one of several points which have suggested to European scholars that the development of Islamic theology was largely influenced by Christian theology' [56, p. 65]. Once an idea begins, under some impulse, to float around, it can be turned into an antibody to fight off invading innovations or into a vehicle for promoting other influences. The eternality of the Qur'ān and the allied belief that certain attributes of God mentioned in the Qur'ān stand for real incorporeal beings which have been coeval with God did not appeal to the Muʿtazalites, because to them it smacked of the Christian doctrine of Trinity and undermined Islam's uncompromising stance on monotheism. Their motto, if they had one, must have been *Away with the Attributes of Allāh! Away with the eternality of His speech!* To their conservative opponents, acceptance of the doctrine of the createdness of the Qur'ān must have seemed like opening the floodgates to endless subversive innovations. To say that the Qur'ān was created implied, they feared, that God might conceivably have created it otherwise, in another language, in some other era, and that an individual believer or a charismatic ruler might claim that he is entitled to revise its commandments now or later. To insist that the Qur'ān is the uncreated word of God seemed, in their eyes, the most effective inoculation against innovation, the securest means of forestalling attempts to undermine the universality and permanence of God's words.

After Mā'mūn became the Commander of the Faithful (CoF, for short) he took many decisions whose purpose will remain opaque to those who differentiate between facts and speculations. In 827 he proclaimed that, next to the Prophet, 'Alī bin Abū Ṭālib was the best of mankind and that the Qur'ān was a creation of Allāh. I agree with the view, ably put forward by Gutas [57, Ch. 4], that Mā'mūn must have been motivated more from political considerations than religious fervour, and if this thought makes you exclaim "How does all this accord with Mā'mūn's well-known religiosity and learning, with his emulation of the way of life of his forefathers, the rectitudinous 'Abbāsid caliphs, and of those pillars of Islam, the first four caliphs, with his respect for the religious scholars, or with his observance of daily prayers and adherence to other religious injunctions!", I will respectfully remark "How curious! These are just the words Ibn Khaldūn used [41, Vol. 1, pp. 39–40] to defend Mā'mūn against what he thought were baseless accusations of licentious behaviour". In fact, Ibn Khaldūn used similar reasoning (also) for dismissing aspersions cast on the characters of Mā'mūn's father and aunt, Hārūn and his sister 'Abbāsah [41, Vol. 1, pp. 29–34]. The penetrating mind of Ibn Khaldūn overlooked the fact that 'Abbāsī VI, who had both a noble father and a noble mother, presented a devastating counterexample to his *ad hoc* argument.

ad hoc: arranged for this purpose, special

During the last years of his reign, Mā'mūn assigned important positions in his administration, including that of chief *qāḍī*, to persons sympathetic to Mu'tazalite views, and toward the very end he mounted a merciless campaign for extirpating religious orthodoxy by asking the religious leaders in the community to conform to his brand of Islam or face the consequences. The first step taken by Mā'mūn towards creating the 'Brave New Muslim World' was to send a letter to his deputy in Baghdad, Isḥāq ibn Ibrāhīm, ordering him to summon before him the qāḍīs and traditionists, and to ask them to undergo a test (*miḥnah*) concerning the creation of the Qur'ān. A slightly amended version of the

qāḍī: judge practising Islamic law

English translation of the letter, published by Patton [34, pp. 56–61], appears in the next section. In general usage, the term *miḥnah* means a 'testing', 'trial' or 'ordeal', whether due to the vicissitudes of fortune or to the malice of men. It is often used as an equivalent of 'inquisition', particularly when applied to the process inaugurated by Mā'mūn.

miḥnah: inquisition

The first letter of Mā'mūn

Allāh has placed the imāms and caliphs of the Muslims under an obligation to do their utmost to maintain the religion which He has placed in their custody; to preserve the heritage of prophethood which He has granted them to inherit; to transmit the knowledge which He has consigned to their charge; to govern their subjects in accordance with what is right and just, and to induce them to obey Allāh. The CoF begs Allāh to bestow on him firmness and proper resolution in carrying out his duties with success.

The CoF knows that the bulk of the people all over the world (*hashw al-ra'iyyah wa siflat al-āmmah*, the riffraff and the insignficant), lack insight and the capacity to ponder; are ignorant of Allāh and too blind to see Him, too much in error to know the reality of His religion, the confession of His unity and the belief in Him; perverted, also, so as not to recognize His clear tokens, and the obligation of His service; unable to grasp the real measure of Allāh, to know Him as He really is, and to distinguish between Him and His creation, because of the weakness of their views, the deficiency of their understandings, and their turning aside from reflection and recollection; for they put on an equality Allāh and the Qur'ān which He has revealed. They are all agreed and stand unequivocally in accord with one another that it is eternal and primitive, and that Allāh did not create it, produce it, or give it being; while Allāh Himself says in His well-ordered Book, which He appointed as a healing for what is within the breasts and as a mercy and right guidance for the believers, 'We have made it an Arabic Qur'ān' (43:3), and everything which Allāh has made He has created. He says, also, 'Allāh has *created* the heavens and the earth and *made* the darkness and the light' (6:1). He speaks also *alif-lām-rā'*: disjointed letters (see p. 178 for more details)

thus, 'We will tell thee tidings of that which went before' (20:99); He says here that it is an account of things *after* whose happening He *produced* the Qur'ān. Then He says, *alif-lām-rā'*, 'A book whose verses were well-ordered, and, then, were divided by order of a Wise and Knowing One' (11:1). Now, for everything that is ordered and divided there is one who orders and divides; and Allāh is the one who orders well His Book and the one who divides it, therefore, He is its creator and producer.

There are also those who dispute with false arguments, and call men to adopt their view. Further, they claim to be followers of the Sunnah, while in every chapter of Allāh's Book is an account, which may be read therein, that gives the lie to their position, declares their invitation [to adopt their opinions] to be false, and thrusts back upon them their view and their religious pretensions. But they maintain, in spite of that, that they are the people of the truth and the [real] religion and the communion of believers, all others being the people of falsehood, unbelief and schism; and they boast themselves of that over their fellows, so deceiving the ignorant, until persons of the false way, who are devoted to the worship of another God than Allāh, and who mortify themselves for another cause than that of the true religion, incline toward agreement with them and accordance with their evil opinions, by that means getting to themselves honour with them, and procuring to themselves a leadership and a reputation among them for honorable dealing. Thus they give up the truth for their falsehood, and find apart from Allāh a supporter for their error. And, so, their testimony is received, because they [sc. the ignorant or people of the false way] declare them [sc. those who pretend to be the people of the truth] to be veracious witnesses; and the ordinances of the Qur'ān are executed by them [sc. those who pretend to be the people of the truth] notwithstanding the unsoundness of their religion, the corruption of their honour, and the depravation of their purposes and belief. That is the goal unto which they are urging others, and which they seek in their own practice and in [their] lying against their Lord, though the solemn covenant of the Book is upon them that they should not speak against Allāh except that which is true, and though they have learned what the condition is of 'those whom Allāh has made deaf and whose eyes He has blinded. Do they not reflect upon the Qur'ān? or are there locks upon their hearts?' (47:25–6) The CoF considers, therefore, that those men are the worst and the chief in error, being deficient in the belief in Allāh's unity, and having an incomplete share in the faith—vessels of ignorance, banners of falsehood, the tongue of *Iblīs* [Satan], who speaks through his friends and is terrible to his enemies who are of Allāh's religion; the ones of all others to be mistrusted as to their truthfulness, whose testimony should be rejected , and in whose word and deed one can put no confidence. For one can only do good works after assured persuasion, and there [really] is assured persuasion only after fully obtaining a real possession of Islam, and a sincere profession of the faith in Allāh's unity. He, therefore, who is too blind to perceive his right course and his share in the belief in Allāh and in His unity, is, in other respects, as to his conduct and the justness of his testimony, still more blind and erring. By the life of the CoF, the most likely of men to lie in speech and to fabricate a false testimony is the man who lies against Allāh and his revelation, and who does not know Allāh as He really is; and the most deserving of them all to be rejected when he testifies about what Allāh ordains and about his religion is he who rejects Allāh's testimony to his Book and slanders the truth of Allāh by his lying. Now, gather together the qāḍīs under thy jurisdiction, read unto them this letter of the CoF to thee, and begin to test them to see what they will say, and to discover what they believe concerning the creation of the Qur'ān by Allāh and its production by Allāh. Tell them, also, that the CoF will not ask assistance in his government of one whose religion, whose sincerity of faith in Allāh's unity, and whose [religious] persuasion are not to be trusted; nor will he put confidence in such a man in respect to what Allāh has laid upon him and in the matter of those interests of his subjects which he has given into his charge. And when they have confessed that [sc. that the Qur'ān is created] and accorded with the CoF and are in the way of right guidance and of salvation, then, bid them to cite the legal witnesses under their jurisdiction, to ask them in reference to the Qur'ān, and to leave off accepting as valid the testimony of him who will not confess that it is created and produced, and refuse thou to let them [the qāḍīs] countersign it. Write, also, to the CoF the reports that come to thee from the qāḍīs or thy province as to the result of their inquisition and their ordering that these things be done. Get acquainted with them and search out their evidences, so that the sentences of Allāh may not be carried out, except on the testimony of such as have insight into real religion and are sincere in the belief in Allāh's unity, and then, write unto the CoF of what comes of it all.

The last four months of Mā'mūn

Mā'mūn's letter, written in the month of Rabīʿ I, 218 AH, before he set out on his last expedition to the frontiers, and about four months before his death, was sent to all the provinces. Those who seek more details would do well to consult Patton [34], the first Western scholar to write a history of this calamity, or to read the *EoI* article on *miḥnah* and some of the references cited therein. Suffice it to say here that most people behaved as did Galileo when he was shown the instruments of torture. Among the handful who refused to abandon the orthodox doctrine of the uncreatedness of the Qur'ān, the most notable was AbḤ. When the news of this defiance reached Mā'mūn, then at Ṭarsūs, the latter ordered that AbḤ, together with one Muḥammad bin Nūḥ, be sent to him. They were put in chains and sent off to Ṭarsūs, but soon after they had left Raqqa, the news of the caliph's death arrived, and they were sent back to Baghdad. Ibn Nūḥ died on this leg of the journey. How Mā'mūn died and how AbḤ was treated after his arrival in the capital by ʿAbbāsī VIII, a half brother to both Mā'mūn and ʿAbbāsī VI, are among those episodes on which historians are not unanimous.

Mā'mūn died under circumstances that would seem highly mysterious to a modern reader, but not to the contemporaries of Ṭbarī, to whom we owe the Arabic text of the above letter, since sudden deaths among the high and mighty during the first two dynasties of Islam (and presumably also other dynasties throughout the ages) were quite common, and Muslim historians often left it to the imagination of their readers to infer when foul play was the most likely cause of death. Whether Mā'mūn's life was brought to an abrupt end by the person who succeeded him, or by someone who believed in the uncreatedness of the Qur'ān, or, as the *ahl al-ḥadīth* would have us believe, by the Creator Himself, because AbḤ had prayed to Allāh, on his way to Ṭarsūs in fetters, to spare him a face to face meeting with the tyrant.

The cause of Mā'mūn's death may not be an open-and-shut case, but it can hardly be denied that he held in contempt anyone whose opinions differed from his own, and was prepared to terrorize the orthodox, securing acquiescence with his own views from such as were weak enough to be intimidated, and exterminating the tougher nuts (or simply nuts, in his opinion) without remorse. Given his domineering character, there is no reason to make the mitigating assumption, as does Ibn Khaldūn (see below), that Mā'mūn was coaxed into composing the letter by someone else.

Mā'mūn's successor presses on with the persecution of AbḤ

The popular account, accepted by Patton [34, pp. 85–113], represents AbḤ as a steadfast believer who refused, even after he was severely beaten, to change his belief, and claims that a crowd of his followers had gathered outside the palace where the test and the beating took place, and that they would have revolted and stormed the palace had the ruler not asked AbḤ's uncle Isḥāq to tell the people that his nephew was not being tortured. A rather different version is given by the *EoI* article on *miḥnah* [58]. In reproducing the relevant passage from this article, I have replaced all its references by [...] and "Aḥmad" by AbḤ:

> That AbḤ was flogged is not in doubt, for all that *the incident is ignored by al-Ṭabarī* [my italics] and Ibn Miskawayh; the sources give as the date of this event both Ramadan 219/Sept. 834 and Ramaḍan 220/Sept. 835, the second of which is to be preferred if it is correct that the total period of his detention was about two-and-a-half years [...]. There are, however, certain respects in which the received Sunnī account may in fact be questioned, in view of what some of the sources have to say. In the first place, these sources are under the impression that AbḤ was flogged until he actually acknowledged the created Qur'ān: al-Yā'qūbī knew this to be the case [...], and AbḤ's contemporary al-Jāḥiẓ tells us that it

took only 30 strokes [...]; al-Mas'udī thought that it took 38 strokes [...], while Ibn al-Murtaḍā opts for 68 [...]. Secondly, these sources know nothing about AbḤ's release having been occasioned by a public commotion; for them, his release was the consequence of his acknowledgement, although Ibn al-Murtaḍā would have us believe that it took place only after he had acknowledged the created Qur'ān before the assembled population of Baghdad. Thirdly, what these sources have to say provides an alternative explanation of why AbḤ was subsequently left alone by the authorities; it was not because they lacked the nerve to test him again, but because he had capitulated. None of these sources can be regarded as other than more or less hostile to AbḤ, but even so it is difficult to explain away the essence of what they have to say. The *en passant* remark by al-Jāḥiẓ, in particular, with its casual and matter-of-fact tone, has a convincing ring to it; Ibn al-Murtaḍā's reference to AbḤ's public acknowledgement of defeat may well be dismissed as an embellishment, although it would have made good sense from the point of view of Ibn Abi Du'ād, who was by this time *qāḍī al-quḍāt* and thus in effect chief inquisitor; and even Ibn al-Jawī was aware of such accounts, for all that he eschewed them [...].

recrudescence: a new outbreak after a quiescent period (especially of something dangerous or disagreeable)

The Mā'mūnian madness *miḥnah* was repealed in about 849 by 'Abbāsī X, whose reign may be identified as the time for the retreat and political extinction of the Mu'tazilah movement and the recrudescence of unenlightened orthodoxy. The long-term impact of the failure of the *miḥnah* has been well summed up by Hinds. It dealt a fatal blow to the notion of caliphal participation in the definition of Islam, let alone total caliphal control over it, and "it permitted the unchecked development of what in due course would become recognisable as Sunnism". Hinds goes on:

> It was now unquestionably the *'ulamā'* [see below], rather than the caliphs, who were "the legatees of the prophets" (*warathat al-anbiyā'*), and henceforward it would be they who, armed with this spiritual authority, and at a distance from those who held temporal power, elaborated classical Islam [58].

Millions of men and women living in the twenty first century continue to believe, as did AbḤ, that the Qur'ān and the *ḥadīth*, interpreted literally, provide the only correct guide for all humanity.

Who/what are *'ulamā'*?

The word *'ulamā'* (or *'ulemā'*) is the plural of the Arabic word *'ālim*, which means a learned man, a scholar, someone who has acquired *'ilm* (learning). This is how al-Khwārizmī[12] interpreted the word *'ilm* in the preface to his immortal booklet on algebra [59]. Let us glance at Rosen's rendering of a short passage from that preface [59, p. 2]: "The learned in times which have passed away, and among nations which have ceased to exist, were constantly employed in writing books on the several departments of science and on the various branches of knowledge, bearing in mind those that were to come after them, and hoping for a reward proportionate to their ability, and trusting that their endeavours would meet with acknowledgment, attention, and remembrance—content as they were even with a small degree of praise; small, if compared with the pains which they had undergone, and the difficulties which they had encountered in revealing the secrets and obscurities of science." The phrase *the learned* stands for *'ulamā'* (عُلَمَاْ) and *science* for *'ilm* (عِلم).

Although the title *'ālim* (عَالِم) could be given to a scientist, or a jurist or a linguist, it is usually reserved for a religious scholar, and the plural form *'ulamā'* is invariably used, as in the above quotation from Hinds (p. 22), for those learned in theological matters. This holds for both *'ālim* and *'ilm*, as may be judged from the following passage [60, p. 49]:

> When 'Umar [bin Khaṭṭāb] died, ibn-Mas'ūd exclaimed, "Nine-tenths of all *knowledge* have vanished." He was then told, "How do you say such a thing when we still have among us most of the Companions?" To which he replied, "I did not mean the *science* of legal opinions and decisions; rather I mean the *science* of knowing Allah."[13]

---

[12] I have made an exception here, because the prefix *al* has become an integral part of the great algebraist's name in the Western world.

[13] The emphasis is not in Faris's translation of Ghazālī's Arabic text. Each word italicized here stands for the same Arabic word, namely *'ilm*. Ibn-Mas'ūd's remark is considered sufficiently important by Ghazālī to deserve a repetition [60, p. 77].

The disastrous consequences of this restricted interpretation of the word *'ilm* will be discussed in Chapter 2.

Who is a great Muslim?

I do not know if there is any truth in the proverb 'Better a blow from a wise man than a kiss from a fool', but I do know that a book that reinforces the prejudices of a reader, since it does more harm than good, is worse than a kiss from a foolish friend. One (fool-friendly?) book of this type is *Hundred Great Muslims* [61]. Both Mā'mūn and AbḤ are among the hundred people chosen by the author. We know that sudden death prevented a tête-à-tête between Mā'mūn and AbḤ, but the author begins his sketch of AbḤ with a vignette in which the two come face to face in Ṭarsūs [61, p. 99]:

> The grand Durbar [royal court] of the greatest of the Abbaside Caliphs, Mamun ar-Rashid [*sic*], at Tarsus, was packed to its capacity. A frail bodied person, with a resolute look and a calm countenance, was carried forward by the guards, through a long row of distinguished courtiers, officials and religious scholars. The person was Ahmad ibn Hanbal who had been summoned by the Caliph, an exponent of the Mutazellite doctrine of the creation of Quran.
>
> The Caliph asked him if he accepted the Mutazellite doctrine about the creation of Quran.
>
> "No", replied Ahmad ibn Hanbal firmly, "The Quran is the world of God. How can it be treated as a creation?"
>
> The Caliph tried to argue with Ahmad bin Hanbal supported by several religious scholars but the Imam was adamant and refused to change his views, which were in conformity with the faith of the Prophet and his Companions. He was, therefore, put behind the [sic] bars.

I will abbreviate *Hundred Great Muslims* as *100GM*, and will refer to its author by his initials, namely KJA. That KJA did not use any diacritical marks is not deplorable in a book of this nature, but spelling the name of the scholarly caliph sometimes as Mamun and sometimes as Mamoon is. Mā'mūn's personal name was 'Abd Allāh, which means that if one wants to mention his full name, one should write 'Abd Allāh al-Mā'mūn. Someone who pays great attention to detail or correct behaviour is called *punctilious*, and it is not unreasonable to expect that an author who wants to gain the respect of his readers would pay attention to detail and to an author's responsibilities to the readers. KJA fails in both aspects of scrupulousness. He insists on calling 'Abbāsī VII "Mam□n ar-Rashid" (where □ stands for "oo" or "u"), which, though unprofessional, is but a peccadillo when compared with falsifying a quotation. Let us see what KJA says about the death and burial of AbḤ [61, p. 100]:

> He returned to Baghdad and ...died at the age of 75 in Rabi-ul-Awwal of 241 A.H. (July 855 A.C.). He was buried in the Martyrs' cemetery, near the Harb gate of Baghdad. "His funeral was attended by millions of mourners and his tomb was the scene of demonstrations of such ardent devotion that the cemetery had to be guarded by the civil authorities and his tomb became the most frequented place of pilgrimage in Baghdad" *(Encyclopaedia of Islam).*

Millions of mourners? KJA has not provided any bibliographic information about his source, other than naming it as *Encyclopaedia of Islam*. I have good reasons to believe that he means *EoI*. On consulting *EoI* [33], I found the following account (in which [...] indicates, as before, references that have been omitted):

> Aḥmad b. Ḥanbal died in Rabīʿ I 241/July 855, at the age of 75, after a short illness, and was buried in the Martyrs' cemetery (*Maqābir al-Shuhadāʾ*) near the Harb gate. The traditions which surround the account of his funeral, although partly legendary in character, convey the impression of a genuine popular emotion, and his tomb was the scene of demonstrations of such ardent devotion that the cemetery had to be guarded by the civil authorities [...]. His tomb became one of the most frequented places of pilgrimage in Baghdad.

You may no longer be curious to know what KJA says about Māʾmūn; accordingly, I will be brief. He praises the caliph's love of learning, describes him as an able administrator and a wise statesman [61, p. 377]: "Mamoon was a very kind-hearted ruler, reputed for his forbearance and humanitarianism. He used to say that if people could know of his kind nature, they would commit more crimes. He would often say that he got greater pleasure in forgiveness than in awarding punishment". After painting this portrait, KJA did not have the heart to mention the *miḥnah* or AbḤ in the same chapter!

Finding both AbḤ, whose views 'were in conformity with the faith of the Prophet and his Companions', and Mā'mūn, the tyrannical ruler who placed the pious AbḤ behind bars for holding fast to the faith of the Prophet, is like finding both Pope Leo X and King Henry VIII in a book entitled *Hundred Great Catholics*. Why this particular analogy?

Soon after Luther startled Christendom with his bold theses on the Roman Catholic Church and her beliefs, Henry VIII (1491–1547) prepared (May 1521) a rebuttal in the form of a book titled *Assertio Septem Sacramentorum* (Defence of the Seven Sacraments). The Pope of the time, Leo X, was so pleased with the *Assertio* that he bestowed upon its author the title *Fidei Defensor* (Defender of the Faith). At the time of writing this book Henry was, or thought he was, a devout Catholic, but all this changed when he wanted to divorce his wife Catherine of Aragon, whose prayers for producing a male heir had remained unanswered, so that he could marry Anne Boleyn. The Popes had long established their prerogative to grant divorces, and had granted several to reigning monarchs for reasons which Jesus Christ might well have found dishonourable. Pope Leo X also had his reasons for refusing to annul Henry's marriage. Whether for this reason or not, the king persuaded a compliant and anticlerical Parliament to pass legislation permitting the separation of the Church of England from the Church of Rome, making the king himself the Supreme Head of the English Church.

There was a time when I wondered whether Henry VIII wrote the *Assertio* himself or had it written for him, and I learnt subsequently that even Luther's response implied a doubt concerning the authorship of the book, but, after reading about Henry's education ("intended to prepare him to be Archbishop of Canterbury") and overabundance of talents [62], I have no difficulty in accepting that Henry and Mā'mūn were formed in the same mould; Henry VIII was, according to Duff [63], "a singularly well-educated man, and keenly interested in the ecclesiastical turmoils of the times". Henry responded to Luther's innuendo in a letter [64, p. 490]: "Although ye fayne your self to thynke my boke nat myne owne, but to my rebuke (as it lyketh you to affyrme) put out by subtell sophisters: yet it is well knowen for myn, and I for myne avowe it".

Though Henry cast aside the trammels of Papal authority, he was keen to retain the title bestowed on him for defending the pontiff's doctrines, and so have been all his successors, Protestant as well as Catholic. The title did not change but the faith professed by the title holder did. In *God Save the King*, William Renwick Riddell remarked [65, p. 16]: "I do not know that any more curious circumstance can be cited than this—and one scarcely knows how to characterize it—perhaps, as loyal subjects, the best thing we can do is to let it alone and say nothing about it."

I think the circumstance of an *Amīr al-Mominīn* (Commander of the Faithful) inflicting severe punishment on a man who became a pillar of orthodox Islam is decidedly more curious than Henry's decision to hang on to his title, and still more curious is the fact that both AbḤ and Mā'mūn are counted among great Muslims, and not only by the author of *100GM*.

The ingenious Ibn Khaldūn, having panegyrized Mā'mūn's piety in the early part of the *Muqaddimah*, may have wanted to follow Ṭabarī's example (p. 21), but total silence would have deprived him of the opportunity to condemn the Mu'tazilah for their heretic views. He found a way out by using another principle of parsimony, which can be stated, unlike Occam's razor, in plain language: Don't tell the whole truth. Ibn Khaldūn, who did not allow his ingenuity to be restrained by the thought that the *Muqaddimah* might be read by someone who has looked at the skeletons in the 'Abbāsī cupboard, chose to be selective [52, Ch. 6, § 14]:

> Thus, the Mu'tazilah decided that the Qur'ān was created. This was an innovation. The early Muslims had openly expressed the contrary view. ... Certain leading Mu'tazilah indoctrinated certain caliphs with it, and the people were forced to adopt it. The Muslim religious leaders opposed them. Because of their opposition, it was considered permissible to flog and kill many of them. This caused orthodox people to rise in defense of the articles of faith with logical evidence and to push back the innovations.

The orthodox people who rose in defense of the uncreatedness of the Qur'ān (and related articles of faith) used more than logical evidence to push back the innovations. They used unrestrained physical violence and made Mā'mūn look like mild-mannered, if not exactly kind-hearted.

Interlude

It is interesting to see how a Muslim historian of comparatively recent times viewed the *miḥnah*. Muḥammad Shiblī (1857–1914), usually called Shiblī Nu'mānī, was (and continues to be) counted among the most influential and distinguished Muslim scholars in the Indian subcontinent. W. Cantwell Smith did not exaggerate when he chose these words to describe Shiblī's stature [66, pp. 38–41]: "This man is another genius of commanding importance: few would rank a fourth along with Ḥālī, Shiblī, and Iqbāl, as the great literary figures in modern Indian Islam. He was the founder of modern literary criticism in the vernacular, was a poet, and was outstanding as an historian and biographer." Shiblī planned a series of biographies under the general heading "Royal Heroes of Islam", and chose Mā'mūn as his first subject; later, he revised the plan and wrote biographies of 'Umar ibn Khaṭṭāb and other nonroyal heroes, including Ghazālī (whom we will meet in the next chapter). The foreword to the second, revised edition of Shiblī's *Al-Mā'mūn* [24] was written by Sir Syed Ahmad Khan (see p. 110).

I was astonished that both Sir Syed and Shiblī referred to the biographee as 'Mā'mūn al-Rashīd', and baffled by the fact that, instead of using the standard terms, namely *makhlūq* (created) and *ghayr makhlūq* (uncreated), which would be immediately intelligible to an Urdu reader, Shiblī opted for the adjective *ḥādith* and the noun *qidam* (meaning sempiternity), which would make, in the absence of some explanatory text, as little sense to the typical Urdu reader as would 'entities' on p. 2 to those who have not heard of Occam's razor; disappointed to see that Shiblī devoted only one and a half page (out of about 170 pages dealing with Mā'mūn) to *miḥnah*,[14] treating it as merely a hiccup in Mā'mūn's

sempiternal: eternal [L. *sempiterus*—*semper*, always

[14] In a book of comparable size (132 pages of text), Cooperson [27] needed five pages for the same purpose.

magnificent reign. Shiblī begins the concluding section (entitled *Maestri of Mā'mūn's era*) of his biography with the comment that a historian dealing with an epoch is duty-bound to provide an account of the top experts and virtuosi of the period, so that the reader may assess the state of culture and civilization and the ruler's munificence towards scholars and artists, and this would require, Shiblī asserts, several volumes if one were to do justice to the court of Mā'mūn. Shiblī, who has to content himself with just a few pages, includes AbḤ among the theologians and divines mentioned in the last section, and adds [24, p. 180]: "the writings of these traditionists and jurisconsults are scholarly relics the likes of which would be hard to match by any other period of history".

Why Mā'mūn failed

The desire on the part of the Mu'tazilah to reconcile religion with reason, however laudable we may call it, turned into a catastrophe when Mā'mūn tried to impose his brand of Islam as the state religion. This misguided move failed because it took no account of the pitifully cramped mental horizon of the average Muslim, the butcher, the baker, the cobbler, the candlestick-maker, the camel rider, the concubine owner.[15] The *miḥnah* was an attempt to ram a highbrow religious outlook down the throats of people who found the createdness of the Qur'ān incomprehensible and utterly repugnant. Mā'mūn and the next two caliphs made a monumental mistake by ignoring the fact that, in the opinion of those they classified as the riff-raff, the anthropomorphic creed of AbḤ was consistent with the language of the Qur'ān, and that opinion remains, sadly, the majority view in the Muslim world even today, where AbḤ's piety continues to command the same reverence as it did in the time of Mā'mūn. Notwithstanding the claims made in defence of Mā'mūn's character by Ibn Khaldūn,

[15]It seems that concubines were rather common in those days, and one did not have to be opulent to own one. Even the impecunious AbḤ, described by Patton as a great saint [34, p. 5], had one. I quote Laoust [33]: "By each of his two legitimate wives AbḤ had one son, Ṣāliḥ and ʿAbd Allāh, besides six children by a concubine, who are not otherwise known."

neither Mā'mūn nor any of his top functionaries was regarded as a paragon of piety by the common man, to whom it was evident that AbḤ, not an 'Abbāsid caliph, least of all Mā'mūn, was the person who strove to emulate 'Umar.

It will be convenient to introduce the abbreviations: *BaḤ* for *Bayt al-Ḥikmah*, which means *House of Wisdom*, and *XaḤ* for the closely related word *Khizānat al-Ḥikmah*, which may be translated as *Storehouse of Wisdom*. The Arabic word *ṣāḥib* has many meanings, including *inhabitant*, *owner*, *master*, *lord*; in what follows, the compound word *Ṣāḥib al-*□ may be translated as *Head of* □.

Mā'mūn is credited with building an academy in Baghdad called *BaḤ*, which comprised a well-stocked library, an astronomical observatory, and a gigantic translation bureau, and I can support this claim only by saying "and so say all of us". Well, not *all* of us, and among the doubting Thomases I will only mention Gutas, who insists [57, p. 59]: "It was certainly not a center for the translation of Greek works into Arabic; the Graeco-Arabic translation movement was completely unrelated to any of the activities of the *bayt al-ḥikma*. Among the dozens of reports about the translation of Greek works into Arabic that we have, there is not even a *single* one that mentions the *bayt al-ḥikma*". Speaking for myself, I cannot even tell if the name *BaḤ* signified a conglomerate of institutions or the entire city of Baghdad, just as the name *Bayt al-Maqdis* is applied to Jerusalem. In either case, *BaḤ* would have subsumed a state-supported library [67], and *XaḤ* would have been an appropriate name for such a collection. I hesitate to assert that it must have been so, because the compiler of *Fihrist* [12, 68], our only source of information about the authors and books of that era, has described Sahl bin Hārūn as *Ṣāḥib al-BaḤ* (p. 10) and also as *Ṣāḥib al-XaḤ* (p. 20).

There can be no doubt, despite our meagre knowledge of *BaḤ*, that the encouragement of scholarly activity in Baghdad spurred other amīrs and sultāns and shāhs and viziers to vie with one another for "signing up" scholars to their courts—much as managers of modern football (both soccer and gridiron) clubs compete for the signing of accomplished and promising players. In the article on Mā'mūn, the author of *100GM* refers to this healthy contagion and recalls a long passage in which Robert Briffault describes the frenzy of demand for scholars [69, p. 188]. The excerpt in *100GM* begins with the following words [61, p. 175]: "The incorruptible treasures and delights of intellectual culture were accounted by the princes of Baghdad, Shiraz and Cordova, the truest and proudest pomps of their courts. But it was not as a mere appendage of princely vanity that the wonderful growth of Islamic science and learning was fostered by their patronage." The second sentence may sound slightly wonky to you, because KJA changed (surreptitiously!) "appanage" to "appendage". Let us shrug off not only this solecism but also its cause (an excess of self-confidence) and let us also overlook Briffault's proclivity for occasional exaggeration, which I find affable even when it fails to convince me, and see what he writes, when he has finished describing the rise of Arabic science, about the causes of its decline [69, pp. 217–8]:

appanage: grant awarded by a monarch for the support of a member of the royal family

> The culture of the courts of Damascus and Baghdad had been eyed askance by the zealots of Islam; and when al-Mā'mūn established his famous school of translators, the Dār al-Ḥikmet or 'Home of Science,' he had to placate the pietist conscience by assurances that it was merely a college of household physicians. To the Muslim faithful and their 'Ulamā', the whole cultural movement remained from first to last a thing accursed; Hārūn and al-Mā'mūn had sold their souls; and in Moorish Spain there were constant outbursts of fanatic zeal in which the books of science were consigned to the flames. The attitude of religious ardour towards intellectual culture was precisely the same in the Muslim as in the Christian world. Only there was this difference, that in the former it was the intellectuals and heretics who for a time held the whip-hand of power; the pious had perforce to rest content with sour looks and suppressed growls, and to wait patiently until the Turk, the Berber, and the Spaniard came to their assistance, and plunged Islam back into the purity of faith and the darkness and ignorance of barbarism. If, while in the tenth century European aspirants to knowledge sought the schools of the learned Moors, in the twentieth century Professor Westermarck [Edvard Alexander Westermarck (1862–1939)] journeys to Morocco to study the ways of primitive barbarism, it is because in the two worlds the contest between light and darkness had opposite issues; in the one case dogma was defeated by rational thought, in the other it prevailed over it.

The last four words of the above passage show how easy it is, even for a skilled writer, to fall, if he lets his guard down, to the level of the sender of a text message hastily composed on a cellular phone. It seems worthwhile to rephrase Briffault's last clause: In Europe, dogma was defeated by rational thought; in Islam, dogma defeated rational thought.

I have spent this much time on Briffault because he is perhaps the only Western author who has been ungrudging in placing Arabic science well above the Hellenic. Not surprisingly, he is frequently quoted by those who believe that Islam is not hostile to science. Which version of Islam, I would like to know? That preached by AbḤ, which has held the upper hand for more than a thousand years? Or that practised by the wayward Hārūn and Mā'mūn? Let us call "o-Islam" the orthodox version which requires belief in an uncreated Qur'ān, and the other "h-Islam" (the heterodox version, the heresy, according to which the Qur'ān is a creation of Allāh). Those who claim that Islam is compatible with science and cite history and Briffault in support of this claim should re-read the relevant chapters (V and VI) of his book, and add a suffix ("o-" or "h-") where they find the word "Islam"; they would discover that it was the h-version which ushered in the halcyon days, and that Briffault often uses the word "Arab" (or "Arabian" or "Arabic") for "h-Islam". In fact, his main message is already stated in the second paragraph of his fifth chapter:

> No conception could be remoter from the truth than that which commonly pictures the coming of Islam as a sort of Mahdi rising, a jihad of wild darvishes fired to frenzy by religious fanaticism. The experiences from which such a picture is drawn, Muslim fanaticism, one might almost say Muslim faith, all belong to a subsequent age, when Islam's civilization had sunk to dust and its creed had become transformed by Ash'arite theology. Its origin and its halcyon days were far different.

Ab'ul Ḥasan al-Ash'arī (died 935), commonly regarded by his admirers as the person who rescued orthodoxy from the clutches of Mu'tazalism, founded the school to which belonged Ghazālī, whose attitude to science is discussed in the next chapter. These two, along with AbḤ, are of cardinal importance in the history of Islamic theology. An English translation of al-Ash'arī's book

Al-Ibanah ʿan Uṣūl ad-Diyānah (The Elucidation of Islam's Foundation) with a commentary has been provided by Klein [70].

Ibn Khaldūn did his best to rewrite history by brushing under the carpet the ugly fact that the inquisition inaugurated by Mā'mūn resulted in the flogging of AbḤ (and execution of others?), but who can rewrite fiction and dethrone the legendary caliph of *Thousand Nights and a Night*.

The question raised in the title of this chapter can only be answered by asking another question. Which Islam? The liturgical and literalist creed preached by the *muḥaddith* "Imām of Baghdād" or the stillborn version that captured the affection of the heretic and half-Persian caliph of Baghdād? I sum up by borrowing some words from Macdonald [71]. The caliph who succeeded in bringing science to his court and the corridors of the *House of Wisdom*, but failed in planting its seeds in the streets and mosques of Baghdād, was "a very indifferent Muslim who favored Greek and scientific studies to the utmost of his powers, [who] published a decree that the Qur'ān was to be regarded as created, and that such should be the doctrine taught from all public pulpits".

Dogma can no more be dispelled by a decree than bad weather be outlawed by an act of parliament.

2 *Who Banished Science from Islam?*

Those who spearheaded the scientific advance during the glorious era of Islam are usually called Muslim (or Arab) scientists, though not every knowledge-seeker was a votary of Islam and only a handful of them were native Arabs. Even so, each descriptor has some justification: all the scholars of this period used Arabic as the medium for recording and disseminating their discoveries, and nearly all the potentates who patronized these scholars professed, at least nominally, the faith of Islam.

votary: a devoted adherent or follower

potentate: a ruler or monarch, especially an autocratic one

Everyone who writes about the intellectual advances made in the Islamic era struggles with the problem of finding apt labels, and no one has yet succeeded in coining the right phrase to displace what we grudgingly call Islamic or Arabic science. In preparing the text for his *Venture of Islam*, Hodgson [31, pp. 57–60] was driven to invent a double-adjectival term, 'Islamicate', in analogy with 'Italianate' (in the Italian style, showing the influence of Italian art or culture). To my ears, this term raises a twofold difficulty. In the one ear, it immediately evokes the nouns *Caliphate* and *Imāmate*, but, in the other, it rhymes with countless verbs, like *abdicate*, *educate*, and so on. I think we have better precedents in the terms *Anglophone* and *Francophone*, which have been applied to persons, countries, cultures, authors and literatures, and I prefer therefore the adjective *Arabophone*, which is already in use [72], and includes both Arabs and non-Arabs, Muslims and non-Muslims. All we need in addition is a substitute for the Arabic term *Dār al-Islām*, and I will use *Islāmica* for the vast part of the globe that was under the sway of Islamic/Muslim rulers; he who resided is *Islāmica* was an *Islāmican*, and also, if he studied philosophy or science, an Arabophone.

Specifying the decades during which the decay of Islamican science became manifestly irreversible is a little harder than naming the principals who led the struggle against the spirit of inquiry, and one of them, there can be little doubt, was the person whose name appears in the next sentence as Alghazzālī, but I will call him Ghazālī, though many other variants also exist. Sachau, who viewed the fourth century (Ḥejira) as the turning-point and the close of the century as the time when the triumph of orthodoxy sealed the fate of independent research for ever, did not hesitate to identify the culprits [73, p. x]: "But for Alashʿarī and Alghazzālī the Arabs [Islāmicans, in my terminology] might have been a nation of Galileos, Keplers, and Newtons." The Darwins are not mentioned because Sachau wrote this in 1879.

Abū Ḥāmid Muḥammad ibn Muḥammad ibn Muḥammad al-Ṭūsī al-Ghazālī (*ca.*1058–1111) was a religious philosopher and jurisprudent, the most prominent of his time and, according to his many admirers, of any time. Ghazālī has been lavishly praised by both Muslims and non-Muslims. Among the Christian authors who have paid him tributes, two in particular stand out: Macdonald and Zwemer. Macdonald, the first to publish a biographical account of Ghazālī in English [74], devoted a chapter to him in *Development of Muslim Theology, Jurisprudence and Constitutional Theory* [75], wherein he described Ghazālī as 'the greatest, certainly the most sympathetic figure in the history of Islam, and the only teacher of the after generations ever put by a Muslim on a level with the four great Imams' [75, p. 215]. Zwemer went a step further by calling him the greatest of all Muslims since the days of the Prophet, and he even saw Ghazālī as a potential ally [76, p. 11]: "There is a real sense in which Al-Ghazali may be used as a schoolmaster to lead Moslems to Christ. His books are full of references to the teaching of Christ. He was a true seeker after God".

The purpose of the chapter

I propose to look at Ghazālī from the eyes of a scientist and a citizen of the modern world. As a result of studying some of his most important books, I have been led to conclude that Ghazālī should be called the Pied Piper of Islamica, that he was the doyen of the countless pipers who lured Muslims away from science, that his books pose a threat to those who swear by the spirit of free inquiry, that he was a true believer in the innate inferiority of women, in the immense power of magic, in the efficacy of severe punishments. His views on the status of women and flogging, though in keeping with the spirit of his times, are a stumbling block to progress in the Muslim world, where he is still revered as *Imām* Ghazālī.

Ghazālī, "because of whom the lame walked briskly"

Biographical material concerning Ghazālī, especially his childhood and early education, is rather sketchy and, as might be expected, difficult to verify; for a critical examination of the available sources, the reader is referred to a recent book on his philosophical theology [77]. It will be enough for us to know that he was born in Ṭūs, lived during the Seljūq period, taught in Baghdad and Nīshapūr, travelled widely in the region, and participated more in the rough-and-tumble of politics-and-pulpits than the average reader might think after reading his autobiography.

Ghazālī offered to lead others to the paradise reached by himself, and earned in return the illustrious title of *Ḥujjat al-Islām* (Proof of Islam). The oft-heard remark, now an expression of "public opinion" in the Muslim world, "Could there be another Prophet after Muḥammad, surely it would have been al-Ghazālī" is attributed to 'the learned Suyūṭī' by the learned Browne [78, p. 293], but such remarks tend to have multiple attribution.

A website (http://www.ghazali.org/) provides an excellent on-line collection of electronic texts on Ghazālī's life and works; the following verse is printed at the head of the webpage:

> Because of him the lame walked briskly,
> And the songless through him burst into melody.

Who are the former lame and songless? Where are they walking to, and what songs are they singing? Have any women joined them? And are there (among those who did not join this melodious mob) any whom *he* has silenced with the threat of death? I will attempt to answer these questions by examining his major works.

Ghazālī's output

A prolific author of considerable talent, Ghazālī wrote more than fifty books. I will focus on three of his books, listed here in chronological order: *Tahāfut al-Falāsifa*, *Iḥyā' 'Ulūm al-Dīn*, which is regarded as his masterpiece, and a booklet, *Al-Munqidh min al-Ḍalāl*, that may be called his intellectual autobiography; I will refer to these books as *Tahāfut*, *Iḥyā'*, and *Munqidh*, respectively.

Munqidh came to the notice of European readers in 1842 with the publication of a work (henceforth called *Essay*) on Arabian philosophy by Schmölders [79], which included Ghazālī's Arabic text of *Munqidh* as well as its French translation. I will be using the translation of Montgomery Watt [80] without any comments other than those dealing with the English equivalents of some scientific terms.

Translations of the three titles

The titles of *Tahāfut* and *Munqidh* are usually translated as *The Incoherence of the Philosophers* and *The Deliverer from Error*, respectively.

The first word in the title of *Iḥyā'* has been translated as *revivification* by Schmölders [79, p. 216], as *revitalization* by Zidan [81], and as *revival* by Zwemer [82, p. 177] and Farah [83]; Macdonald [74] chose *revivifying*, but Gianotti [84] preferred *reviving*, and I have no strong opinions about whether the sense of Ghazālī's title is better captured by a noun or a gerund. The second word in the title has been invariably (and inappropriately, in my opinion) translated as *sciences*, which means that if one wants to keep the three significant words in the same order as in the Arabic title, its English rendering becomes *Revivification of the Sciences of Religion*.

As I explain later, it would be far more appropriate to translate the last two words in the title as *Teachings of Islam* or *Islamic Teachings*. In my opinion, *Reanimation of Islamic Teachings* captures the title as well as the contents of his book, and there is room only for replacing the first word by one of many alternatives.

Iḥyā' extolled as a *philosophical* work?

Shiblī, a highly respected Muslim historian who has already been mentioned (p. 28), published a biography of Ghazālī in 1902 [85], which contains a section entitled *Philosophy of Akhlāq and Iḥyā' al-'Ulūm*; the word *Akhlāq* can be translated as *morality* or *ethics*, and the phrase *Iḥyā'al-'Ulūm* is simply Shiblī's (undeclared!) abbreviation for *Iḥyā' 'Ulūm al-Dīn*. Shiblī explains the uniqueness and popularity of *Iḥyā'* by remarking that Ghazālī freely appropriated a great deal of material from existing Arabic books on moral philosophy, blended it with selections from various religious texts, and presented the mixture in limpid, exoteric prose. The result, according to Shiblī [85, p. 47], was a faultless book that became highly popular and so impressed (on the one hand) Muslim imāms, who believed it to be a divinely inspired work, and (on the other hand) Henry Lewes, who paid the following tribute in his *History of Philosophy* (hereafter *HoP*): "Had a French translation of *Iḥyā'* existed in the days of Descartes (who is regarded as the founder of modern moral philosophy in Europe), everyone would have said that Descartes had plagiarized it."

Now, if one has studied *Iḥyā'*, and is also familiar with the thoughts of George Henry Lewes and René Descartes, one would immediately suspect that something is amiss here. Imagine my surprise when I did find, upon consulting *HoP*, the following statement [86, p. 50]: "It bears so remarkable a resemblance to the *Discours sur la Méthode* of Descartes, that had any translation of it existed in the days of Descartes, every one would have cried out against the plagiarism." Was Shiblī right after all? The answer, as I explain below, is a resounding 'No', since the 'It' and 'it' in the above quotation do not refer to *Iḥyā'*. Let us first read some sentences which precede the above quote. Speaking of Ghazālī, Lewes wrote [86, p. 50]:

> So great was the admiration he inspired, that the Mussulmans some times said, 'If all Islam were destroyed, it would be but a slight loss, provided Algazzāli's work on the "Revivification of the Sciences of Religion" were preserved.' [⚠] This work, probably owing to its originality, was never translated into Latin during the Middle Ages, and remained a closed book to all but Arabian scholars until M. Schmölders published his version. It bears so remarkable a resemblance to the ... cried out against the plagiarism.

If one stops here, Shiblī would seem to be vindicated, but a little perseverance is needed to discover that Lewes has misled his readers by omitting—inadvertently—a remark that would have informed them that the phrase 'This work' in the second sentence refers to *Munqidh*, the booklet translated by Schmölders, not *Iḥyā'*, the tome mentioned in the first sentence. Lewes's lapse, indicated in the above by the danger sign, can be rectified by replacing the icon by a new sentence that correctly identifies the work to which the second sentence refers. We may add, for example: "Ghazālī recounted his skirmishes with philosophers in *Munqidh*, his intellectual autobiography, which has been translated into French by Schmölders. This work ...".

Any lingering doubts that Lewes might have been talking of *Iḥyā'* will be dispelled if I inform my readers that Schmölders did not publish a translation of *Iḥyā'* in his *Essay*. Lewes reviewed *Essay* in 1847 [87], and cited this review in the chapter on Arabian philosophy in *HoP*; a scrutiny of the 1847 review is rewarded by some information not supplied in the book chapter. We pick up the thread at the point of our interest:

> So great indeed was his renown, so ardent the admiration he inspired, that the Mussulmans sometimes said, 'If all Islam were to be destroyed, it would be but a slight loss, provided Algazzāli's work on the *Revivification of the Sciences of Religion* were preserved.' Of this remarkable man, we have now before us a remarkable treatise [namely *Munqidh*], for the first time translated, wherein is given the history of his mind in the pursuit of truth; and for which we can find no better title than that affixed to the posthumous work of Coleridge: 'Confessions of an Inquiring Spirit.' It bears a very striking resemblance to the 'Discours sur la Méthode,' and 'Méditations' of Descartes ...

To summarize what has been said so far (by Lewes and myself): Lewes noted an uncanny similarity between *Discours* of Descartes and *Munqidh* of Ghazālī. *Iḥyā'* may be a great book in the eyes of many Muslim saints (listed by Shiblī), but Lewes expressed no opinion about it.[1]

To discuss the contents of *Iḥyā'*, we must turn our attention to the topic that forms the heading of the next section.

Arabic and English words for *knowledge*

The Arabic word that comes closest to knowledge is *'ilm*. Here, for instance, are two Arabic terms that will be mentioned later (p. 44): *'ilm al-ḥisāb* for arithmetic and *'ilm al-jabr* for algebra. The usual English rendering for *'ulūm*, the plural form of *'ilm*, is 'science', but Lane has given 'sciences, or several species of knowledge' [89, p. 2141]; indeed, the faculty (or college) of science in an Arabic university is often called *kullīyāt al-'ulūm*. The plural form did not exist in classical Arabic [89, p. 2141], and does not occur, for instance, in the Qur'ān [90, p. 41].

To those who would like to know the difference between *'ilm* and two other Arabic words with a similar meaning, namely (*'arafa* and *sha'ra*), I recommend Lane's *Arabic-English Lexicon* [89] or Rosenthal's book on the concept of knowledge in medieval Islam [90]. Here it would be enough to quote one paragraph from the latter work (p. 45):

> In given passages of Muslim literature, it is often difficult to be certain whether the use of the term *'ilm* is meant to refer to knowledge both secular and religious, or only to the latter kind. It is also often difficult to decide whether *'ilm* is meant to denote abstract "knowledge" or the singular of *'ulūm*, the individual discipline. In the Muslim mind, these distinctions rarely if ever loomed as important as they do in our own way of thinking. This by itself is a characteristic aspect of the Muslim concept of *'ilm* in general and of the Muslim approach to its plural in which abstract knowledge finds its concrete expression.

---

[1]Some familiarity with the philosophical works of Descartes, who is often called the father of modern philosophy, might have prevented Shiblī from assuming an overlap between the ethical principles enunciated in *Iḥyā'* and the contents of a book whose full title has been translated as *Discourse on the Method of Rightly Conducting the Reason and Seeking Truth in the Sciences* [88].

The English term 'science' originates, as the reader of this book is likely to be aware, from the Latin word 'scientia' whose root (*scire*) means 'to know'; literally speaking, one may say that science is simply what we know—the sum total of all human knowledge. Such a definition would include all the 'logies' and the 'ics', but it would also embrace, unless we insist on a stricter definition, much that we do not commonly associate with science. It has become customary to use the word *science* for a branch of knowledge acquired by a systematic study. We use the English words 'science' and 'sciences' rather promiscuously, for we have not just one science but many: astronomy, botany, chemistry, economics, geology, mathematics, physics, zoology, and so on, are each regarded as a science. Oddly enough, we speak not only of the science of physics, the science of chemistry, etc, but also of the physical sciences, the chemical sciences, the social sciences, and so on. The word *science* now stands both for the product—the entire corpus of organized knowledge that we have now built up—and for the very process whereby the store of systematized knowledge is gradually enlarged.

Physic, physics and philosophy

Theology and philosophy have vied with each other for public attention and allegiance throughout history. For aeons the supremacy of theology was absolute and undisputed, but philosophy gradually gained ground and eventually it was able to assert its independence; while these two rivals struggled for wresting ascendancy, science was quietly and imperceptibly inching its way to autonomy.

As a preliminary to reading Ghazālī's pronouncements on science, it is necessary to become acquainted with the branches of knowledge mentioned by him, and to agree on the English equivalents of their Arabic names.

Let us begin with *al-ṭib* and *al-ṭabī'īyāt*. The former still carries the same connotation as in Ghazālī's time: *ṭib* is equivalent to the archaic word 'physic', and may be confidently translated as 'medicine', and one who practices *ṭib* is a *ṭabīb*, a 'physician'.

A contemporary Arab is likely to translate the term *al-ṭabī'īyāt* as 'physics', but to Ghazālī it meant 'natural science(s)', and he classified it as a branch of philosophy. There was a time, no further back than about a century, when 'physics' was called 'natural philosophy'; William Thomson (Lord Kelvin), the archetypal physicist, occupied the chair of natural philosophy in the University of Glasgow for more than half a century [91], and co-authored, together with his opposite number in Edinburgh, an authoritative textbook on physics [92] whose preface began with the following definition: "The term Natural Philosophy was used by Newton, and is still used in British Universities, to denote the investigation of laws in the material world, and the deduction of results not directly observed." If we go all the way back to the ancient Greeks, natural science and philosophy become indistinguishable.

It is scarcely necessary to point out that in Ghazālī's lifetime, and even long afterwards, astrology and astronomy were jumbled up and regarded as a single science, covered by the term, *'ilm al-nujūm* (the science of stars), and the word *najm* (star) itself was meant to include a planet, a comet, or any other luminous celestial body. To make sure that this twofold confusion is not lost in translation, I will render *'ilm al-nujūm* as *nujūmology*, which seems no more improper than the Greek-Latin hybrid *television*.

Ghazālī's condemnation of natural sciences

Much has been written about Ghazālī, but I have not come across a thorough appraisal of his views on natural sciences and mathematics; Appendix C is intended to fill this gap. Macdonald stated that Ghazālī's early education embraced "theology, dialectic, science, philosophy, logic" [74]. Concerning Ghazālī's attitude to science, we are told: "he never speaks disrespectfully of philosophy and science" and that his views on science

> were the same as those of the contemporary students of natural philosophy. Their teachings he accepted, and, so far, can be compared to a theologian of the present day who accepts evolution and explains it to suit himself. His world was framed on what is commonly called the Ptolemaic system. He was no flat-earth man like the present 'Ulamā'of Islam; God had "spread out the earth like a carpet," but that did not hinder him from regarding it as a globe.

Macdonald must have based his appraisal of Ghazālī's views on science and mathematics on a book other than *Iḥyā'*, perhaps *Tahāfut* or *Munqidh,* which—so far as Ghazālī's description of the sciences is concerned—is merely an abridgment of *Tahāfut.* In these books, Ghazālī is not quite as rabid as in his magnum opus, but is still not at ease when he speaks of mathematicians and philosophers; the tune and the melody sound slightly different, but the attitude is far from congenial. In *Iḥyā'*, he is uncompromisingly anti-scientific; in the other two books, he speaks like the solemn man whose anxiety and insecurity were well described by Galbraith [93, p. 13]: "Change and new evidence have a way of making previous convictions seem odd, even ridiculous. The reasonably relaxed man can accept correction without too grievous loss of dignity. But the solemn man cannot. He may have heard that the truth will set him free. But he rightly senses that it might also make him seem silly."

inimical: unfriendly, hostile, adverse

That Ghazālī *learnt* any science seems doubtful to me, but I have no doubt whatsoever that he regarded advanced mathematical investigations as unquestionably inimical to faith, and that no one who is not actually insane could oppose science more vehemently than did the author of *Iḥyā'*. There can be no greater disrespect than attaching the label 'ignorance' or 'folly' (*jahl*) to those parts of natural science which he adjudged as contradictory to the true religion (see p. 195).

In *Munqidh,* Ghazālī divides the philosophical sciences into six categories, amongst them mathematics and natural sciences. Mathematics deals with three topics: *arithmetic* and *geometry* (*'ilm al-ḥisāb wa al-hindasa*) (علم الحساب والهندسة) and *astronomy* (*the science of the shape of the world* علم الهيئة العالم).[2] Since *'ilm al-jabr* (algebra) is not mentioned, we must suppose that, in Ghazālī's classification, arithmetic subsumes algebra. He adds that mathematical investigations, which lead to incontrovertible results, have no bearing on religion *per se,* but great danger lurks in these investigations [80, pp. 33–5]:

> None of its results are connected with religious matters, either to deny or to affirm them. They are matters of demonstration which it is impossible to deny once they have been understood and appre-

[2] Watt writes "arithmetic, plane geometry and solid geometry" [80, p. 33].

hended. Nevertheless there are two drawbacks[3] which arise from mathematics.

(a) The first is that every student of mathematics admires its precision and the clarity of its demonstrations. This leads him to believe in the philosophers and to think that all their sciences resemble this one in clarity and demonstrative cogency. Further, he has already heard the accounts on everyone's lips of their unbelief, their denial of God's attributes, and their contempt for revealed truth; he becomes an unbeliever merely by accepting them as authorities (*bi'l-taqlīd al-maḥḍ*), and says to himself, 'If religion were true, it would not have escaped the notice of these men since they are so precise in this science'. Thus, after becoming acquainted by hearsay with their unbelief and denial of religion, he draws the conclusion that the truth is the denial and rejection of religion. How many have I seen who err from the truth because of this high opinion of the philosophers and without any other basis!

Against them one may argue: 'The man who excels in one art does not necessarily excel in every art. It is not necessary that the man who excels in law and theology should excel in medicine, nor that the man who is ignorant of intellectual speculations should be ignorant of grammar. Rather, every art has people who have obtained excellence and preeminence in it, even though stupidity and ignorance may characterize them in other arts. The arguments in elementary matters of mathematics are demonstrative whereas those in theology (or metaphysics) are based on conjecture. This point is familiar only to those who have studied the matter deeply for themselves'.

If such a person is fixed in this belief which he has chosen out of respect for authority (*taqlīd*), he is not moved by this argument but is carried by strength of passion, love of vanity and the desire to be thought clever to persist in his good opinion of the philosophers with regard to all the sciences.

This is a great drawback, and because of it those who devote themselves eagerly to the mathematical sciences ought to be restrained. (My italics.) Even if their subject-matter is not relevant to religion, yet, since they belong to the foundations of the philosophical sciences, the student is infected with the evil and corruption of the philosophers. Few there are who devote themselves to this study without

---

[3]Ghazālī uses the word *āfatān* (آفتان), plural of *āfah* (آفة); *drawback* does not quite express the venom implied by the Arabic word, and *scourge* might be a better choice.

being stripped of religion and having the bridle of godly fear removed from their heads.

(b) The second drawback arises from the man who is loyal to Islam but ignorant. He thinks that religion must be defended by rejecting every science connected with the philosophers, and so rejects all their sciences and accuses them of ignorance therein. He even rejects their theory of the eclipse of sun and moon, considering that what they say is contrary to revelation. When that view is thus attacked, someone hears who has knowledge of such matters by apodeictic demonstration. He does not doubt his demonstration, but, believing that Islam is based on ignorance and the denial of apodeictic proof, grows in love for philosophy and hatred for Islam.

A grievous crime indeed against religion has been committed by the man who imagines that Islam is defended by the denial of the mathematical sciences, seeing that there is nothing in revealed truth opposed to these sciences by way of either negation or affirmation, and nothing in these sciences [is] opposed to the truths of religion. Muhammad (peace be upon him) said, 'The sun and the moon are two of the signs of God; they are not eclipsed for anyone's death nor for his life; if you see such an event, take refuge in the recollection of God (most high) and in prayer'. There is nothing here obliging us to deny the science of arithmetic which informs us specifically of the orbits of sun and moon, and their conjunction and opposition. (The further saying of Muhammad (peace be upon him), 'When God manifests Himself to a thing, it submits to Him', is an addition which does not occur at all in the collections of sound Traditions.)

This is the character of mathematics and its drawbacks.

The incoherence of the the above passages and the insecurity of the author is truly pathetic. Ghazālī regards mathematics as the scourge of Islam, and feels, on the one hand, that mathematicians must be quarantined, but admits, on the other hand, that 'there is nothing in revealed truth opposed to these sciences'.

The difference between mischief and mathematics

According to Ghazālī [94, p. 119], 'Umar bin al-Khaṭṭāb said, "From the stars learn that by which you can be guided on land and sea; then hold back." I don't believe it. Why would 'Umar, who was opposed to sea voyages (p. 6), mention both land and sea? Even Ghazālī's admirers admitted his laxity in citing the sayings of the Prophet, but they have not found it embarrassing; the Urdu translator of *Iḥyā'* has added that, for the purpose at hand, Ghazālī's use of dubious *ḥadīthes* was entirely justified [95, p. 24]. Appendix C bears out Macdonald [74], who chose to be charitable in discussing this aspect: "His quotations are exceedingly careless, and it was one of the great charges brought against him by his assailants that he falsified Traditions; the fact was that he quoted from memory and very freely."

Ghazālī gives other reasons why Muslims are forbidden to indulge in nujūmology; the reasons include, we will find out upon reading Appendix C, that it pulls men away from God and that it is based on mere guesswork.

Both Christianity and Islam decried astrology, but both failed, for reasons that are not hard to grasp, to curb its hold on the masses and even on most of the highly educated. If we leave Ghazālī, and leap forward some five centuries to examine the views of the great Danish astronomer Tycho Brahe (1546–1601) and his brilliant assistant and successor Johannes Kepler (1571–1630), we will see how far they had come by taking the route sternly rejected by Ghazālī and his followers, the path of rational enquiry. Another century or two was needed to subdue astrology and banish it to the dark corners inhabited by charlatans, horoscopists and the superstitious; lamentably, though, this iron grip on the imagination of society nevertheless continues to persist, even in the most secular of contemporary company; with better education, it may suffer further marginalization, but its complete disappearance seems as unlikely as the peaceful abolition of constitutional monarchy.

It is no secret that Tycho and Kepler, both great astronomers, believed in astrology, but astrology meant to them far more than horoscope-casting. Tycho's attitude towards astrology was rather refined, tempered by his grasp of astronomy and alchemy [96], and he knew the difference between astrology and astronomy, as did many others before him, including Ptolemy [97, pp. 80–4]. He saw astrology as an aid to medicine and as an adjunct to meteorology and weather-forecasting, and vigorously defended it, in his inaugural lecture, against the attacks made on it by theologians, and we can think of his lecture even as a response to Ghazālī's denunciation of astrology; Dreyer [96, pp. 74–8] gives an account of Tycho's lecture, delivered in the French legation in Copenhagen. Thoren describes what happened after Tycho's lecture ended [98, p. 84]:

> Immediately after the lecture, Albert Knoppert, professor of law, came up to Tycho and Dançey and said, "When I heard your attacks on the philosophers and physicians, and even the theologians, I was afraid that you would also launch into us jurists—so afraid that I broke into a sweat." Tycho remembered enough from his legal studies to guess that Knoppert was alluding to a well-known section of the Justinian code (Roman law) entitled "Against Mischief-Makers and Mathematicians (Astrologers)." So he replied (in the same collegian vein) that he had once studied law himself in Leipzig but that he had abandoned it when he discovered that jurists did not know the difference between mischief and mathematics.

Justinian's prohibition of the teaching of astronomy and philosophy was only the final blow in a long struggle between the Platonists and Christians of Athens. The events leading to the closure of the Athenian school have been described in detail by Watts [99]. Two years after the edict, Damascius (the head of the school) and six members of his inner circle decided to emigrate to Persia because their pagan religion made it impossible to live without fear of the laws in the Roman Empire; that they returned and passed their remaining days in pagan communities [100] is not relevant here.

What Saint Justinian did for Christianity, Imām Ghazālī was to do for Islam: blot out the spirit of free enquiry and gag the philosophers.

We pause to examine Ghazālī's views on some other matters which he found fit for inclusion in *Iḥyā'* .

Ghazālī's views on some mundane matters

Volume 2 of *Iḥyā'* is a homily dealing with the conduct of everyday life. It begins by laying out a set of recommendations about eating and drinking, useful for those who have been brought up without such guidance, but—unfortunately—one also finds a mass of useless, even misleading, recommendations.

The first precept is that food should be lawful (both in itself and in how it was acquired). It should be placed on the ground, for that was the way of the Prophet; however, placing food on a dining cloth or on a table is permissible, even though it is an innovation. We know that Ghazālī abhors innovations, and this is about the only one that does not bring a frown to his face. One should wash one's hands before one begins eating, clean one's teeth (by using a tooth pick and rinsing one's mouth out thoroughly) after one is finished. Amidst a medley of sense and nonsense, one is informed that the Prophet said that one should not cut bread or cooked meat with a knife, but use one's teeth for this purpose; one should eat only an odd number of dates, raisins and other countable items. Much praise is showered on meat as an item of food. Cow's meat, on the other hand, causes illness, but cow's milk is beneficial, and cow's fat curative. One should not drink water when one is standing. An odd number of stones should be used for performing an abstersion. When someone enters a house to urinate he should advance with the left leg first and when he leaves he should advance with the right. If one reads the rest of Volume 2, one cannot but be astounded at the man's temerity in offering advice on every conceivable aspect of daily life, including how to urinate, copulate and chastise one's wife (or wives). If the reader's appetite has been whetted by this brief sketch, he should read the whole volume and find out the difference between our era and Ghazālī's time.

abstersion: the act of absterging (here cleansing by wiping with pebbles after a substance is excreted from an orifice in the lower part of the body)

Ghazālī and gender equality

It is highly instructive to become familiar with the contents of the section devoted to the etiquette of marriage [83]. Since I cannot go into all the details here, I have chosen to concentrate on matters dealing with the difference in the status of men and women in a society run according to the precepts advocated by Ghazālī.

Beating other people (including one's wife, children, subordinates and domestic servants) has become socially unacceptable in some parts of the world, including the West, where it is regarded as a grave offence, but many patriarchal cultures still condone such behaviour on account of tradition and religious beliefs. Muslim men and women who venerate Ghazālī should become better informed about his views on these matters. They should read *Iḥyā'* before they accept its relevance to the their own daily affairs and to the modern world in general. Two comments, attributed by Ghazālī to the second Caliph 'Umar, are reproduced below, and would suffice to convey the obsolescence of his teachings.

1. 'Umar scolded his wife when she talked back to him saying, "You are no more than a toy in a corner of the house; if we have need of you [we take you], otherwise, you sit as you are." [83, p. 96]
2. 'Umar said, "Disagree with your wives, because disagreement with them is a blessing." It was also said, "Consult them, then disagree with them." [83, p. 97]

I prefer to let the reader discover the brazen misogyny of Ghazālī by reading Volume 2 of *Iḥyā'*, since I find the drudgery of reproducing his words too distasteful, and the effect unjust to an author who was expressing views held by nearly all men of his time.

Revival of the secular sciences and useful knowledge

The author of *Iḥyā'* knew that over four centuries had elapsed since the demise of Caliph 'Umar, but he saw no need to dissent from the latter, and most contemporary Muslims are eager to agree with both—about everything. If *Iḥyā'* presents, as Muslims generally believe, authentic Islam, one cannot avoid the conclusions that Islam is hostile not only to astrology but also to natural sciences, and the rulers who believed in horoscopes and patronized scholars whom Ghazālī condemned as infidels (see below) did so in defiance of the theologians.

The material presented in Appendix C makes it abundantly clear that Ghazālī's version of Islam demands a society in which science is made to play the role of a handmaiden, a system in which the jurisprudent makes all the important decisions; we need, according to the Imām, a few medical men to cure those who fall ill now and then, we might go so far, but only so far, as to allow a handful of numerate Muslims to count our camels and cows and goats, and to divide a man's inheritance between his children, and on no account should we encourage anyone to acquire more knowledge of the stars than is necessary for crude navigation in a desert or along a familiar coastline. One proof of the Pythagorean theorem is acceptable, for who knows when one might need it, but more than 360 proofs, as we proudly claim to have amassed by now [101], is a reprehensible waste of time, which could be more piously spent in memorizing the *Iḥyā'*. He is mortally afraid of innovations, and his greatest fear is that the feeble-minded members of the flock—meaning perhaps the unlearned, the sceptics, the free thinkers—would be led astray by the practitioners of the seductive secular sciences. He would have been horrified if someone had asked, 'Isn't it desirable that scholars of religion should also take a *serious* interest in some of the secular sciences?' In my opinion, what sets apart, more than anything else, post-Renaissance Europe from the Islamic world (both before and after Ghazālī's time) is the voluntary participation of the Christian clergy in scientific research and the fateful abstinence of Muslim priests from this activity. Ghazālī lacked the knowledge, and therefore the vision, to realize that, by exhorting his followers to shun the secular sciences, he was directing them to an abyss deep and dark enough to prevent escape for centuries.

It is odd that even Macdonald, who is expected to know the difference (according to English usage) between 'knowledge' and 'science' uses the latter word in his biography of Ghazālī [74], a choice that can easily befuddle a non-expert, as may be judged from the following example. Before his death, the father of Abū Ḥamid and his brother Aḥmad entrusted his sons and whatever little money he had to a friend, who turned out to be faithful and taught the boys and cared for them till all the money was exhausted. Macdonald continues the story: 'Then he [the friend] advised them to go to a Madrasa and become students there, "seekers of science", in the Arabic phrase.' The Arabic phrase for a student is *ṭālib al-ʿilm*, and 'ṭalib', which means 'a seeker' has a plural familiar to nearly everyone on this planet: *Ṭālibān*. If you find it acceptable to use the label 'seekers of science' for the

madrasa: a place where lessons are given.

Ṭālibān, go on translating the last two words in the title of *Iḥyā'* as *Religious Sciences* or as *Sciences of the Faith*.

If we apply it to our times, Ghazālī's idea of *knowledge* is found to be hopelessly outdated. All sciences are now interlinked, and progress in one field depends on, and leads to, the development of the other fields. Starve one discipline, and you will arrest the growth of all the others. Where would modern medicine be without electrocardiography, radiography, angiography, computer tomography, ultrasonic and magnetic resonance imaging, pacemakers, transplants, antibiotics, anaesthetics, not to mention routine measurements of temperature, blood pressure, blood glucose level, RBC count, etc, etc. Contemporary Muslims should stop reading, citing and memorizing Ghazālī and embrace instead science and scientific attitude; for this to happen, contemporary Muslim scientists will have to start writing books entitled *Iḥyā' 'Ulūm al-Dunyā*, which may be roughly translated as *Revival of Useful Knowledge*.

The concept of *useful knowledge* began to occupy educational reformers in Britain and the USA around the end of the eighteenth century. The best known, but not the first, organization to promote the idea was the *Society for the Diffusion of Useful Knowledge* (SDUK), founded in Britain by Lord Brougham in 1826 [102, 103]. Three years later, Noah Webster and his friends founded the *Boston Society for the Diffusion of Useful Knowledge* [104]; in the 1770s, societies with similar names had been founded in Virginia [105] and in Philadelphia by Benjamin Franklin [106]. These pioneers realized that mass education was the key to making their societies more fair and progressive, that affordable self-education through reading low-priced authoritative books and attending scholarly lectures was the most effective means of raising the educational standards of the underprivileged people. The term 'useful knowledge' was defined very liberally, and it could include Hebrew and horticulture, mathematics and manure.

I would like to end this section by quoting a passage from the introduction to the works of Jeremy Bentham, written by Thomas Southwell Smith [107, p. iii]: "Not only is it now generally admitted, that the subject-matter of instruction for these classes [middle classes] should consist of the physical sciences, as well as of language, but it is, moreover, beginning to be perceived, that some advantages would result to the community from opening the book of knowledge to the very lowest of the people; that everything which it is desirable to teach even the masses, is not comprehended in the facts, that there is a devil, a hell, a so-called heaven, a Sunday, and a church, but that there are things worthy of their attention connected with the objects of this present world,—the properties and relations of the air they breathe, the soil they cultivate, the plants they rear, the animals they tend, the materials they work upon in their different trades and manufactures,—the instruments with which they work,—the machinery by which a child is able to produce more than many men, and a single man to generate, combine, control, and direct a physical power superior to that of a thousand horses. There is a growing conviction, that the communication of knowledge of this kind to the working classes would make them better and happier men; and that the possession of such knowledge by these classes would be attended with no injury whatever to any other class. The want of elementary books is therefore becoming every day more urgent; nothing has yet been done to supply them; and yet here, in the Chrestomathia, there is a mine from which any competent hand might dig the material, and fashion the instrument." The writer of these lines was a Christian, who gave up Calvinism (the faith of his parents, who cast him off) to embrace Unitarianism, because it denied salvation to none, whether (s)he be Christian, Jew, Muslim, Buddhist or whatever [108, 109].

chrestomathy: useful knowledge [Gr. *chresto*, useful| *mathein*, to know]

Ghazālī and Khayyām

Trattner has commented on the contrasting personalities and conflicting views of Ghazālī and his contemporary Khayyām, who were both Persian. He describes with poetic brilliance Ghazālī's mission and its impact on the world of Islam [110]:

> In 'Umar Khayyām's youth (middle of eleventh century) the schoolmen still paid a weary and half-conscious tribute to truth. The forces of reaction, like creeping sands of the desert, had already begun to crawl with inexorable deadliness to blot out the fair gardens of cultivated liberalism. In contrast to the bright tiles of their

> mosques, the Persians began to paint life in gloomy colors, for they were now at work on the task of bringing liberalism to an end and setting up in its stead a stern devotional mysticism. Such was the avowed purpose of al-Ghazālī (d. 1111), the leading theologian of the age and 'Umar's contemporary. Through al-Ghazālī's efforts the revolt against growing liberal thought mounted into a tidal wave. Even the possession of philosophical books soon became no longer safe. Frequent burnings of libraries emphasized the anti-liberal spirit. Belief now became a duty; inquiry a heresy.

According to Persian rumours [78, p. 251], there was no love lost between Ghazālī and Khayyām. It has been reported [111, p. 21], for instance, that Ghazālī used the call of a muezzin as a pretext for ending his meeting with Khayyām, quoting, as he rose to his feet, the following verse from the Qur'ān [17:83]: 'Truth has come and falsehood vanished; verily what is false is bound to vanish.' In view of what Ghazālī has written about the pernicious influence of mathematicians, there is no reason to doubt the rumour, even if *this* story is a fabrication.

By following the solemn Ghazālī instead of the irreverent and innovative Khayyām and his like, the Muslim world took the road to ignorance and superstition, and their potentates, unable to see any immediate benefits resulting from the patronage of secular scholarship and unaware of developments in Europe, lost interest in science without losing their faith in horoscopes and other frivolous interests. To adapt Robert Frost's words, the road not taken, sometime ages and ages ago, was the one that led to science, and that has made *all* the difference.

Ghazālī's verdict: Death to al-Fārābī and Ibn Sīnā

The theologians, it has been said, profess to *know*, where the philosophers only *speculate*, and this divergence is well illustrated by the following joke. A theologian, locked in a contest with a philosopher, derided his opponent for the uncertainty of his quest. "You," he said, "are like a blind man looking in a dark room for a black cat that is not there." "Perhaps," quipped the philosopher, "but *you* would have found it."

One thing for which we can admire Ghazālī, however, is providing readers of *Tahāfut* with a feeling of mental exhilaration and challenging them to think clearly on the relation between philosophy and theology. After all, the chief purpose of provocative discourse is to compel one's opponents to re-examine the logical basis of their views. It is unlikely that the disputants will abandon or even materially modify their stance, but they will be forced to refine their arguments before the next bout.

Unfortunately, Ghazālī was not one of those who would be content with a verbal ding-dong. He wanted to expose infidelity (*kufr*) and smoke out the infidels. In *Munqidh*, one finds a section with the heading *The schools of philosophers, and how the defect of unbelief affects them all* [80, p. 30], wherein Ghazālī charges Socrates, Plato and Aristotle with infidelity, and decides to give them no quarter: "We must therefore reckon as unbelievers both these philosophers themselves and their followers among the Islamic philosophers, such as Ibn Sīnā, Fārābī."

kāfir: an infidel
kuffār: infidels

A few pages later, he states, after exposing three principal errors of the above-named philosophers [80, p. 38]:

> On the further points—their denial of the attributes of God, their doctrine that God knows by His essence and not by a knowledge which is over and above His essence, and the like—their position approximates to that of the Mu'tazilah; and the Mu'tazilah must not be accounted infidels because of such matters. In my book, *The Decisive Criterion for Distinguishing Islam from Heresy*, I have presented the grounds for regarding as corrupt the opinion of those who hastily pronounce a man an infidel if he deviates from their own system of doctrine.

These liberal remarks, denouncing impulsive imputations of *kufr*, have won Ghazālī much praise, but it should not be forgotten that *The Decisive Criterion* [112] was written when Ghazālī himself was charged with unbelief, and that he was no against denouncing someone as an infidel so long as due deliberation precedes the indictment. He became obsessed with 'the laxity of men's belief in the principle of prophecy and in its actuality and in conduct according to the norms elucidated by prophecy'; 'ascertained that this was widespread among the people'; identified four principal causes for this laxity; confronted, for quite a while, 'individual men, questioning those who fell short in observing the Law' [80, p. 71]; their replies are divided in five categories, the last and longest of which is the response of the philosophers:

> A fifth man says: 'I do not perform these acts out of obedience to authority (*taqlīdan*). I have studied philosophy and I know that prophecy actually exists and that its achievement is wise and beneficial. I see that the acts of worship it prescribes aim at keeping order among the common people and restraining them from fighting and quarreling with one another and from giving rein to their desires. But I am not one of the ignorant common people that I should enter within the narrow confines of duty. On the contrary I am one of the wise, I follow wisdom, and thereby see clearly (for myself) so that I do not require to follow authority. This is the final word of the faith of those who study the system of the theistic philosophers, as you may learn from the works of Ibn Sīnā and Abu Naṣr al-Fārābī. [80, p. 72]
>
> These are the people who show politeness to Islam. Often you see one of them reading the Qur'ān, attending the Friday assembly and public Worship and praising the sacred Law. Nevertheless he does not refrain from drinking wine and from various wicked and immoral practices! If someone says to him, 'If the prophetic revelation is not genuine, why do you join in the prayers?' perhaps he will reply, 'To exercise my body, and because it is a custom in the place, and to keep my wealth and family. Or perhaps he says, 'The sacred Law is genuine; the prophetic revelation is true'; then he is asked, 'And why then do you drink wine? and he replies, 'Wine is forbidden only because it leads to enmity and hatred; I am sufficiently wise to guard against that, and so I take wine to make my mind more lively'. Ibn Sīnā actually writes in his *Testament* that he swore to God that he would do various things, and in particular that he would praise what the sacred Law prescribed, that he would not be lax in taking part in the public worship of God, and that he would not drink for pleasure but only as a tonic or medicine. Thus the net result of his purity of faith and observance of the obligations of worship was that he made an exception of drinking wine for medical purposes!
>
> Such is the faith of those philosophers who profess religious faith. Many have been deceived by them; and the deceit has been the greater because of the ineffectiveness of the criticism levelled against the philosophers, since that consisted, as we have shown above, in denying geometry and logic and others of their sciences which possess necessary truth. [80, p. 73]

Since previous critics of philosophy had been ineffective, and even counterproductive (because they were imprudent enough to deny the validity of all their opponents' arguments and results, including the latter's unassailable mathematical and logical demonstrations), Ghazālī decided to demolish in *Tahāfut* the philosophers' case and their reputation by attacking their philosophical arguments. The concluding section of *Munqidh* opens with the spine-chilling question, "Now that you have analysed the theories of the philosophers, will you conclude by saying that one who believes in them ought to be branded with infidelity and punished with death?", and he answers it himself [113, p. 249]:

> To brand the philosophers with infidelity is inevitable, so far as three problems are concerned—namely:
>
> 1. The problem of the eternity of the world, where they maintained that all the substances are eternal.
>
> 2. Their assertion that Divine knowledge does not encompass individual objects.
>
> 3. Their denial of the resurrection of bodies.
>
> All these three theories are in violent opposition to Islam. To believe in them is to accuse the prophets of falsehood, and to consider their teachings as a hypocritical misrepresentation designed to appeal to the masses. And this is blatant blasphemy to which no Muslim sect would subscribe.

Both Fārābī and Ibn Sīnā were dead when this was written, and *may* have come to no harm even if they had been alive in Ghazālī's days, because not all the rulers were as devout as Imām Ghazālī wanted everyone to be, but a similar statement from a contemporary cleric who wields some influence would induce his devotees to take action against the offender.

Indifferent selection of heroes

If you are making a hall of fame for Muslim heroes, it would be as well to begin with a more stringent criterion for selection than that used by John Donne in choosing his "harem" of females, as described in his playful poem *The Indifferent*:

I can love both fair and brown,
Her whom abundance melts, and her whom want betrays,
Her who loves loneness best, and her who masks and plays,
Her whom the country formed, and whom the town,
Her who believes, and her who tries,
Her who still weeps with spongy eyes,
And her who is dry cork, and never cries;
I can love her, and her, and you, and you,
I can love any, so she be not true.

We saw in the first chapter that Caliph Māʿmūn, a heresiarch *par excellence* and Imām Aḥmad bin Ḥanbal, a diehard orthodox, were both included in *100GM* [61]. If we pick up this book again, we will find many other anomalous heroes in its pages. Ghazālī appears there, but so do al-Fārābī, Ibn Sīnā, Khayyām, and Ibn Rushd (known to the West as Averroes). Ibn Rushd, who was born shortly after Ghazālī's death, challenged the latter's condemnation of philosophy in two works, entitled *Incoherence of the Incoherence* and *Decisive Treatise*, and ought to deserve, in the eyes of anyone who agrees with Ghazālī, a death sentence as well.

I cannot say much about Ibn Rushd here, and leave the curious to consult other sources. A few sentences from *HoP*, though, seem worth quoting [86, p. 60]: "Aristotle became infamous in Islam; all the philosophers were proscribed, and their works destroyed. Hence it was that Ibn Rushd, venerated for centuries by Jews and highly esteemed by Christians, has left scarcely any trace on the minds of Arabs. Hence also the extreme rarity of his great works in the original; while Hebrew and Latin versions abound in all great collections of manuscripts. The published Latin versions are very numerous. From 1480 to 1580, Renan tells us, scarcely a year elapsed without some new edition appearing. In Venice alone more than fifty editions were published, of which fourteen or fifteen are more or less complete." I am pleased to report that many of his works are now available online [114].

Knowledge, science and present-day Muslim clergy

I will examine *Iḥyāʾ* in Appendix C; here I only want to remind the reader that Ghazālī's original (Arabic) title is, as a matter of fact, not really misleading, for his book is concerned essentially with religious knowledge. The same cannot be said for an institution that is regarded, among many Muslims, as one of the world's most revered schools of religious learning, the so-called *Dār al-'Ulūm* (usually written as Darul Uloom), which was founded in Deoband on 30 May 1866 [115]. The Urdu translation of *Iḥyā'*, to which I have referred above, came from a Deobandī scholar. The fabulous stories reported in the translator's preface provide a glimpse into the credulity of this circle of scholars and their followers, who seem to inhabit the same world in which Ghazālī lived. One finds here a story that is recounted also by Macdonald [74]:

> ... Abū Bakr ash-Shāshī [who died, according to Macdonald, a little more than two years after al-Ghazzālī] has a story that is worth telling. "In our time there was a man in Egypt who disliked al-Ghazzālī and abused him and slandered him. And he saw the Prophet (God bless him and give him peace!) in a dream; Abu Bakr and 'Umar (may God be well pleased with both of them!) were at his side, and al-Ghazzālī was sitting before him, saying, 'O Apostle of God, this man speaks against me! 'Thereupon the Prophet said, 'Bring the whips!' So the man was beaten on account of al-Ghazzālī. Then the man arose from sleep, and the marks of the whips remained on his back, and he was wont to weep and tell the story." The Muslim imagination was evidently tickled by this kind of dream, for a similar story is told, with a long *isnād*, of Ibn Ḥirazaham al-Maghribī, another assailant of al-Ghazzālī.

The Ghazālī critic who was whipped is identified in the Urdu translation as Abu'l Ḥasan 'Alī ibn Ḥirazaham, and the first narrator of the story, also named, is reported to have added that the marks of the whip lashes could be seen when ibn Ḥirazaham was given his ritual pre-burial ablution [95, p. 21]. I hope to escape scourging in my dream if I remind Macdonald that in those pre-scientific days even the Christian imagination was tickled by such dreams. In one of his most famous letters, Saint Jerome described a similar dream and wrote [116, p. 211]: "I profess that my shoulders were black and blue, that I felt the bruises long after I awoke from my sleep, and that thenceforth I read the books of God with a zeal greater than I had previously given to the books of men". The western reader may be surprised to know, however, that the majority of Muslims are still willing to accept the truth of these tales.

Though one reads the words 'arts and sciences' more than once in the official description, the author(s) of the text must be among those who still follow Ghazālī and believe that all genuine knowledge is derived from the *'ilm* handed down by the Prophet, that everything else is either useless or not an *'ilm* at all, even if it is called by that name. The resources at the web site deal, as anyone can verify, only with religious issues. One wing of this institution, known as Darul Fatwa, issues fatwas (edicts) on islamic matters, including the life-and-death matter of deciding who is a *kāfir* (infidel).

Understandably the material and intellectual resources available to Deobandī scholars are meager compared to those within easy reach of Western academics, and one does not expect, therefore, that the Deobandīs would be conversant with the thoughts of George Henry Lewes or the contents of *HoP*. It appears, however, that they do not even read Urdu books written by someone with a different opinion. As it happens, *Munqidh* was translated into Urdu in 1890 by a Syed Mumtāz 'Alī [117], who is stated on the front page to have worked as a translator for the Chief Court of the Punjāb in Lahore. One can see, from the extensive footnotes added by the translator, that he was rather learned and capable of thinking for himself, a rare bird among his fellow Muslims. A footnote at the appropriate place informs the reader of the similarity between the views of Descartes and those expressed by Ghazālī in *Munqidh*, and adds a comment similar to that made by Shiblī, without mentioning Lewes or *Iḥyā'* explicitly [117, p. 12]: "It has been speculated that if the writings of Imām Ghazālī had reached France during the days of Descartes, it would have been generally assumed that Descartes had borrowed his ideas from the Imām."

Mumtāz 'Alī's asides provide some insight into his thoughts and the views on either side of his mode of thinking, which makes his translation a little more valuable than other renderings and—for that matter—even the original itself. He was evidently a man of deep faith, but no bigot, as one would expect from someone who shows himself to be an ardent admirer of Sir Syed Ahmed Khan. Let us note in passing that, in one of his footnotes, Mumtāz

'Alī takes issue with Ghazālī for imputing *kufr* to Fārābi and Ibn Sīnā [117, pp. 32–3]. A rough translation of this footnote is worth presenting here: "Charging Ibn Sīnā and Fārābī with infidelity is sheer bigotry on the part of Imām Ghazālī, who is concerned that the writings of these two scholars might mislead some readers and corrupt their minds. If a work is to be condemned on the basis of this criterion, what are we to say about this statement of the Almighty where the phrase *yuḍillu bihi kathīran* is used about the Qur'ān?[4] Furthermore, it is extremely timid and diffident of a scholar with the stature of Imām Ghazālī to dread a confrontation between Islam and philosophy. Is Islam really such a feeble religion that it cannot face the philosophical sciences? Is it really possible to buttress the edifice of Islam by suppressing freedom of opinion and expression by issuing edicts of infidelity? Certainly not! Such measures always fail in achieving their aim and result in giving a boost to the opposition." When I look at the stagnation of Islamica, I find it difficult to share Mumtāz 'Alī's optimism, and am tempted to replace his "Certainly not!" with "Apparently yes".

kufr: infidelity

The Deobandīs, who may be called the early Jihādī's in the subcontinent, were revitalized in this role, after the Soviet invasion of Afghanistan, as a result of receiving support from many sources in and outside Pakistan. The Ṭalibān sprang from a Deobandī *madrasa* in Akora. The vast majority of sectarian killings in Pakistan have been attributed to Deobandīs [118]. They rejoice in fomenting sectarian hatred because, as noted (in the context of racism) by Ashley Montague in *Man's Most Dangerous Myth* [119] and by Aldous Huxley in the preface to the book, human beings have a desire to act aggressively, and the members of other sects (or ethnic groups) are convenient victims, whom one may attack, when egged on by a religious decree, without any qualms. The pleasure delivered by such acts of extreme agression is comparable to that derived from a drinking bout or sexual orgy, whereas toleration, cooperation and altruism can at best provide a gentle emotional uplift.

---

[4]My footnote: The phrase *yuḍillu bihi kathīran* (يُضِلُّ بِهِ كَثِيرًا) occurs in verse (2:26) of the Qur'ān, which speaks of Allāh making many go astray and leading many to the right path.

We have now answered the question, "Who are those whom Ghazālī inspires to stand up and be counted, and what songs do they sing?" There was enough diversity in early Islam for Ibn Sīnā and Ibn Rushd to be able to find patrons who did not demand devoutness and purity of faith in addition to thirst for knowledge. But the philosophers have lost the ideological battle, and the vast majority of contemporary Muslims have inherited Ghazālī's zeal, his ideals and his intolerance, his uncompromising faith and his deep distrust of innovations. Their world view is impregnated with the dogma and superstition left by Ghazālī in the pages of *Iḥyā'*. The devotees of Khayyām and the fans of Ab'ul-'Alā al-Ma'arrī [78, pp. 289–93] have been silenced—for the moment.

Any school of thought which finds it necessary to create hatred between its followers and other sections of the society or other nations and religions, instead of encouraging their common development through cooperation and coalescence of interests to the benefit of all, is misguided, for the world of today needs, as much as or more than it ever has, constructive ideas of development and cooperation, not antagonism and destruction.

Ghazālī—the Imām of the unlearned

What seems to weigh most heavily on Ghazālī's mind is his fear that inquisitive young persons with impressionable minds might desert his camp and join the party of the philosophers—all infidels and heresiarchs, in his opinion—and he also knows that the zealots on his side, when they argue with the philosophers, are not properly equipped for the battle. He feels that he has saved Islam by proving conclusively that the philosophers "are infidels and that the killing of those who uphold their beliefs is obligatory" [120, p. 226].

Ghazālī was wrong to think that the pursuit of mathematics and logic inevitably leads to a loss of faith. Leonhard Euler, one of the great mathematicians of all times, "was a believer in God, downright and straightforward" [121, p. 250], and so was Kurt Gödel, a super heavyweight logician [122, p. 56]. The real antidote to desertion and the only means of preventing well-intentioned but ignorant Muslims from giving a bad name to Islam, it need hardly be said, is to produce, within the faithful, scholars who command the respect of their adversaries. Since conditions in Ghazālī's time, and even several centuries after him, were not particularly conducive to converting the ignorant masses into learned logicians, skilled scientists, and proficient physicians, he opted for the easier alternative of proscribing philosophy, and welcoming the masses to his camp. They came—in their hundreds of millions, but the Islam he revived is the faith of the unlearned, of those who define *'ulūm* as he did; their Islam includes neither al-Fārābi, nor Ibn Sīna, nor Ibn Rushd, nor Khayyām; nor is there any place in this Islam for the great Ṣūfī Ibn al-'Arabī [123], for he does not believe in the physical hell which so terrifies Ghazālī and his flock. If we apply Ghazālī's criteria for deciding who is a true believer, deniers of miracles must also be left out, and we must be willing to excommunicate well-nigh all the scientific grandees currently counted as Muslims. The gallery of Islamican scientists of the glorious past would be left, like the present gallery, with pygmies whose traces are all but lost in the shadows of their towering, excommunicated intellectual giants.

Senescence and demise of Arabophone science

The scientific enterprise of Islamica, a colossal international activity, could hardly be expected to have withered in the brief span of one or two decades, but would it have taken as long as four centuries for Ghazālī's influence to wipe out science from the minds and courts of Muslim potentates? Ghazālī died in the beginning of the twelfth century, and Islamican science lingered for another four centuries, although great scientists became extinct much earlier; the demolition of the Istanbul observatory in 1580, ordered not by an enemy conqueror but by the resident Ottoman Sultan (see p. 70), was the last nail in the coffin of Arabophone science. In Sabra's opinion, Ghazālī's role in the decline of science in Islamica has been exaggerated, and blaming Ghazālī diverts attention from what still requires an explanation [124]: "the fact that science and philosophy continued to exist and develop in Islam for many centuries, despite the uninterrupted opposition." Solving this mystery is much easier than restoring a Rubik's cube to its starting, perfectly ordered, configuration. Sabra's opinion is shared by many others, amongst whom I will only mention Gutas and Walbridge.

One of the longest sections in the *Muqaddimah* is that dealing with forecasting the future of dynasties and other predictions of this nature [41, Vol. 2, pp. 200–31]. The first paragraph of Rosenthal's translation ends with the remark 'Stories of soothsayers being approached by rulers and commoners alike, with the request for prediction are well known', and the third starts with the comment 'Rulers and amirs who want to know the duration of their own dynasty show the greatest concern for these things and the greatest curiosity in them'. Though the Arabs had their own soothsayers and diviners, astrologers joined this group, the *Muqaddimah* tells us, only after the first wave of translation [41, Vol. 2, p. 203]: "Matters concerning royal authority and dynasties and all other matters of general importance were considered as depending on the conjunctions of the stars. Nativities and interrogations and all other private matters were considered to depend on people's "ascendants"—that is, on the constellations of the firmament at the time when (these matters) were brought up." Ibn Khaldūn's own attitude may be inferred from the following remark [41, Vol. 2, pp. 224–5]: "I have also heard that in the East there are other prediction works. They are attributed to Avicenna and Ibn ʿAqb. They contain no indication whatever that (their contents) are correct, because (correct predictions) can be derived only from astral conjunctions."

It does not seem outrageous to suggest that all the Islamican rulers, however cultured or however barbaric, patronized profane scholarship because each such ruler wanted to have at his beck and call experts in two specialities: one, a medicine man, for preparing curative potions, and the other, a mathematical wizard, for predicting the future, and often the same man performed both roles. That nujūmology and medicine (the lion's share of science and philosophy in that era) continued to be patronized long after Ghazālī's departure is hardly a matter for surprise. As pointed out by Browne [125, p. 5], science (which meant mainly alchemy, nujūmology, and mathematics) and philosophy "were so closely connected with medicine that the title *Ḥakīm* was, and still is, indifferently applied alike to the metaphysician and the physician". The study of medicine was intimately linked with the motions of the sun and the planets, because a mystic link was believed to exist between the various bodily organs and the signs of the zodiac. A man's complexion, his character and temperament, his success or failure, all depended upon where the sun and planets were in a particular sign of the zodiac. Furthermore, because health and disease were also dependent on the stars and planets, nujūmology was a fundamental study for anyone who wanted to become a physician. Indeed, most remedies were administered according to the planetary configurations. By observing the stars a physician was supposed to be able to tell whether a patient was likely to recover, and by the phases of the moon whether or not he should be bled.

According to E. G. Browne, Ghazālī was the theologian who did more than anyone else to bring to an end the reign of philosophy in Islam, and to replace it with a 'devotional mysticism which is at once the highest expression and the clearest limitation' of the orthodox Muslim doctrine [78, p. 293]. Elsewhere Browne also stated that while the Golden Age of Islamican science and literature was the "first century or two of the ʿAbbāsid Caliphate of Baghdad (i.e. from a.d. 750 onwards), a high level of culture continued to be maintained until the awful catastrophe of the Mongol or Tartar invasion of the thirteenth century inflicted on it a blow from which it has never recovered".

Since this diagnosis of the decline of Arabophone science has been disputed by Walbridge and Gutas, it seems necessary to examine their arguments for dissension. Walbridge dismisses the devastation caused by the Mongols [126, p. 98–9]:

> [**1**] The barbarian invasion theory is undermined by the fact that one of the greatest efflorescences of Islamic science took place precisely under the barbarians who had inflicted the greatest damage on Islamic civilization: the Mongol Īl-Khānid state, which supported the Marāgha observatory in the third quarter of the thirteenth century. Naṣīr al-Dīn Tūsī, the great Shiʿite philosopher and scientist, was able to convince the Īl-Khān Hülegü to underwrite the compilation of a new set of astronomical tables to allow more accurate astrological predictions. These funds allowed Ṭūsī

efflorescence: a flowering or bursting forth

> to bring together the finest team of scientists ever assembled in the Islamic world. These astronomers and mathematicians revolutionized Islamic mathematical astronomy, creating a tradition of mathematical astronomy that lasted for at least two hundred and fifty years in the Islamic world and were the sources for Copernicus's mathematical methods. [**2**] Finally, although Western Europe was largely free of barbarian invasions, at least after the Vikings had become rulers rather than plunderers, the Middle Ages saw constant feudal warfare, and the Scientific Revolution itself took place amidst the religious warfare of the Reformation.

I have inserted numbers within square brackets to enable me to refer individually to the two points in the above text.

The argument against the barbarian invasion theory presented under point **1** simply does not hold water. I have already explained why nujūmology was not neglected by most rulers, and Ṭūsī's example illustrates my point so well that I feel justified in spending some time on him. True, the Īl-Khān Hülegü (also Hulāgu) established for Ṭūsī in 1259 the observatory of Marāgha in Adharbaijān, equipping it with the very best instruments and an immense library, but Ṭūsī was not any old astronomer whom the Mongol war-lord happened to spot on the banks of a river.

Quhistān: literally mountain-land, at present the southern part of eastern Iran; the region was the heartland of Isma'īlī rule

Born in Ṭūs, Naṣīr al-Dīn (hereafter NaD) Ṭūsī (1202–1274) entered the employ of the Isma'īlī governor in Quhistān, and was later sent by him to Alamūt to work for Imām 'Alā' al-Dīn Muhammad, the Grand Master of the Isma'īlī faith, and his successor Rukn al-Dīn (RaD) Khūrshāh. He remained at Alamūt as an honoured (albeit involuntary) guest until the Mongol invasion of the region. During his stay at Alamūt, he is supposed to have converted from Shī'ism to the Isma'īlī faith. Ṭūsī persuaded RaD that his best plan was to avoid bloodshed and surrender himself and his fortresses to Hülegü. Soon after the surrender, RaD was put to death, but Ṭūsī won the respect and confidence of Hülegü, on whom he seems to have exercised enormous influence. Hülegü used to consult Ṭūsī as to whether or no the stars were favourable for an undertaking. Before ransacking Baghdad in 1258 Hülegü commanded the astrologer whom the Grand Khan, his brother, had given him, to choose days propitious for action of all sorts. This man, a co-religionist of the Caliph, predicted six great calamities should Mongols lay siege to the capital of Islam [127, pp. 96–8]. Hülegü summoned NaD Ṭūsī and asked him if these predictions would come true, and the sage assured him that no heavenly retribution would ensue if the Caliph were put to death. The continuation of the astronomical tradition of Islamica was the result of this extraordinary conjunction of a worldly-wise scientific genius and a heathen despot who, in his eagerness to procure sound astrological advice, was willing to provide unstinting support for the collection of more reliable astronomical data.

As a preamble to examining the merit of point **2**, I recall that Nicolaus Copernicus (1473–1543), though not an ordained priest, was a churchman, the canon of Frauenberg [128, p. 42]. He procrastinated with the publication of his book *De Revolutionibus* because he feared ridicule rather than ecclesiastical censure. In fact, he had been encouraged by the top brass in the Vatican to publish his hypothesis; he dedicated *De Revolutionibus* to Pope Paul III, and included an appreciative letter from Cardinal Schönberg (written in November 1536) in which the Cardinal urged Copernicus to publish his new theory of the universe. Initially, only the Protestants heaped insults on the heliocentric scheme. The Catholic church was not opposed to the study of astronomy, and was prepared to accept any hypothesis or theory which accounted satisfactorily for the observations, so long as its proponent did not confuse its verisimilitude with verity, which was to be found only in the Scriptures. Christopher Clavius, the driving force behind the 1582 calendar sanctioned by Pope Gregory XIII, was a Jesuit priest and a leading astronomer of his time. Though Clavius remained opposed to the heliocentric model, he admitted, after confirming Galileo's revolutionary findings through his own telescopic observations, that the Ptolemaic arrangement of the planets was untenable [129].

To address the thrust of point **2**, let us note that Putnam's *Four Hundred Years of Freethought* provides an explanation (plausible, in my opinion) of why the Reformation, lurid and destructive as it was, turned out to be a stroke for liberty [130, Ch. 5]. Putnam writes: "The Reformation was as relentless as Rome in its own way—but still it was better, and also by its opposition made Rome better. I doubt if science could have so grandly won its way if the despotic unity of Rome had not been destroyed and its very existence involved in a life-and-death struggle for political power" [130, p. 47]. He offers several reasons, among them the three discussed below.

First, the Reformation helped science not so much by explicitly supporting it, but by precipitating the world of Europe into a mortal struggle on theological questions, thereby diverting the attention of authority to a certain extent from the happenings in the theater of science, where the actors pursued their enquiries, as in the case of Newton, somewhat unobtrusively, and won their splendid victories without the Church apparently realizing their vast significance—and when the Church fathers finally found the time to turn their gaze on these fields and wanted to supervise the proceedings as of old, it was too late, the genie was out of the bottle, the scientific genii had won their independence, and the *Principia* had already taken the intellectual world by storm.

Second, the Reformation came after the invention of the printing press, which became an instrument of war in the hands of Luther, who used it to strike a terrific blow at Rome from which it has never recovered. Rome, which would have burned every printing press if it had had the power, wanted no channel of communication with the people other than the pulpit mounted by an accredited priest. The power of the pulpit was the bulwark of Rome, whereas the printing-press was the salvation of Luther, and he could not have won without its power to arouse vast masses of people—and to give them an opportunity to judge for themselves. The Ottoman Empire opposed the printing of texts in Arabic script until 1729, and even then the permission excluded religious texts [131].

Third, Luther's decision to translate the Bible into the common language and give it to the pople was a master stroke, an immense advance for liberty. No matter what the Bible is in itself, its wide distribution in the time of Luther, accompanied by an appeal to private judgment was the source of a tremendous agitation. It brought into play forces of revolution that Luther and his princes could not control. As Luther dissented from Rome, and Zwingly dissented from Luther, it was inevitable that there should be dissent and protest everywhere. The era of individuality had set in, and Luther could not direct its currents according to his wishes. It swept beyond him, beyond the power of any man, any church. There arose numberless sects, divisions, separations, strifes, quarrels, which made it plain that there were plenty of private judgments, more than Luther ever bargained for; but it was the logic of the situation. Luther himself might retreat, but the tide went on, and the waves of controversy multiplied, and there was no knowing what course the river of human thought was going to take. One of the earliest versions of the Qur'ān for the use of non-Arab Muslims was published in 1790, and a Turkish translation was not available even as late as 1915 [132].

Since Walbridge has more to say, let us continue examining the case presented by him [126, p. 98–9]:

> The second theory, positing an innate Islamic hostility towards science, has similar problems. Those advocating it tend to contrast Eastern scholastic rationalism with a supposed antirationalism in Islam. **[3]** As evidence, they cite a small set of well-known texts, especially Ghazālī's *Deliverer from Error* [*Munqidh*], in which Muslim theologians condemn science and philosophy. Because of this hostility, they claim, natural science and mathematics were excluded from the *madrasa* curriculum. But it is difficult to argue that Ghazālī's book was either typical or decisive, and **[4]** the pinnacle of Islamic astronomy came after, not before, Ghazālī. Few other such texts exist, and in contrast to the situation in Europe, prosecutions for heresy were rare. **[5]** The Islamic world produced no martyrs for science like Bruno and Galileo. Muslims, by and large, cared more about whether people practiced the laws of Islam than about the nuances of their beliefs. **[6]** Moreover, as later recorded curricula show, science actually was taught—on a basic level at least. **[7]** Mathematics was needed to divide inheritances, which religious lawyers were required to do, and astronomy was needed for mosque timekeeping. Manuscripts on geometry, arithmetic, algebra, basic astronomy, advanced mathematical astronomy, and the construction and use of astrolables are common. Manuscript anthologies of *madrasa* textbooks routinely contain works on astronomy and mathematics. **[8]** Medical manuscripts are everywhere. **[9]** As we will see in Chapter 9, Islamic reformers, Islamic revivalists, and colonial administrators of the nineteenth century were united in their complaints that *madrasa* education was too rationalistic and scholastic.

Had the author of the above passage been a Martian, it would have been easy to sympathize with his ignorance of the *madrasa* tradition on a far off planet, with his inability to differentiate between the contents of a syllabus adopted by an institution and the knowledge acquired by students trained by that institution. The author, nominally from our planet, is hopelessly out of touch with history and present reality, and has somehow convinced himself that he understands Islam's difficult, ambivalent relationship with science and secular knowledge. Some facts, listed below as replies to points **3–8**, might serve as the antidote to this delusion:—

3 For exposing Ghazālī's antipathy to science, I have chosen *Iḥyā'*, one of the most important books in the world of Islam.

acme: culminating point, apex, peak

4 The acme of "Islamic astronomy" was reached in the custom-built Marāgha observatory, funded by the Mongol infidel Hülagü, and the director of the laboratory was Ṭūsī, the regenerate Twelver Shī'ah (who pretended for a while to be a Sevener Isma'īlī), judged to be an infidel by Ibn Taymiyyah, in whose eyes the *Twelvers* and the *Seveners* (Appendix E defines these terms) were equally eligible for decapitation.

5 It would be more correct to say that we have no properly documented cases of Islamican persecution of secular scholars. This is absence of evidence, not evidence of absence. What happened, at the instigation of the then *Shaykh al-Islam*, to the Ottoman astronomer Taqī al-Dīn (Takiyuddin) [133] in the late sixteenth century [134–136] bears a close parallel to how Galileo was treated by the Church of Rome. Furthermore, Ghazālī did pass death sentences on Fārābī and Ibn Sīnā and whoever agrees with them.

6 As for the curricula, there is a world of difference between including a subject in the syllabus and laying stress on it, making it plain to the students that it has not been put there as an embellishment, a ploy for fooling a gullible onlooker who lacks first-hand experience of the distinction between shadow and substance and scans through the syllabus.

7 A calculation involving inheritance matters does not always reduce to solving a purely mathematical problem, which always has a unique answer. Consider a man who leaves behind seventeen camels, three sons and the following will: "Divide my camels in such a manner that my eldest son gets one-half of them, the second gets one-third, and the youngest gets one-ninth of the total number of camels." Mathematically, the problem admits no solution (at least, if no camel was to loose its life) because seventeen, being a prime number, is divisible only by itself and by unity, but a *qaḍī* or an *imām* must come up with a solution that appears to be in accordance with both the terms of the will and the rules of arithmetic.[5]

When Muḥammad bin Mūsā al-Khwārizmī wrote, at the behest of Mā'mūn, a popular book on algebra, he wisely decided to confine it "to what is easiest and most useful in arithmetic, such as men constantly require in cases of inheritance, legacies, partition, law-suits, and trade, and in all their dealings with one another, or where the measuring of lands, the digging of canals, geometrical computation" [59, p. 3], and he was aware of the fact, not fully appreciated by his English translator [137], that the rules of religion must take precedence over those of arithmetic. Someone who could understand this book and calculate legacies was engaged in accountancy, not mathematics.[6] Advances in mathematics often come by asking and answering questions which have no obvious applications at first. Was the *madrasa* climate such as to keep its students and teachers abreast of the latest developments in mathematics, astronomy and physics (see below)? Only those who keep abreast can make advances, leaving the others to either atrophy or to petrify. Precise time-keeping (chronometry) is

---

[5]I have not made up this problem. If you type *hazrat ali mathematics*, you will find that the "solution" of this conundrum is widely attributed to ʿAlī bin Abū Ṭālib. If the attribution is correct, one must admire the great man's presence of mind and feel sorry at the puerility of his admirers.

[6]Shiblī, whose admiration for the scholars patronized by Mā'mūn knew no bounds (see p. 29), reveals his limitations by the following remark [24, p. 48]: This book [of al-Khwārizmī] is so exhaustive and well-organized (*jāmiʿ aur murattab*) that later Islamic scholars, though they wrote hundreds of excellent books on algebra, made no further progress in solving real problems (*aṣl masā'il*).

not to be equated with determining the times of prayer. There is no room for astronomical calculations in the orthodox view of fixing the times of sunrise and sunset, important for fasting purposes; this aspect will be discussed in Chapter 3.

Sufi has traced the evolution of the Islamic curriculum in the madrasas of the Indian subcontinent [138], and Robinson [139, 140] has compared the curricula followed in the Ottoman empire (around 1600) and in the Safavid and Mughal empires (both around 1700). I leave it to the reader to verify that the astronomy and mathematics texts do not go beyond NaD Ṭūsī. This means that the students did not hear of Copernicus, nor did they know that some Bolognese algebraists had succeeded, by finding the general solution to the cubic equation, in solving a problem that no Islamican mathematician of the time was capable of doing; that by solving quartic equations, the Europeans had entered a territory whose existence was inconceivable to Khayyām.[7] Did anyone think of including Kepler, Galileo and Newton in the madrasa curricula. According to Adnan Adivar [143], only Muḥammad II (1432–81) showed a genuine interest in science, but dogma gained the upper hand after him: "During the two and a half centuries that passed between the conquest of Constantinople [by Muḥammad II] and the Treaty of Carlowitz (1699), Turkish armies marched on to central Europe, establishing contacts with Western nations; but these military incursions failed to bring about intellectual contact between the two worlds. On the contrary, the critical spirit of modern times, that is of the Renaissance, retreated before the dogmatic spirit which then reigned supreme in the lands of Islam." Safavid and Mughal kings were no more inclined towards the sciences than their Ottoman counterparts.

Had a late sixteenth century Muslim monarch realized that the need of the hour was a second round of translation in the Mā'mūn manner, Macaulay would have been de-

[7]Guided by a geometrical outlook, Khayyām considered the square of a square to be a quantity that is not measurable [141, 142].

nied the opportunity to jeer at Oriental learning by speaking of "medical doctrines, which would disgrace an English farrier,—astronomy, which would move laughter in the girls at an English boarding-school,—history, abounding with kings thirty feet high, and reigns thirty thousand years long,—and geography, made up of seas of treacle and seas of butter" [144, p. 402].

8 Medical manuscripts might have been *everywhere*, but Muslim physicians were *nowhere* in evidence. Even Ghazālī lamented the dearth of Muslim men of medicine (see p. 194). In his discussion of the various branches of knowledge, Ibn Khaldūn includes medicine [41, Vol. 3, pp. 148–51], mentions four great Mulsim physicians, remarks that in "contemporary Muslim cities, the craft of medicine seems to have deteriorated", and warns against relying on what has come to be called *ṭibb al-nabawī* (Prophet's Medicine). E. G. Browne quoted these remarks approvingly, and added [125, p. 13]: "I am informed that a manual so entitled is still one of the first books read by the student of the Old Medicine in India, along with the abridgment of Avicenna's *Qānūn* known as *Qānūncha.*"

9 Why would an Islamic *reformer* oppose a rationalistic curriculum? Whether this is true or not, the reformers (from eighteenth century onwards) were as ignorant of the scientific advances as the people they wanted to reform. How could the blind lead the blind?

Walbridge has suggested that "mysticism played a role in directing the attention of Islamic scholars and philosophers away from physical science" [126, p. 101]. And, pray, who made mysticism respectable in Islam? We already know what E. G. Browne had to say about this issue (see p. 65), but I'll now let Walbridge answer the question [126, p. 101]: "[Ghazālī] found . . . peace and certainty in Sufism. Retiring to his home town, he wrote his greatest work, *The Revival of the Sciences of Religion*, an explanation of Islamic law in which the legal concepts are explained in terms of Sufism. Although Ghazālī can scarcely be given credit for an intellectual development that probably was inevitable, he does symbolize the integration of mysticism into the mainstream of Islamic intellectual life." Now, can Walbridge, who suggests that mysticism played a role in removing the limelight from science, and concedes that it was Ghazālī who integrated mysticism and Islam, escape the conclusion that Ghazālī contributed to the decline of Islamican science?

I turn now to Gutas, who mentions, among other factors, the following [57, p. 171]:

> The Mongol invasions of Syria after 1258 and especially their siege of Damascus in 699/1300, which simply exacerbated a bad situation and called for a more aggressive ideological attitude—hence Ibn-Taymiyya, who played an active role in the Mongol-Syrian negotiations, and hence the return to a "conservative" traditionalism, championed by the Ḥanbalīs and the reconstructed or reformed Ash'arism of Shāfi'ī scholars after al-Ghazālī.
>
> Why, then, are these scholars identified as members of the "old" orthodoxy, and why are such views, generated in societies under extreme pressure, supposed to represent "Islamic" orthodoxy? For the historical record, consulted in its entirety, is otherwise, and [we are told about the flourishing, in the heartland of orthodoxy, of a brilliant physician and a consummate astronomer, whose models reappear two centuries later in the work of Copernicus] ...

I must say that if I could differentiate between the old and the new orthodoxy, I would not be complaining about the stagnation of the Muslim world. How can anyone tell a stick-in-the-mud literalist of the ninth century from a diehard literalist of the fourteenth or even the current century? They all insist on the etrnality of the Qur'ān, and on interpreting its text literally, which means that the bulk of the Muslim population regards the Qur'ān not only as an ethical book but also a scientific treatise and a record of history (see the next two chapters). As for the facts listed by Gutas under the "historical record", it would be enough to recall what has been said above concerning the patronage of physicians and astronomers (in response to similar statements by Walbridge).

Gutas finds it unreasonable to decry the utterances of leaders in times of intense political excitement, especially if the community sees itself as under siege, but what is one to do if the leaders are always under pressure. Ghazālī thought that Islam was taking its last breath in front of his eyes, Ibn Tamiyyah felt beleaguered two centuries later [145], and no Muslim leader today feels differently from the boorish boatswain in the following story, related in a different context by De Morgan [121, p. 40]: The officer reproved the boatswain for perpetual swearing, and the latter replied that he heard the officers swear. "Only in an emergency," said the officer, which elicited the rejoinder *"That's just it, a boatswain's life is a life of emergency"*.

boatswain: a petty officer in a ship

The soma of Islamica?

The people of *Brave New World* avoided glumness with the help of *soma*, a psychoactive drug described as having all "the advantages of Christianity and alcohol [but] none of their defects" [146, p. 53]; a double dose of the drug was sufficient to raise "a quite impenetrable wall between the actual universe and their minds" [146, p. 69]. What nostrum kept the Islamicans of the sixteenth and seventeenth centuries smug and satisfied, inebriated with the military and intellectual achievements of their Muslim forbears, blissfully oblivious of what was happening outside Islamica? A soporific mixture of "pastoxication" (a morbid occupation with past splendour) and an insouciant insularity (the belief that whatever was taking place outside Islamica was not worth taking note of) became the *soma* of Islamica.[8]

As interest in genuine scientific learning waned, an obsession with pseudo-scholarship and the occult filled the vacuum. It is interesting to read Ibn Khaldūn's discussion of "various kinds of intellectual sciences" [41, Vol. 3, pp. 111–227], and to see what he includes and how much space is devoted to each "science". One is not surprised to find there mathematics, physics, medicine, agriculture, and metaphysics, and these topics occupy fewer than fifty pages; some seventy pages are devoted to the occult sciences, described under sections on "the science of sorcery and

[8]Muslims are not the only victims of pastoxication. During a visit to Greece (around 1980), the physicist Richard Feynman noted that the Greeks seemed to live under the yoke of ancestor worship, and had still not managed to shake off their adulation of the past [147, pp. 94–5].

talismans" and "the science of the secret of letters", the first of which discusses the evil eye, and the second provides a detailed description of magic squares. No observatories or laboratories were needed for cultivating the occult sciences; nor was royal patronage necessary. Their practitioners provided their services to grateful clients for payment in cash or kind. The science of magic squares reached its zenith around 1100, and subsequent "progress" consisted mainly in exploiting the putative magical properties and applications of these squares [148]. An excellent record of the mingling of magic squares, alchemy and stone-age superstition may be seen in an early nineteenth century book by a Muslim author [149], later re-issued in 1921 [150].

The spell of Ghazālī

Karl Popper gave the title "The Spell of Plato" to the first volume of *The Open Society and its Enemies* [151], and began his preface with some sombre words: "If in this book harsh words are spoken about some of the greatest among the intellectual leaders of mankind, my motive is not, I hope, the wish to belittle them. It springs rather from my conviction that if we wish our civilization to survive we must break with the habit of deference to great men." He put Plato at the head of those leaders of the past whose ideas have provoked perennial attacks on freedom and reason, whose influence, too rarely challenged, continues to mislead large sections of mankind and divide them. Writing at the end of the Second World War, Popper was evidently thinking of only the Western world.

When I ascribe the demise of Arabophone science and the stagnation of Islamica to one individual, namely Ghazālī, the author of *Iḥyā'*, I do not mean that it was all Ghazālī's doing. The lessons taught in *Iḥyā'*—antipathy to science and rationality, respect for and belief in superstitions, magic, talismans, and the evil eye, advocacy of intolerance, aversion to freedom of expression, avowal of harsh punishments and denial of equal status to women—did not originate with Ghazālī. The purpose of *Iḥyā'* was to *revive*, not invent, what its author thought to be true Islamic teachings.

To say, as Sabra and others have done (p. 64), that Ghazālī's role in the decline of Islamican science has been exaggerated is to miss the point. Ghazālī is merely the most successful exponent of a cluster of regressive and divisive ideas, the most-listened-to performer in a long line of pipers, who, by playing the same tenebrous tune, have led successive generations of Muslims into the abyss where superstition and ignorance pass for faith and learning. The stagnation and putrefaction of the Muslim world should be imputed to all these pipers, every one of whom is a reincarnated Ghazālī. These protectors and preservers of traditions, whom I will henceforth call *priests*,[9] are found in all echelons of a Muslim society, even though, in theory, formal priesthood and Islam are as immiscible in practice as oil and water are. In the next chapter, we will meet one representative of this group, and we will find that, though he "flourished" in the twentieth century, he thought like Ghazālī.

tenebrous: dark, gloomy, shadowy

Macdonald, who held Ghazālī in high esteem, began winding up his chapter on Ghazālī with the following words [75, p. 141]: "So much space it has been necessary to give to this great man. Islam has never outgrown him, has never fully understood him. In the renaissance of Islam which is now rising to view his time will come and the new life will proceed from a renewed study of his works".

I would like to finish with exactly the same words, but then I would risk, for want of some additional remarks, misleading my readers, and it is a writer's obligation not to do so consciously; I must therefore add some comments of my own to each of Macdonald's sentences.

So much space it has been necessary to give to this great man of the past. Much to its detriment, Islam has never outgrown him, has never fully understood how damaging his influence has been. In the renaissance of Islam which everyone has been waiting for (and heralded by the optimist Macdonald already in 1903), the time for judging him will come, but a better new life will proceed only from a proper study and critical evaluation of his works, which cannot but condemn his books to the dusty shelves of history.

---

[9]Some of their more common titles and appellations are listed and explained in Appendix D.

3 — *To Regress or to Egress?*

Nearly all Muslims who give any thought at all to the dismal state of the Ummah (worldwide community of Muslims) agree that Islam is in need of a major reform. However, their prescriptions for curing the current ills of the Muslim world cover the widest possible spectrum, ranging all the way from a return to the pristine faith preached and practised by the Prophet (and the first four Caliphs) to the other extreme of forging a new version compatible with the values shared by all the great religions, at peace with science, and mindful of human rights, as enshrined in the Universal Declaration of Human Rights.[1] Since everyone who has examined the ailing body of the Ummah thinks of himself as a potential or real reformer, a term based on the root 're-form' will lead to ambiguity, which can be avoided if I call those who favour the first remedy *regressionists* and label those at the other extreme as *egressionists*.

egress: going out, emergence (applicable also to a celestial body exiting an eclipse).

Under the influence of indoctrination and in response to the complexity of modern life and the malaise engulfing Muslim societies, the regressionists believe that other Muslims, gone astray from the simple and straight path shown by the Prophet, should patch up their differences, return to the roots of Islam and create, as did the Prophet and his companions, a society that follows the guidelines laid down in the Holy Qur'ān. Many of them make no bones about emulating, when the circumstances become propitious, their forebears, the early *Mujāhedīns* (or Jihādists, in the current parlance), who offered three choices to the non-Muslim communities they chose to confront [152, p. 141]: convert to Islam and become our equals, or pay a poll tax for keeping your faith while living under Muslim domination, or engage in a battle, and

[1] http://www.un.org/en/documents/udhr/

let the sword be the arbiter. This policy could not continue indefinitely: an expansion that relied solely on the sword had to perish by it in the end, which came when the Muslims could no longer compete with the Christians in mastering the high seas and making powerful, mobile artillery. No one would quarrel with the regressionists if the resurrection of the Caliphate were to involve replacing the sword with the pen and the poll tax with persuasion tempered with a good-humoured acceptance of failure. The use of non-coercive means of converting the misguided into law-abiding co-religionists would endear the regressionists even to those who fail to be persuaded, and the regressionists' success, even if it is stupendous, would not be viewed as a threat—unless the viewer happened to be a competing proselytizer.

To examine the eggressionist viewpoint, we may turn to one of its advocates, S. Khuda Bukhsh, and quote from his essay *Thoughts on the Present Situation*, published in 1912 [153, pp. 219–20]: "The world moves and we move, or, at all events, we should move, with it. ... [we cannot have] any sympathy with the class of men (unfortunately the larger portion of our community belongs to that class) who take it for granted that our religion and our social system admit of no corrective, or call for no improvement. ... It would be the merest affectation to contend that religious and social systems, bequeathed to us thirteen hundred years ago, should now be adopted in their entirety without the slightest change or alteration. This is exactly the battlefield on which for the last fifty years a relentless war has been waged in India between the party of light and hope, and the party which is wedded to the old order of things. Though the God of battle has not yet pronounced His verdict, the signs of the times are clear enough. It is certain that the party opposed to progress has not a very long lease of life left to it. It is doomed and dying, and it might as well reason with the winds or threaten the waves of the sea. New ideas, large formative conceptions, are seething in the intellectual and emotional cauldron of our day."

Regrettably, Khuda Bukhsh's prognosis—that the party opposed to progress was doomed and dying—has turned out to be no more than wishful thinking; whether we like it or not, the opponents of progress are still with us, in large numbers and in no mood to throw in the towel; if anything, they seem to have become, for reasons that are not hard to fathom, more vociferous. The failure of the prognosis and the enduring hold of Muslim priests and pious scholars on the psyche of the Muslim masses owes as much to the inertia of the human mind and the intellectual stagnation of the Islamic world as to the ambivalence of the so-called moderate Muslims towards those who claim to be men of religion.

Secular-religious apartheid

Egypt gained independence in 1922, and became a republic some thirty years later. The British Raj in India ended in 1947 with the partition of the country and the creation of Pakistan, the largest Muslim country in the world until its two wings suffered another partition in 1971. The Dutch accepted Indonesian independence as a *fait accompli* in 1949. The Federation of Malaya, the precursor of Malaysia, became an independent state in 1957. No formal date of independence can be assigned to Iran, but we may take the formation of the Mossadegh government in 1951 as a sign of independence. The period 1950 ± 10 may be called the Dawn of Freedom, the years in which the dream of home rule was fulfilled for most of the Muslim states that had previously been under the yoke of Christian colonialism. In other words, the Muslim world has been running its own affairs for nearly sixty years.

Since India had, until 1947, the largest Muslim population in the world, a portrait of the Indian Muslims in the 1940s would provide at least a rough description of their contemporaries in other Muslim states, if we set aside the contentious issue of the Caliphate in Istanbul, that was dear to many Indian Muslims but anathema to their Arab brethren. A reader curious to become acquainted with Indian Muslims, their attitudes and intellectual movements before independence, is referred to Cantwell Smith's tract *Modern Islam in India* [66]. To form an idea of the social composition of the Muslim world some fifteen years later, we may take the pre-1971 Pakistan as a typical example. In *Research on the Bureaucracy of Pakistan*, Braibanti, who studied the period 1947–65, described the state of affairs in the following words [154, pp. 15–16]:

> The reason for this [lack of a deep respect for scholarship among the bureaucrats] is probably the separation of Muslim intellectual life from secular bureaucratic life. At least three important elites can be identified in Pakistan. They are (1) a religious elite which holds Islamic tradition above other values, (2) the secular oriented military and civil public bureaucracy, and (3) a non-bureaucratic intelligentsia. The latter comprises the professions (of which the most articulate is law), the business community, and those politicians who are secularly oriented. *In Pakistan, there is very little interaction among these three elites; membership in one does not confer membership in another and may even preclude it. The sphere of influence of each of the three elites is detached from the others.* Therefore, the disposition toward intellectuality and respect for learning which may prevail in any one or two of these elites will have minimal influence on the others. (My italics.)

I have interrupted Braibanti to insert a few comments. First, the words *secular* and *secularly oriented*, as used above, should be placed in the local context, where a secular person is one who does not wear his faith on his sleeve, someone who does not wear a long beard for fear that it may be confused with an emblem of his faith. Secondly, the term *elite* is to be interpreted as the power elite rather than the social elite. Lastly, to the best of my knowledge, the gulf between these elites existed also in the Arab world. We return to Braibanti now and continue [154, p. 16]:

> The venerable and sophisticated intellectual tradition of Islam became, on the subcontinent, oriented exclusively to Qur'ānic and Persian scholarship. It sought to preserve its identity by isolating itself from Western learning ... But the significant fact is that the Muslims who entered [civil] service were not themselves the religious elite. The *maulana* and *maulvi* of the traditionalistic Qur'ānic culture was not part of the same elite which wielded bureaucratic power. Hence the intellectuality which characterizes the Muslim component of the ICS and the present bureaucracy of Pakistan derives its strength from the more recent British influence unsustained by the Islamic tradition of learning which continues to flow in a separate stream. Only in the lower clerical reaches or among superintendents and assistants are *maulana* and *maulvi* types to be found. The designations *maulana* and *maulvi,* while highly regarded as

For the meanings of *maulānā* and *maulvī*, see pp. 203–204.

symbols of a traditional way of life, seldom command the same eminence of respectability among the Western-oriented elites as does the term *sensei* among the Japanese.

A few changes, too obvious to require elaboration, are needed before these remarks can be taken over and applied to Muslims outside the subcontinent. The essential point—a premise, if you will—is that the bureaucratic and military elites wielded, in all Muslim states (except Arabic kingdoms, emirates and sultanates), more power than the religious leaders. Looking ahead, Braibanti wrote:

> However valid for the period under discussion, the foregoing description may be made obsolete in a decade or so by significant social changes now taking place. The need for Islam to withdraw and look inward and backward to the real and imagined glories of caliphates of the Middle East disappeared with partition in 1947. Insulation and retrospection as means of preserving Islamic culture in the face of an overwhelming Hindu majority are no longer necessary.

Braibanti's caution cannot be criticized, since the future defies prediction, but we can see, given the benefit of hindsight, that his observations remain valid, on the whole, even after more than four decades. However, we may note some new features that have crept in. First, lawyers and judges may still be the most vocal when we look at the professionals, but they are seldom the smuggest, who are to be found among the managers and directors of multinational corporations. Secondly, in the last four decades, particularly during and after the reign (1977–88) of General Ziā'al-Ḥaq, a part of the military elite must have become de-secularized, and it cannot be ruled out that, within the armed forces, the secular and the non-secular senior officers might bump into each other now and then. In the civilian section, the paths of the religious and secular elites still do not cross (not just in Pakistan but elsewhere also), partly due to the difference in their attitudes to religious matters, but mainly because they inhabit disparate pecuniary strata; the opportunities to exchange views and influence each other during a friendly get-together are really so few and so far between as to be utterly inconsequential.

Does the secular-religious divide have any detrimental consequences for a society where it is endemic? Yes, because it is, or creates, a barrier to the education of one elite by the other, making a society more closed than it need be.

Cricketer and Priest. Cricket and French politics

Readers who happen to be cricket fans and old enough to have taken a keen interest in the game during the 1950's, but not so old as to have suffered severe senile dementia before reading these pages, might recall the name of David Sheppard. Here is a brief sketch of this remarkable individual: David Stuart Sheppard, cricketer and priest: born Reigate (Surrey) 6 March 1929; played cricket for Sussex 1947–62 (Captain 1953) and England 1950–63 (Captain 1954); ordained deacon 1955, priest 1956; Assistant Curate, St Mary's, Islington 1955–57; Warden, Mayflower Centre, Canning Town 1957–69; Bishop of Woolwich 1969–75; Bishop of Liverpool 1975–97; retired in 1997 and received a life peerage the following year; died West Kirby, Merseyside 5 March 2005. His obituary in the *Independent* stated [155]: "Of the 13 clergymen known to have made a mark in English cricket history, including one who was the great-grandson of Charles II and Nell Gwyn and another who founded the Hambledon club, only David Sheppard achieved an England cap, writes Derek Hodgson. While he might have become Primate of All England [that is, Archbishop of Canterbury and the principal leader of the Church of England] he could also have captained England for a long spell [instead of only two matches] and been elected President of MCC."

Now, the citizens of an open society get their formal education (or training for a vocation) from schools and colleges and their informal education from other sources: family, friends, neighbours, colleagues, travel companions, media. During the course of one's life, one can learn, from these sources, a little about some of the things which others find interesting: mushroom picking, music, philately, photography, fishing, rock climbing, party politics, ...

In the 1970s, the members of the research group to which I belonged (as a postdoctoral fellow) used to visit a local pub for lunch, where one could eat and watch whatever was being displayed on the screen of a large television set, usually some sporting event. In the summer of 1974, a visiting cricket team played a series of test matches against England, and we all intently watched the proceedings as we munched our sandwiches and gulped our drinks. Out of my loyalty to the game and to my friend Jean-Paul, a French postdoctoral fellow (the only member of the group who knew nothing about the game), I did my best to explain, day in and day out, the mysteries of this arcane ritual to him. Towards the end of the summer, with scores of such lunch time lessons stored in his head, an incident, perhaps a run-out or a stumping, no longer vivid in my memory but consequential for those who were playing or following the match, caught his attention, he turned towards me and, before I could make any comments, exclaimed, "You know, I now *understand* the rules of cricket!".

I also used to discuss with Jean-Paul (but not when we were absorbed in cricket) the likely outcome of another engrossing contest, the French presidential election, which turned out to be a very close run between Valéry Giscard d'Estaing, and François Mitterrand. Although I was ineligible, both I and Jean-Paul, who was going to cast his vote, hoped for a socialist victory. One day, Jean-Paul told me that his father had come round, after a lifelong aversion to socialism, to voting for the socialist Mitterand. When I asked the reason for this change of heart, he told me that his father felt that if his son was going to vote for them, the socialists could not have been such demons as he had imagined them to be.

One seldom concedes an argument, especially when it does not lie in the scientific domain, after a tedious and heated debate with an adversary, and probably no one changes his mind if an issue is examined in a gathering where everyone starts with the same opinion, and there is no incentive for revising this opinion. A change of opinion is more likely to occur gradually, after one has repeatedly discussed a contentious matter in the relaxed atmosphere of a home, a cafeteria or a cricket pavilion.

David Sheppard, an ardent opponent of apartheid, must have discussed the sports boycott of white South Africa and many other matters related to theology, politics and sports with his fellow cricketers, and carried their opinions, at least subconsciously, to his fellow clergymen. Eventually he and other advocates of the boycott succeeded in persuading the British public to ostracize South African sports, and this boycott did help in some measure towards the eventual downfall of the apartheid regime.

The twenty-first century regressionists

Any reader of this book can easily find reports that would substantiate my claim that the regressionists abound even in the current century. Since Khuda Bukhsh was concerned with the Indian situation, it would not be improper to continue with the subcontinent, and refer to a news item that appeared in the *Hindustan Times*. As late as 2006, Dr Kalbe Sadiq (Kalbé Ṣādiq), a reform-minded Muslim cleric in India, blamed the "Mullahs" for destroying Islam [156]. He stated, while delivering a lecture on 'Islam versus Muslims', that these tradition-bound priests had tarnished the image of Islam in the past and were still hampering progress by issuing "ridiculous fatwas".

fatwa (or *fetwa*): religious edict

An example of the divide between Dr Sadiq and his regressionist opponents is the dispute concerning the implementation of a purely lunar religious calendar.

Sighting of the crescent

The months of the Islamic calendar being lunar and the first day of each month being ascertained by the actual appearance of the new crescent on the night sky, uncertainty as to the true day on which the month began might and indeed does arise, culminating occasionally in bitter disputes. In principle a disagreement about the visibility of the crescent need not ruffle anyone's feathers, because every believer who trusts his eyesight is free to place more confidence in his observation than that of a neighbour, but since the observance of important religious occasions (a festival or a period of mourning) depends on the sighting of the crescent, communal cohesion is threatened when Muslims fail to agree on a common date. When Dr Sadiq, an advocate of fixing the Islamic calendar by using astronomical calculations, announced the dates of the first and the last day of *Ramaḍān* (the month of fasting), the Lucknow Moon Committee opposed him, and called his standpoint "un-Islamic", since, the General Secretary of the committee explained, "there were certain guidelines in Islam about sighting the moon and these could not be ignored". The Secretary revealed his antipathy to science by stating that visual evidence was paramount because "scientific predictions might prove wrong"; one cannot tell whether he meant human error (in performing the calculation) or the imprecision of observations, and he probably did not know that the former can be made highly improbable by taking the necessary precautions, and the latter is too small to be of any practical significance. He may even have meant (perish the thought!) that the moon might rebel against Newton's law of gravitation. The traditionalists support their stance by referring to the *ḥadīth*, according to which a visual sighting of the new moon is a *sine qua non*. Believing means seeing, they insist.

A Muslim is entitled to maintain that visual sighting of the moon is an indelible part of his faith, but such a Muslim should resist the temptation of adding his voice to the oft-heard claim, rather loud because it is made by so many of the faithful, that Islam is valid at any place and at all times. There are places on this earth where the moon cannot be seen for long periods because the sun does not set for weeks or months.

To watch the sky or to use a watch?

According to the literal interpretation of the Qur'ān, a Muslim is required to fast from dusk to dawn (in the ninth lunar month). In Maudūdī's translation of verse 2:187 we find [157, Vol. 1, p. 147]:[2] "...eat and drink at night until you discern the white streak of dawn against the blackness of night,[193] then (give up all that and) complete your fasting until night sets in.[194]" His comments in the two footnotes (numbered as in Maudūdī's text) are reproduced below:

193. In fixing the time of obligatory rites, Islam has been mindful that these timings should be so clear and simple that people, at all stages of development, should be able to follow them. This is why Islam bases its timing on conspicuous natural phenomena and not on the clock.

[2] This is in fact a translation of Maudūdī's Urdu text.

Some people object that this principle of timing is untenable in areas close to the poles, where night and day each last for about six months. *This objection is based on a very superficial knowledge of geography.* In point of fact neither day nor night lasts for six months in those areas—not in the sense in which people living near the Equator conceive of night and day. The signs of morning and evening appear at the poles with unfailing regularity and it is on this basis that people time their sleeping and waking, their professional work, their play and recreation. *Even in the days before watches were common, the people of countries like Finland, Norway and Greenland used to fix the hours of the day and night by means of various signs that appeared on the horizon.* Just as those signs helped them to determine their schedules in other matters, so they should enable them to time their various Prayers, the pre-fast meal and the breaking of the fast. (My italics.)

194. 'Complete your fasting until night sets in' means that the time of fasting ends with nightfall, i.e. sunset marks the breaking of the fast. The precise time of the end of the pre-dawn repast is when a lean strip of aurora appears at the eastern end of the horizon and begins to grow. The time to break one's fast starts when the darkness of night seems to have begun to appear over the eastern horizon.

I include myself among those who 'object that the principle of timing is untenable in areas close to the poles'. Maudūdī gives the dissenters short shrift by saying that their objection is based on a very superficial understanding of geography, but his own defence of the use of visual signs (instead of clocks) shows, I claim, *no* understanding of geography, and—what is even more reprehensible—no desire to seek and examine the relevant evidence, which is presented in the following sections.

Living at high latitudes

Lying between the 57th and 81st parallel, Norway is rather slender and long, shaped almost like a battered teaspoon (if one is looking at a small size map). Trondheim, a university town, lies between the 63rd and 64th parallel, whereas Tromsø, another university town, is situated between the 69th and 70th parallel. In other words, Trondheim is just below, but Tromsø significantly above, the Arctic Circle, the imaginary circle which marks the southern extremity of the polar day (24-hour sunlit day, loosely called the "midnight sun") and, likewise, the polar night (24-hour sunless night). In Trondheim one can tell, for the greater part of the year, the day from the night, provided that clouds do not block direct sunlight, and this proviso is met less often than not. At the height of the summer, the nights, so called, are not pitch dark, and a pedestrian can easily read the road signs. The converse becomes true towards the end of December, when the sun, so sorely missed at this time of the year, makes only a brief appearance every day, drenched in golden yellow and looking utterly unfit for worship by a Zoroastrian, incapable of acting its role as the provider of light and warmth, the sustainer of life on earth. The days are very long (20 hours or so) during midsummer and very short (barely 4 hours) around the winter solstice. Around the summer solstice, Tromsø has midnight sun for months. In June or July, fasting in Trondheim from sunset to sunrise is *just* possible, with the repast and the breakfast merged into a single meal, but out of the question if one happens to be living in Tromsø. Human beings and other animals are endowed with what are popularly known as *biological clocks* [158], but such clocks, you will find out in the following story, are not trustworthy at all.

A passenger commits suicide

The macabre heading of this section is taken from a collection of letters written by Lord Dufferin (to his mother) while on a trip to Iceland in the summer of 1856. The editor of his letters has provided several headings for each letter, and the above heading appears in Letter V [159].

Before it set sail from Stornaway in the Hebrides, Lord Dufferin's ship had taken some poultry on board for the journey. I interrupt the story to remind my city-dwelling readers, most of whom are awakened by their preset alarms, that a cock (or a rooster) and other animals have also provided wake-up services in their neighbourhoods, and still do for a large section of humanity. An "English-speaking cock" is traditionally believed to utter the sound "cock-a-doodle-do", but in general the word *cock-crow* refers to the piercing noise made by a cock of any nationality.

> Shortly after this a very melancholy occurrence took place. I

> had observed for some days past, as we proceeded north, and the nights became shorter, that the cock we shipped at Stornaway had become quite bewildered on the subject of that meteorological phenomenon called the Dawn of Day. In fact, I doubt whether he ever slept for more than five minutes at a stretch, without waking up in a state of nervous agitation, lest it should be cock-crow. At last, when night ceased altogether, his constitution could no longer stand the shock. He crowed once or tiwce [sic] sarcastically, then went melancholy mad: finally, taking a calenture, he cackled lowly (probably of green fields), and leaping overboard, drowned himself. The mysterious manner in which every day a fresh member of his harem used to disappear, may also have preyed upon his spirits [159, p. 32].

The biological clock of this bird was evidently disturbed by the persistence of sunlight, and human beings are not excepted in this respect. Even if one insists, in the face of all the evidence, that the native dwellers of high latitudes have acquired, through some evolutionary adaptation, the ability to tell the time even when clouds block direct sunlight, a Muslim who emigrates to Norway after attaining adulthood would not be able to do much better than Lord Dufferin's cock.

Night and day

The earth, a nearly perfect sphere, spins as it goes round the sun in an almost circular orbit; the axis around which the earth rotates is not perpendicular to the plane of the orbit. Let us begin by defining the term 'year' as the time that the earth takes to go round the sun once. The orbital motion and the tilt of the axis of rotation give rise to the four seasons, and the spinning motion accounts for the apparent rising and setting of the sun. Let us simplify matters by introducing and defining, for the purpose of this discussion, a *doy* as the time it takes for the earth to make one revolution around its axis. There is no such word in English, which uses the word 'day' both for *the time of light*, the interval between sunrise and sunset, and for what I have called a *doy*, a twenty-four hour period from midnight to midnight (or from sunrise to sunrise, or from sunset to sunset, or for that matter from midnight to midnight, non to noon, etc). The Urdu language, with its enormous appetite for borrowing foreign words (especially from Arabic and Persian) has three words for both *day* (the time of light) and *night* (the time of darkness), but no single word for a *doy*. The Norwegians are blessed with two national languages (both Norwegian), and they can boast of having not only *dag* (day) and *natt* (night) in each language but also *døgn* (for my *doy*). Necessity became, for the Norwegians, the mother of invention. Had they not been so inventive, they would have been as befuddled as Lord Dufferin's cock, and done who knows what.

I grew up in the Northern hemisphere in a city located just below the 25th parallel—that is, closer to the equator than to the Arctic Circle. We all knew that days became slightly shorter in winter, but the difference in the daylight hours during summer and winter was not large enough to disrupt our daily routine or to make us wonder why that was so. 'Return home before it gets dark' was one of the rules that I (and my playmates) had to obey, and no one needed a wrist watch to comply with this rule. If my family had emigrated to Norway when I was a child, my mother would have had the good sense to say 'Return home before ... pm'. But now I must return to Maudūdī.

I suspect that Maudūdī never came close to the Arctic Circle in the summer time, and who would blame him for not venturing so far north during the winter time, let alone for not crossing the Antarctic Circle at any time of the year. If he had taken the trouble to acquire a thorough knowledge of physical and human geography, he would not have presented his surmise as a fact. I am driven to the conclusion that the canard which was his footnote 193 is just a bluff, and that what he wrote there was motivated by his determination to defend *his* interpretation of the meaning of Qur'ān.

canard: a hoax, a deliberately misleading report

A Turkish geographer of the seventeenth century

The Turkish territorial expansion reached its acme in the sixteenth century, during the reign of Suleiman the Magnificent, but their contact with the Western nations did not incline the Turks towards cultivating science and philosophy. The first Turkish book to mention the heliocentric view of Copernicus (1473–1543), the translation of Joan Blau's *Atlas Major*, appeared in 1685 [143]. Kātib Chelebi (1609–57), bibliophile, author and geographer, lamented the Turks' neglect of science in *Mīzān al-ḥaqq* (*Balance of Truth*), his last book [51, p. 28]:

Sheykh al-Islam: title of the chief cleric in the Ottoman empire (see p. 205)

> While engaged in the study of mathematics, three problems occurred to me. Regarding them as problems in jurisprudence, I asked for a fetwa [religious edict] from the then Sheykh al-Islam, Bahā'ī Efendi.[3] No answer was forthcoming. After I had composed a treatise containing an exposition of the problems, he wrote an answer to one of the three. This answer, in the Sheykh al-Islam's own handwriting, turned up in the possession of Sheykhzade Efendi, the official responsible for reviewing and issuing fetwas. It was a piece of raving lunacy. I transcribed it and appended it verbatim to that treatise, under the heading 'Correction of Answer'. He who wishes may see the treatise. The problems are these:
>
> 1. Is the rising of the sun in the west reconcilable with the laws of astronomy?[4]
>
> 2. How does one perform the five daily prayers and keep the Fast in places where there are six months of daylight and six months of night?
>
> 3. Is there any place other than Mecca where the *qibla* can be any of the four directions?[5]
>
> So you see that men of ability should make great efforts to understand abstract thought and mathematics, so that one may not be full of surmise and uncertainty on the road of speculation, and end up a misguided ass.

We are told [51, p. 8] that Kātib Chelebi "died in October 1657, peacefully and suddenly, while drinking a cup of coffee". Was

[3] Translator's footnote: Bahā'ī Mehmed Efendi (b. 1004/1595-6) was Sheykh ul-Islam from 1649 to 1651 and again from 1652 till his death in 1654.

[4] Translator's footnote: It is believed that the rising of the sun in the West will be one of the Signs of the Hour, the precursors of the Judgment. See [160, p. 132]: '...the rising of the sun from the place where it sets, ...as well as the other eschatological signs according to the description thereof in authentic Tradition, are a reality that will take place'.

[5] Translator's footnote: The *qibla* is the direction Muslims face when praying, towards the Ka'ba, the shrine at Mecca.

it just coffee? With some imagination, one could write a semi-fictitious and semi-biographical work, suggesting that someone was so outraged by the above passage that he decided to have Kātib poisoned.

Maudūdī, an unofficial Shaykh ul-Islam, would have greatly benefited from reading *Mīzān al-ḥaqq*.

Why Kātib Chelebi's word fell on deaf ears?

What motivated Kātib Chelebi to write his last book can be described by using his own words from the preface to the book: "Like the fanatical wars in the olden time, the futile wrangling of these stupid people [his contemporaries] has well-nigh led to bloodshed. For this reason these few lines have been drafted in order to demonstrate the method of proof in the questions at issue, and the name *Mīzān al-ḥaqq fi'khtiyār al-ḥaqq* ('The Balance of Truth in Choosing the Most True') has been given to them, so that ordinary people may know what the matters of strife and dispute are, and what manner of fruit they yield." When one goes through the book, it becomes clear that the book is addressing ordinary priests, and his principal aim is to breathe a spirit of liberalism and moderation into his readers. For us his book is valuable because it allows us to see what the ordinary people were wrangling about. Let us take a look at the first eight chapters.

1. *The 'Life' of the Prophet Khiḍr*. Khiḍr, the patron of travellers in Turkish folklore, is generally identified with the mysterious Servant of God whose encounter with Moses is described in the Qur'ān (18:64-81). For his identification with Elias and St. George, see Hasluck's *Christianity and Islam under the Sultans* [161, 319–36]. He is said to have been the Vizier of Alexander the Great and to have discovered the Fountain of Immortality. In Kātib's time, and even today, people believe that they have encountered Khiḍr, which is consistent with the myth of his immortality. The counterargument is that Khiḍr's immortality is proved false by the Qur'ān (21:35): 'We have not granted to any man . . . eternity.' Kātib tries to get out of the quandary without offending anyone, and offers an hounourable compromise: "Some mystics, when in a state of purity, see the dead before their eyes, . . . later narrators, through ignorance or wilful deceit, present spiritual visions

as objective fact. The common folk do not know the real story, and think this to be true. Such is the erroneous origin of the tales in question. Some lying pretenders claim that these spiritual encounters and dealings are objective, and thereby they frequently attain corrupt ends."

2. *Singing.* Is singing permitted or forbidden? Kātib summarizes the differing viewpoints: "In Islam, the exponents of the sacred law have categorized it as perfectly permissible to listen to the melodies produced by birds, and have allowed those produced by human throats, subject to certain conditions and rules. But, they say, to listen to instruments that are blown or struck is never permissible." He discusses the pros and cons, and takes, in keeping with his peaceful approach, the middle ground: "Every man has his opinion, as the saying goes: the words and deeds of both factions have always had a certain justification, yet the quarrel has never been resolved. The intelligent man will not be so stupid as to hope to decide a dispute of such long standing."

3. *Dancing and Whirling.* It becomes clear that Kātib does not approve of the Ṣufīs and dervīshes, but does not want to wage a war against them because this would amount to taking away their rice bowl. "Only the orthodox Ulema have interfered with them, as is their duty, writing many tracts against them. The dervishes reply, quite unabashed, 'Our profit and means of livelihood is the dervish lodge and the company of disciples. How is it possible for the practices and rites of an Order to be brought to naught? The rites and ceremonies which we have constantly performed for so many centuries are established among us. Though they be "innovation", yet we practise them.'

   "Thus they make it plain that their means of livelihood is folly, which hostile criticism cannot induce them to abandon. Just as they do not desist from whirling, so some of the fanatically orthodox do not cease from carping at them: the tug-of-war between the two parties has brought them into a vicious circle. At no time has there been a break in the chain of contention; it has grown longer and longer."

4. *The invoking of blessings on prophets and companions.* By this is meant the use of such expressions as 'May Allah bless him and give him peace', or 'The blessing and peace of Allah be upon him', when any of the honoured prophets is mentioned, or 'May

Allah be pleased with him' when any of the honoured Companions of the Prophet is mentioned. According to one learned opinion, it is a religious duty to say 'Blessings on the Prophet' once in a lifetime, according to some others, it is only canonically laudable to do so, and there are still others who say that the tradition makes the use of the formula compulsory after every mention of the Prophet. "As for the fact that some preachers enjoin the people to bless the Prophet during their sermons, while others do not: this hardly merits much discussion but is simply a matter of custom. It arises from the differences of opinion that are current among the learned; differences from which they derive much benefit, as will be explained."

5. *Tobacco*
6. *Coffee*
7. *Laudunum, Opium, and Other Drugs*
8. *The Parents of the Prophet*. Kātib remarks, "This topic has been included because it is yet another battlefield of opinions", and discusses the sensitive issue in the form of questions and answers. For this summary, it will be enough to state one question: "Does Abū Ḥanīfa not say in the *Fiqh akbar*, 'The parents of the Prophet died as unbelievers'?" Before quoting Kātib's answer, I would like to add here that this clause does not occur in all texts of the book [160, p. 132]. The question is answered by Kātib in the following words: "Sheykh Bahā'al-Dīn-zāde said that the reason for the inclusion of this clause in the articles of the creed was that some people had gone to the extreme in denying that the Prophet's parents were infidels. As this denial was obviously contrary to the principles of the Faith, Abū Ḥanīfa made this clause one of the tenets of Islam and included it in the *Fiqh akbar* in order to confute those who showed too much respect for the Prophet's parents and too little for the principles of the Faith. As the Imam Fakhr al-Din al-Rāzī mentions in his great Qur'ān-commentary, this excessive respect originated with the Rafidite Shiites in the old days, just as they preached the doctrine of the sinless state of the Prophet. Later some Sunnites imitated them in this."[6] Kātib's advice: Hold yourself aloof from this controversy.

[6]Translator's footnote: The Prophet never claimed to be divinely inspired, except when delivering the revelations, or to be perfect in his everyday life. His followers however have come to credit him with a sinless state and even the power to work miracles, to which he never pretended.

I will limit myself to listing only the titles of some of the remaining chapters: 9. *The Faith of the Pharaoh*; 10. *The Controversy concerning Sheykh Muḥyi'l-Dīn ibn 'Arabī*; 11. *The Cursing of Yazīd*; 12. *Invocation*; 13. *Pilgrims to Tombs* 15. *Shaking Hands*; 16. *Bowing*; 18. *The Religion of Abraham*; 19. *Bribery*; 20 & 21. *The Controversy between ... and ....*

I have no reason to doubt Kātib's claim that tempers ran high when Turks discussed the fidelity (or not) of the Prophet's parents and, even more importantly, of his uncle, Abū Ṭālib, without whose support the Prophet may not have been able to withstand the wrath of his tribe. I trust him because I know that some of these questions, and others equally grave in the opinion of the combatants, continue to cause fights as ferocious as the battles between supporters of rival soccer teams. However, I cannot imagine that the people who quarreled on such matters had the capacity for ruminating on the three brain teasers of Kātib Chelebi.

Advice from Alexander Pope

When Maudūdī wrote his footnote 193, he fell prey to wishful thinking, a weakness that has blighted the lives of many, including scientists and other thinkers. In principle, he could have easily avoided the trap by consulting a few experts. But where were they to be found? Not among other moulvīs and maulanās, at least. It is not inconceivable that a diligent search, launched perhaps with a few advertisements in the national newspapers, would have culminated in a list of real experts, one or two geographers but mainly those who were occupied with observing animal behaviour at high latitudes; some respondents, belonging to the secular elite, may have recalled a travelogue or two. Most, if not all, of the scientists and travelers in the hypothetical list of cognoscenti would have been non-Muslim (since the commentary was written during the period 1942–72). Would Maudūdī have read the travelogues and contacted the scientists, asking each to confirm or contradict his surmise (that the inhabitants of extreme northern latitudes are able to tell the time from the signs in the heavens)?

Alexander Pope's versified *Essay on Criticism* is in three parts, the second of which deals with 'causes hindering a true judgment', and the verses which cover the first two causes ('pride' and 'imperfect learning') are reproduced below (with added emphasis) [162, p. 72]:

> Of all the causes which conspire to blind
> Man's erring judgment, and misguide the mind,
> What the weak head with strongest bias rules,
> Is pride, the never-failing vice of fools.
> Whatever nature has in worth denied,
> She gives in large recruits of needful pride;
> For as in bodies thus in souls, we find
> What wants in blood and spirits, swelled with wind:
> Pride, where wit fails, steps in to our defence,
> And fills up all the mighty void of sense:
> If once right reason drives that cloud away,
> Truth breaks upon us with resistless day.
> *Trust not yourself; but, your defects to know*
> *Make use of ev'ry friend—and ev'ry foe.*
> A little learning is a dang'rous thing;
> Drink deep, or taste not the Pierian spring:
> There shallow draughts intoxicate the brain,
> And drinking largely sobers us again.

A *Pierian Spring* is a mythological spring in Pieria (Macedonia) sacred to the Muses, a source of inspiration to those who drank from it; I have followed modern dictionaries in using an upper case 'S'.

An Islamic Academy of Sciences

The Islamic world needs a single body akin to the *Pontifical Academy of Sciences* for dispensing the water of the Pierian spring to those who are thirsty for knowledge. The members of this academy should be selected according to strict criteria, without prejudice or partisanship; its roles should include diffusion of current scientific knowledge into every nook and cranny of the Muslim world, so that a Muslim who is looking for reliable information about a particular issue, expressed in his own language, can consult a publication of this organ, or direct a question to its secretariat, when a relevant report is not available. If such a body does come into existence, its pamphlets, reports and encyclicals would command more respect than the *fatāwa* (plural of *fatwa*) of individual priests, and it would then become much easier to dispel superstitions from the minds of illiterate individuals [163], many of whom believe, for example, that the birth of a child with a harelip or cleft palate is caused by the pregnant mother's handling of a knife during a lunar eclipse [164].

If an *Islamic Academy of Sciences* is formed in the future and its members are asked, 'Can humans living close to the Arctic Circle tell the time (throughout a calendar year) without the help of a watch?', their response, an unequivocal 'No', should convince the last doubting member of the Ummah that a literal interpretation of the Holy Qur'ān is simply not feasible in regions very much closer to the poles than to the equator.

Maudūdūdī, let us note in passing, was also opposed, like most Islamic scholars whose works or words have reached me, to biological evolution, not because he understood biology better than geography, but because he could not reconcile Darwinism with his interpretation of the Qur'ān.

4 — *An Arabic Qur'ān*

The title of this chapter alludes to the forty-first sūrah (section) of the Qur'ān, which begins with a two-letter code (*ḥā'-mīm*) and then goes straight to the point: "A revelation from the Lord of Mercy, the Giver of Mercy; a Scripture whose verses are made distinct as a Qur'ān in Arabic for people who understand". I have used a recent rendering [165]; in the six freely available older translations [166], *who* is followed by *know* in four, and by *have knowledge* or *understand* in the other two.

ḥā'-mīm: disjointed letters (see p. 178 for more details)

What, apart from Arabic, do the people mentioned in verse 41:2 'understand' or 'know'? That they must know the Arabic language is self-evident and consistent with the opening verses of the twelfth Sūrah [165]: "*Alif lām rā'*. These are the verses of the Scripture that makes things clear—We have sent it down as an Arabic Qur'ān so that you [people] may understand". The Qur'ān also says (14:4) that when a Prophet was sent to any people he preached in *their* language so that *they* may understand him. It stands to reason that when the Apostle of Allāh presented the Qur'ān to the people of Ḥejāz, he spoke in Arabic, and that the imagery and concepts used in the Qur'ān were comprehensible to people around him. No one should be surprised that the Qur'ān refers, when it speaks of the creation of Adam, to the chemical vocabulary then in vogue, and makes no mention of X and Y chromosomes, ribosomes, messenger RNA and mitochondrial DNA. Had Adam been created by mixing components other than the four elements known to the cognoscenti among the Ḥejāzīs, no one would have understood the story of the Creation. Indeed, Ghazālī—all too aware of the limits to human communication—discussed the dangers of ignoring these constraints at least twice in *Iḥyā'*, citing Muḥammad as well as

alif-lām-rā': disjointed letters

Ḥejāz: The region where Islam was first preached.

Jesus on each occasion. According to him, the former is supposed to have said [94, pp. 146–7]:[1] "Talk to people about what they know and leave what they do not know. Do you want to give the impression that Allāh and His Messenger lie?". Genuine or not, the sayings quoted by him are packed with pedagogic wisdom.

The Bible and the Qur'ān. Herman Melville and *The Whale*

The Bible and the Qur'ān use much the same imagery; both speak of heaven and hell, virtue and sin, reward and punishment, angels, Satan, and demons, Noah/Nūḥ and the flood, Jonah/Yunus and the whale. Well, not quite. The sacred books refrained from going into distracting details and did not dwell on the difference, noted already by Aristotle, between the cetaceans (the whales and porpoises) and those other marine dwellers, the fish. Even, Herman Melville (sailor, author of *Moby-Dick—or, The Whale* and self-trained marine biologist), who knew that Aristotle and Linnaeus had laid stress on the difference between a whale and a fish, who knew more about whales than they did, insisted on defining (for all time to come!) a whale as a fish, because he was addressing non-specialist readers, and he chose his words to catch their attention [167, pp. 167–8]: "Next: how shall we define the whale, by his obvious externals, so as conspicuously to label him for all time to come? To be short, then, a whale is *a spouting fish with a horizontal tail*. There you have him. However contracted, that definition is the result of expanded meditation. A walrus spouts much like a whale, but the walrus is not a fish, because he is amphibious. But the last term of the definition is still more cogent, as coupled with the first. Almost anyone must have noticed that all the fish familiar to landsmen have not a flat, but a vertical, or up-and-down tail. Whereas, among spouting fish the tail, though it may be similarly shaped, invariably assumes a horizontal position." (Emphasis in the original.)

Neither the early Christians nor the early Muslims had any reason to feel embarrassed by the cosmology or the biology in

---

[1]Ghazālī refers to these words again when he discusses the duties of a teacher [94, pp. 236–7]. The corresponding passages in Faris's translation [60] are on pp. 87, 143. The veracity of the citation is examined in Appendix C.

their Scriptures. Earth, air, fire and water retained their elemental status until a thousand years after the revelation of the Qur'ān, and the only strata people knew were the earth, and what was above (or below). During the last few centuries, most of the Christian world has been gradually shedding its belief in the literal truth of the Bible, and has adopted what some have called the 'New Theology', but most Muslims continue to believe that the Qur'ān, being the holy word of Allāh, is not only a source of moral teachings but also a record of history and a scientific text; commentaries of the Qur'ān written centuries ago are still regarded as relevant, which is not surprising since the majority of contemporary Muslims have been left untouched by, and have made no contribution to, the intellectual advancement of the world during the last six centuries. Those who are literate and interested in religious matters, revere and regurgitate books written by authors who have long since departed, and see no need for looking at other sources of information and seeking inspiration from scholars and theologians outside their own fold.

Our knowledge base changes with time, and so must our interpretation of the Qur'ān, if it is to retain its unique status and continue to guide contemporary Muslims and their future generations, some of whom will have more knowledge than their parents and grandparents. Had the Christian response to acquiring and assimilating new knowledge (that is, knowledge unavailable to one's forefathers) been duplicated in Islamica, the idea of a God sitting on a celestial throne upheld by eight angels, expressing His rage at the disobedience of His earthly servants by causing every so often disastrous quakes and devastating deluges, would have become untenable to a Muslim who truly comprehends the implications of modern cosmology.

In this chapter I propose to trace the evolution of Christian theology in the last two centuries, focussing attention for the most part on Unitarians; to identify the forces which have humanized Christianity and created a new image of the God of the New Testament; to suggest that similar changes are needed in the world of Islam, and to argue that this transformation can only be brought about by abandoning the attitude that has turned an Arabic Qur'ān into an archaic Qur'ān. For background information about the first civil war in Islam, see Appendix E.

Who is the author of the Qur'ān?

As a rule, orthodox Muslims believe that the Qur'ān is Allāh's word, uncreated or created according as the believer is a Sunnī, or a Shī'ah [160, 168]. I am aware of only one exception to this rule, namely the Urdu littérateur Niaz Fathehpuri (1882–1966), who took issue with the orthodox viewpoint and stated that the Prophet only claimed that the Qur'ān came to him as *waḥī* from Allāh, which does not mean that it is the word of Allāh [169, pp. 424–37]. After examining those verses of the Qur'ān where the word *waḥī* or an equivalent occurs, and finding that *waḥī* was also sent, for instance, to the mother of Moses (28:7), to the bee (16:68), and to each of the seven heavens (41:12), he arrived at the conclusion that the Qur'ān is *waḥī* sent by Allāh, not *kalām Allāh* (God's word); he also presented (without naming it) the M'utazilite argument and the ensuing conclusion that the traditional belief contradicts not only the Qur'ān itself but also the concept of monotheism presented by the Prophet of Islam. Niaz Fathehpuri (henceforth NF) never renounced Islam, but nearly all religious leaders of his time thought of him as a renegade, and it seems incredible now that their vociferous condemnation did not incite others to punish him in this world for his unorthodox analysis. The hostility directed at Nasr Hamid Abu Zayd (1943–2010), whose stance towards the interpretation of the Qur'ān was far less radical [170], shows that a contemporary author would need considerable courage if he happens to hold views similar to those of NF and chooses to make them public. NF's analysis is worthy of serious consideration and it is rather unfortunate that his essay [169, pp. 424–37] remains inaccessible to those who cannot read Urdu.

Niāz Fateḥpūrī

waḥī: inspiration, revelation

Naṣr Ḥāmid Abū Zayd

Whether the Qur'ān is literally the word of Allāh, or a book inspired by Him, makes no difference to my main aim, which is to point out what is obvious but frequently overlooked: so far as giving guidance is concerned, a divine book is no different from one written by a human author who is no longer in this world; a book has to be read and interpreted by other human beings, and when interpretations differ, the dispute cannot be resolved by consulting the author.

Only men can speak through the Qur'ān

While the Prophet was alive, interpreting the Qur'ān remained his prerogative. After his death, the leadership of the community (the Caliphate) came into the hands of Abū Bakr, his intimate friend and the father of 'Ā'ishah, his favourite wife; the next three Caliphs—'Umar, 'Uthmān and 'Alī—had equally close ties with the Prophet. Traditional Muslims grow up with the dogma that since all four Caliphs had been constant companions of Muḥammad during most of his Apostolic years, they were all rightly guided, and interpreted the Qur'ān as the Prophet himself would have done in running the affairs of the community. In fact, the boundary of their deference extends much further, and includes those who are called the Companions of the Prophet: anyone who claimed to be a Muslim and had some contact with the Prophet belongs to this select club, every member of which is held by these traditionalists to be beyond criticism and exempt from reproach.

The comforting view about the inerrancy of the rightly guided Caliphs, and the saintly status accorded to *all* the Companions of the Prophet, cannot be reconciled with the events that took place towards the end of 'Uthmān's life. Most Muslims who did not belong to the influential clan of 'Uthmān became disenchanted with his conduct, and a group, led by Muḥammad (a son of Abū Bakr, half-brother of 'Ā'ishah) demanded his impeachment and, after finding evidence of a double cross on the part of 'Uthmān, eventually murdered him. The assassination ignited the the first civil war of Islam and sowed the seed of the Sunnī-Shī'ah schism that has proved resolutely unbridgeable so far, with no signs of reconciliation in the future. After 'Alī, Muḥammad's cousin and son-in-law, became the fourth Caliph, 'Ā'ishah formed an alliance with Ṭalḥah and Zubayr, her brothers-in-law, and senior Companions, who put their claim to the coveted Caliphate higher than that of the incumbent. The trio led, and lost, a bitter battle against 'Alī, a combat that came to be known as the Battle of the Camel because 'Ā'ishah participated in it, riding a Camel. Clearly, the two sides could not both have been right in their interpretation of the Qur'ān and the teachings of the Prophet; the Qur'ān was interpreted by each party according to its own opinion [171], and no one who knows the difference between humans and angels should be shocked at being told that the Prophet must have been misquoted freely by both sides, and that a Companion was as likely to be a self-seeking scoundrel as a devout man desperate to preserve the new faith and the unity of its adherents.

During 'Alī's Caliphate, belief in the divine authorship of the Qur'ān was put to a novel use in the Battle of Ṣiffīn, which pitched the supporters of 'Ali against those of Mu'āwiyah, who had been appointed Governor of Syria by 'Umar, the second Caliph. Seeing that the battle was turning in favour of 'Alī, Mu'āwiyah's astute general 'Amr ibn al-'Āṣ came up with a creative ruse. He ordered his men to tie pages of the Qur'ān to the tips of their lances and hold them aloft; the gesture was to be interpreted as a proposal to resolve the dispute by seeking arbitration from Allāh. 'Ali saw through the deception and urged his men to fight on, but many of them were reluctant to prolong the combat [172, pp. 70–5]. The fighting stopped but arbitration had to be left to ordinary mortals, and the two protagonists returned to their power bases, 'Alī to Kūfa and Mu'āwiyah to Damascus.

A large group of 'Alī's supporters was highly disgruntled by the turn of events at Ṣiffīn, and adopted the slogan *Lā Ḥukma Illā Lillāh*, meaning, "No Rule except that of Allāh". They may be called the first band of Muslim fundamentalists or the forerunners of the *Ṭālibān*, their fervour and their cruelty to other Muslims even exceeding their ignorance. In trying to win them over 'Alī is reported by Ṭabarī [173, Vol. 1, p. 3333] to have said: "We have not asked men to arbitrate; we have appointed the Qur'ān as the arbitrator. But this Qur'ān, a writing inscribed between two covers, is inarticulate, and only men can speak through it."

The dissidents, who came to be known as the *Khawārij*, were not convinced, and the dispute had to be settled by force. 'Alī was victorious, but not long afterwards a sympathizer of the dissident group struck his head with a sword, and the blow proved to be fatal not just for 'Alī but for the Caliphate itself, which had so far shunned the practice of hereditary leadership of the community.

The early historians of Islam—like Ibn Isḥāq, the first biographer of Muḥammad, and Ṭabarī—were chroniclers rather than analysts. Their modus operandi was the same as that followed by the collectors of the *ḥadīthes* (cf. p. 4): they took particular pains to record the source of their information, mainly oral, by detailing the chain of communication in the following format: "I heard this from Z, who heard this from Y, who heard this from X, who was on the spot".

Abū J'afar Ṭabarī gives Abū Mukhnif as his source, who heard it from Abī Janāb, who in turn heard it from 'Omāra bin Rabī'a. I was not there when 'Alī tried to pacify the *Khawarij*, but I see no reason to doubt the report. 'Alī must have said something close to what has been quoted above, but even if the words attributed to him were fabricated by someone else, the soundness of the claim that the Qur'ān itself cannot speak and must be interpreted by humans is beyond dispute. Readers who *know* or *understand* will concede that this is an ineluctable constraint; others will put the Qur'ān on the rack until they hear Allāh's (or their own) will through its lines.

Translations of the Qur'ān

Muslims believe that, in so far as the Qur'ān is the inimitable Word of Allāh, it is untranslatable, and thus one can only speak of a rendering of its meaning. Translators have been traduced by many, including their own readers, other translators, and even the Italian language, which distilled the difficulties of the thankless task of translation in the merciless adage *traduttore traditore.* Since the first word means "translator" and the second means "traitor", I will only say that two words to the wise are enough. There is some truth—well, at least half-truth—in the adage, but fortunately the literary world has always had the courage and the good sense to defy the half-truth—even when it came to rendering the Qur'ān in a language other than Arabic. When I speak of a translation of the Qur'ān in this book, I mean, of course, a translation of the meaning of its text.

Numerous (over fifty?) English translations of the Qur'ān have been published over the last hundred years, and several versions are now freely available. With few exceptions, the message does not change a great deal when one compares different translations, including that by Dawood [174], which has been revised many times since it was first published in 1956. One such exception is the translation of the word *waḍribūhunna* in Verse 4:34, a derivative of the Arabic verb *ḍaraba* (based on the stem *ḍ-r-b*); traditionally translated as *beat* or *scourge*, this word was recently translated as *go away* [175].

An Arabic word that will be needed later is *kā'ib*, translated by Lane [89] as a "girl whose breasts are beginning to swell, or become prominent or protuberant" and by Wehr [176] as "having swelling breasts, buxom (girl)"; its plural is *kawā'ib*.

Four out of five Muslims are not Arabs

And I don't know how many out of ten are illiterate or just nominally literate. Illiteracy is rife in the Muslim world and fewer than twenty percent of the faithful understand Arabic. A non-Arab Muslim must memorize some verses of the Qur'ān in order to be able to utter them when he prays (worships) alone, and if he prays with a group (congregation), he hears the imām (the prayer leader) recite the same or some other verses, unless he happens to be the imām himself; whatever his role, he does not understand what he is saying (or is being said on his behalf) to the Creator. Those who are curious to find out the meaning of the verses must look for a priest or turn to translations.

I owe to Mark Davie the observation that the Italian adage about translators originally surfaced in the *plural* form *Traduttori traditori* ("translators traitors") in a nineteenth-century collection of Tuscan proverbs compiled by Giuseppe Giusti [177]. Davie prefers to see in it an expression of the wariness in the popular mind of any language that is not readily understood, and more particularly of a lack of trust in those who use unfamiliar language as a ploy for power. In Italy this could have been said about priests, lawyers, and doctors, who used Latin to add mystique to their profession. The plural form in the proverb casts a shadow of suspicion over those who pretend to hold the key to the knowledge that lies locked in a language unfamiliar to the masses. In the non-Arab part of the Muslim world, priests use Arabic to acquire an aura of authority, and invariably quote, regardless of whom they are addressing, passages from the Qur'ān *arabatim* (to coin a phrase) before they oblige the listener(s) with a translation in the local language.

How does an uneducated, non-Arab Muslim relate to the Arabic Qur'ān? Illiterate followers of a religion can venerate their sacred book only by turning each copy into a holy fetish, a portable idol. If you have not spent much time among Muslims who, whether illiterate or educated, do not understand Arabic, examining an analogous situation would help. I recall how the residents of Virginia, who had never set eyes on a book, treated the Bible when Thomas Harriot (see p. 156) attempted to introduce Christianity to them. I have updated his spellings so that the reader is not distracted by the changes which have occurred since 1585 [178]:

> Many times and in every town where I came, according as I was able, I made declaration of the contents of the Bible; that therein was set forth the true and only GOD, and his mighty works, that therein was contained the true doctrine of salvation through Christ, with many particularities of miracles and chief points of religion, as I was able then to utter, and thought fit for the time. And although I told them the book materially and of itself was not of any such virtue, as I thought they did conceive, but only the doctrine therein contained; yet would many be glad to touch it, to embrace it, to kiss it, to hold it to their breasts and heads, and stroke over all their body with it; to show their hungry desire of that knowledge which was spoken of.

Sadly, the gist of Harriot's message needs no updating.

A carefree head is to be found only on a scarecrow

True, if we are speaking of the mortal world! I picked up the above witticism in my early youth and have quoted it more often than any other saying known to me. Conscious that my mind would not be credited with such a sparkling mix of wit and wisdom, I have hoped to earn some brownie points for honesty by announcing that I first read it in a booklet which stated it to be a Turkish proverb.

Some idea of how difficult it is to reach consensus on the meaning of Qur'ānic verses may be had by examining the description of paradise, which is mentioned several times as a place where everyone will have a carefree head, but never as an arena for revelry. Some of the most alluring (but far from licentious) accounts are to be found in Verses 2:25, 36:55–57 and 44:47–59. The claim that "the Qur'ān explicitly denies any carnal pleasures in paradise" [179] is not supported by my reading of Verses (78:33–34), which promise the pious such delights as gardens and vineyards, *kawāʿib*, and a cup full to the brim. There is no doubt, though, that the Qur'ān does not explicitly promise a harem of seventy or seventy two *ḥūr al-ʿain* to each devout Muslim. For those who may be curious as to how the Muslim paradise acquired its seedy reputation as a place for unbridled lechery, I should add here that all such reports are to be found in the *ḥadīth*, and in the many commentaries of the Qur'ān, but nowhere in the Qur'ān itself.

revelry: boisterous or unrestrained merrymaking

Reverend Samuel Shaw, MA (1635–1696, born at Repton) was a school teacher and a writer. I became aware of him accidentally, and only because of my interest in his namesake, George Bernard Shaw. The first volume of his collected works, entitled *The Voice of One Crying in a Wilderness*, is a series of sermons first preached to his own family and later made public. He speaks here frequently about heaven and hell, and tells his listeners that heaven, properly understood, stands for a full and glorious union with God, and conversely, hell means an eternal separation and wandering from the divinity, and that it need not mean a reserve of fire and brimstone. He is filled with indignation that many of his fellow Christians conduct themselves as they do, and tries hard to teach them the proper meanings of heaven and hell [180, p. 153–4]:

> I would therefore bring a reproof against the unworthy conceptions that many christians have of heaven. Christians do I call them! nay, herein they are rather like Mahometans, who place heaven in the full and lasting enjoyment of all creature-comforts, nay, indeed of sinful and abominable pleasures, as one may read in their Alcoran. It may be, that few christians are altogether so sensual; but, sure I am, the far greater part of christians, so called, are very gross and carnal, at least, very low in their conceptions of the state of future happiness. Heaven is a word as little understood as holiness; and that, I am sure, is the greatest mystery in the world. It

> would be tedious to recount the particular various apprehensions of men in this matter, and indeed impossible to know them. The common sort of people understand by heaven either nothing but a glorious name; or at best but a freeness from bodily torment; as nothing of hell affects them but that dreadful word *fire,* so nothing of heaven but the comfortable word *rest* or *safety*. Others, it may be, think there is something positive in heaven, and they dream of *an honourable, easy, pleasant life, free from such kind of toils, labours, pains, persecutions, reproaches, penuries, which men are subject to in this life;* this is a true notion, but much below the nature of that happy state. (My italics,)

The portrayal of heaven in the italicized text does not involve any 'sinful and abominable pleasures' and represents a celibate variant of the paradise depicted in the Qur'ān. Samuel Shaw speaks with no fear of being challenged on the contents of Alcoran, but he knows that an intelligent member of the audience may ask how "tasteless and gross" descriptions of heaven originated in the first place, and he has worked out an explanation [180, p. 155–6]:

> True indeed, the Holy Ghost in scripture is pleased to condescend so far to our weak capacities, as to describe that glorious state to us by such things as we do best understand, and are apt to be most pleased with, and which do most gratify our senses in this world; as a kingdom, paradise, a glorious city, a crown, an inheritance, &c. but yet it is not the will of God that his enlightened people should rest in such low notions of eternal life; for in other places God speaks of the state of glory according to the nature and excellency of it, and not according to the weakness of our understanding, and describes it at another rate, calling it the life of angels, as here [and now many verses are cited where this glorious state is called *the beholding of God, a coming unto the measure of the stature of the fulness of Christ, God's being all things in us, a knowing of God* etc.]. In a word, which is as high as can be spoken, higher indeed than can be perfectly understood, it is called a being like unto God, 1. *John* iii. 21. *We shall be like unto him.* But this use is not so much for reproof, as it is for information.

However holy the Holy Ghost or the Qur'ān, the heavenly state had to be described in words that unholy humans best understood and were apt to be most pleased with. If a reliable translation of the Qur'ān had been available to the Reverend Shaw, he would have realized that his explanation applies equally well to the Qur'ān. He could not have known that his concept of heaven was shared by Muslim mystics, particularly Ibn al-'Arabī [123].

A book in need of enlightened interpreters

Aḥmed Khān
Muḥammad Iqbāl

Voices against a literal interpretation of the Qur'ān have been raised before in the recent past, most notably in the Indian subcontinent, by Sir Syed Ahmed Khan (1817–1898) and the poet Sir Muhammad Iqbal (d. 1938), also called *'Allāma* Iqbāl (p. 203). Both reformers accepted the theory of evolution and understood that a clash between contemporary science and the Qur'ān can be averted only by giving up the literalist approach, and both clearly stated that Adam is a symbol, not a specific individual, that the story of his fall is a legend, that concepts like hell and paradise are states not places. A single quotation from Iqbal's lectures on *The Reconstruction of Religious Thought in Islam* will be sufficient to show the extent of reconstruction [181, p. 123] and his unequivocal rejection of the literal meanings:

> *Heaven and Hell are states, not localities.* Their descriptions in the Qur'ān are *visual representations* of an inner fact, i.e. character. Hell, in the words of the Qur'ān, is 'God's kindled fire which mounts above the hearts'—the painful realization of one's failure as a man. Heaven is the joy of triumph over the forces of disintegration. *There is no such thing as eternal damnation in Islam.* (My italics.)
>
> ...Hell, therefore, as conceived by the Quran, is not a pit of everlasting torture inflicted by a revengeful God; it is a corrective experience which may make a hardened ego once more sensitive to the living breeze of Divine Grace. Nor is heaven a holiday.

How Iqbal's audience, most of whom must have been wedded to the literalist tradition and without an inkling of early twentieth century scientific ideas, reacted to his lectures, in which he mentioned (without pausing to add a few explanatory remarks) Einstein's theory of relativity and Heisenberg's principle of uncertainty and Planck's quanta of action along with making statements like "Thus we see that the Qur'ānic legend of the Fall has nothing to do with first appearance of man on this planet", I can only guess, but I am pretty sure that the overwhelming majority of sub-continental Muslims continue (like those living elsewhere) to think of heaven and hell as places, and they read and admire Iqbal's poetry without any knowledge of the contents of his *Reconstruction*.

Iqbal cited Verse 55:33 in which the inhabitants of the earth are represented as of two kinds, men and jinns, but he did not comment on the latter [181, p. 131], who are made, as my Muslim readers will know, of smokeless fire (Verse 55:15). Those who have not heard of these creatures may consult a comparatively recent report by a correspondent of *The Economist* [182], who commented that hardly a week passes in the Muslim world without a strange story concerning jinns, and the tales are often "foolish and melancholy". Such stories are indeed exceedingly common, and when they do not involve jinns, some other supernatural element serves the same purpose, and their popularity is always attributed (by those who find the stories puerile) to the low educational level of the societies where these stories keep sprouting up. Before deciding whether or not you agree with this explanation, count up to ten, or whatever number conduces to clear thinking in your head, ponder on whom you would regard an educated Muslim, and then resume reading.

An educated Muslim?

Some thirty years ago, I visited an acquaintance, a much respected and competent physician who ran a successful medical practice in the neighbourhood where I grew up. After learning that I was on leave of absence and currently based in Kuwait, his eyes lit up and he asked rather excitedly if I had read the news, published in the *Kuwait Times*, about a man whose head had turned into that of a goat. Suppressing my surprise that this bizarre tale had percolated beyond the deserts of Kuwait and letting tact override a reckless urge to pooh-pooh the story, I replied casually that I had indeed come across the news. Two other occupants of the room, who had dropped in for idle tittle-tattle before I arrived, could not resist probing the doctor, who was happy to play the raconteur, for more details. Here follows the gist of the gripping story.

A Sunnī man, married to a Shī'ah woman, was skinning the head of a goat (for preparing a family meal) during the first ten days of the month of *Muḥarram*, a period of intense mourning for Shī'ah Muslims, a time for commemorating the tragedy of Karbala in which Ḥussayn ibn 'Alī, the younger of the two grandsons of the Prophet and the supreme martyr in Shī'ah Islam, took a defiant stand against an illegitimate reprobate ruler, namely Yazīd (the second Umayyad Caliph), whose soldiers slaughtered Ḥussayn and some seventy of his male supporters on the tenth of *Muḥarram*. While handling the goat's head, the man made an irreverent remark about Imām Ḥussayn, to spite his wife, or perhaps just to tease her; no sooner had these words left his lips than his head turned into that of a goat.

I could sense, from the manner in which my acquaintance, with an imposing list of degrees and diplomas and certificates from prestigious medical schools and professional bodies and a sound knowledge of human anatomy, related the episode and from the relish with which his account was swallowed by the two visitors, that none had any reason for skepticism and they were all keen to join the club of gullible goats, lest a lingering doubt should make them liable to a similar disfiguration.

During the course of writing this book, I have tirelessly surfed and searched and fished and dredged the Internet to retrieve the story of the Kuwaiti man with a Shī'ah wife and a caprine head. Though I failed to net this particular news item, my efforts were rewarded by a report from Nigeria in which a man turned, using his own evil powers, into a goat, an earthbound quadruped—not, as would have fitted the occasion, a crow, a common sparrow, a butterfly, or even a housefly, if this Nigerian Houdini had had sufficient humility. A group of vigilantes reported to the police that they saw, while patrolling their neighbourhood, some hoodlums attempting to rob a car; the gang was pursued, and during the chase one of the suspected criminals turned into a goat, but this did not fool the vigilantes, who arrested the suspect and brought it/him to the police, who took the goat into their custody [183].

The BBC report on the incident [184] put the blame on the low educational level of the ordinary people, and this explanation will satisfy all save those who believe in the powers of magic. How are we to explain the gullibility of my medically qualified acquaintance? Those who insist on interpreting Qur'ānic verses literally know that some Jews were turned into apes when God punished them for ignoring the Sabbath restriction (2:65–6), and the same God has, surely, the power to punish a man for insulting the prince of martyrs. People raised in the literalist tradition develop from their early childhood the capacity to reconcile the supernatural with the natural, and to swallow emulsions, otherwise called superstitions, in which the two immiscible elements may be blended in any proportion.

Absurdities and atrocities

Belief in absurd stories is perfectly acceptable when it does no harm, when the believer is a peace-loving individual, willing to leave in the hands of the Almighty the determination of guilt or innocence and the dispensation of appropriate reward or punishment. My acquaintance, a mild man, followed the live-and-let-live principle. This chapter is concerned with those who are not like him, those who will not let live anyone who wants to follow a different course, those whose absurdities go beyond the circulation of outlandish stories and culminate in atrocities against the villains in these stories, whom they regard as the enemies of God and His allies. Voltaire warned against the venom floating in their concoctions [185, p. 431]: "Formerly there were those who said: You believe things that are incomprehensible, inconsistent, impossible because we have commanded you to believe them; go then and do what is unjust because we command it. Such people show admirable reasoning. Truly, whoever is able to make you absurd is able to make you unjust. If the God-given understanding of your mind does not resist a demand to believe what is impossible, then you will not resist a demand to do wrong to that God-given sense of justice in your heart. As soon as one faculty of your soul has been dominated, other faculties will follow as well. And from this ensue all those crimes of religion which have inundated the world."

Writing in a wilderness

The Bible tells us that God created angels and then made man in his own image. It also speaks of demons and their exorcism (see p. 131). The Qur'ān states that Allāh fashioned angels from light and then created jinns from smokeless fire, and afterwards made man out of clay. Jinns are able to see men, but men cannot see jinns. Unbelieving jinns are the Islamic counterparts of demons.

A Muslim who believes in the existence of jinns and angels, when asked why, will reply that, since these creatures are mentioned in the Qur'ān, denying their existence would be tantamount to casting doubt on the word of Allāh. Those to whom jinns are as real as humans feel that a knowledge of what jinns can or cannot do, and how (and by whom) they can be exorcized, is as important in their daily lives as the knowledge of amperes and ohms and volts and watts is to an electrician, for a jinn, like an electric current, can be a menace as well as blessing, and—who can say—the jinn you know may be better than the jinn you don't know. Some contemporary Muslims, who have learnt a smattering of science, refer to Verse 55:15, and speculate on how one can tap this inexhaustible source of energy. Possession by a jinn would have offered a plausible explanation for spontaneous human combustion (SHC) had the reported cases of possession not grossly outnumbered those of SHC. If someone disappears in the wilderness, it is at once inferred that jinns have abducted the missing person. Any abnormal, inexplicable or unexplained event is credited to them. They are a kind of *deus ex machina* to account for what would otherwise be unaccountable. In this capacity, a jinn is more than an article of faith: it becomes a useful hypothesis, if not quite a theory of everything.

Whereas Iqbal presented his views in six lectures (delivered in English), all laced with philosophic and scientific aroma, Sir Syed's aim was to write a new *Tafsīr-ul-Qur'ān* (detailed commentary on the Qur'ān) for a wider audience, which he did by writing several tomes (in plain Urdu prose); he addressed the reader directly, called a spade a spade, and did not hesitate to call a puerile explanation a load of nonsense. The descriptions in the Qur'ān, he maintains, are meant to be intelligible to anyone who cares to read the Book. One may take the stories literally, and actually believe in a terrible punishment or a toil-free and blissful eternal existence, in angels and devils and other supernatural beings, or one may treat all these as symbols and metaphors, and extract the essence of the text according to one's own knowledge and understanding. Most interestingly, he dismisses the occurrence of miracles and claims that the Day of Reckoning is the instant when one draws one's last breath. He supports all his conclusions through *his own* analysis of the text of the Qur'ān, and on some premises stated in the introduction to his commentary. One of the premises was unpalatable to all but a handful of nineteenth century Muslims, and it remains so even today. In stating this premise, he used two English phrases (transcribed in Urdu letters); he held that there can be no contradiction between the Qur'ān, which is the *word of God* and nature, the *work of God*, which follows immutable laws made by God Himself, and he realized that a conflict between the two cannot be avoided without renouncing the traditional, literalist path to Qur'ānic exegesis.

To explain Sir Syed's approach, I recall an anecdote about the French mathematician and astronomer Pierre-Simon Laplace (1749–1827). According to De Morgan [186, pp. 1–2], Laplace once went to present an edition of his semipopular book *Systéme du Monde* to Napoleon, the First Consul, or Emperor, who had heard that this book did not mention God, and had a penchant for putting embarrassing questions. He received the book with the following remark: "M. Laplace, they tell me you have written this large book on the system of the universe, and have never even mentioned its Creator." Laplace replied, "I have no need of this hypothesis." Napoleon found the comment amusing and related it to Lagrange (also a great mathematician), who exclaimed "Ah, it is a beautiful hypothesis; it explains many things."

In the above terminology, God is a necessity for Sir Syed, but jinns and angels are dispensable hypotheses, being disruptive to his philosophical system. He believed that the Qur'ān is the word of Allāh, but the help of an angel was not needed for communicating it to Muḥammad in the form of an audible message. He is of the opinion that a host of difficulties arise if one assumes that an angel was necessary for taking Allāh's word to His Messenger, and suggests that only a direct transmission, not requiring the emission of a sound or some other signal by Allāh and its reception by *Jibrā'īl* (Gabriel), is consistent with the properties attributed by Muslims to the Creator. To deduce the meaning of *Jibrā'īl*, he examines Verse 2:97, in which Allāh tells His Messenger that "it is he [*Jibrā'īl*] who has brought the Qur'ān down upon your heart, by permission of Allāh", and concludes that *Jibrā'īl* is the name of the Prophetic capacity to receive a Divine message and recite it to others in their language. A Prophet is someone who has the afflatus to *divine* the Divine message. Sir Syed finds it utterly ridiculous that while some people think of angels as winged creatures, floating about in the sky, each responsible for a specific duty, some others are convinced that angels are incorporeal creatures.

Aware that most of his readers would be so shocked by his interpretation as to reject it outright, Sir Syed looks for some support from a commentator with solid credentials, but he can find a kindred soul only among the Ṣūfīs . He informs his readers that his interpretation differs but little from that given by the celebrated mystic Ibn ul-'Arabī in *Fūṣūṣ ul-Ḥikam*, and backs this assertion by quoting a scholar who wrote a commentary on *Fūṣūṣ ul-Ḥikam*. Since the commentary was not available to me, I consulted Nicholson's *Studies in Islamic Mysticism* [187]; Appendix II of the second chapter is entitled "Some Notes on the *Fūṣūṣ ul-Ḥikam*", and here we find:

> The Divine will (to display His attributes) entailed the polishing of the mirror of the universe. Adam (the human essence) was the very polishing of that mirror and the soul of that form, and the angels are some of the faculties of that form ...

Sir Syed reminds his readers that the depth to which the Arabs had sunk was reflected in the name *Saracen*, given to them by other nations, and traces its origin to the Arabic word *Sāriqīn* (meaning thieves, robbers). Muḥammad's task, he explains, was to impose discipline upon a rapacious, vengeful and lewd people, who had been weaned on tribal loyalty and inter-tribal rivalry, who were consumed by extracting violent retribution for real or imaginary wrongs; his task, in other words, was to replace cruelty with compassion, injustice and the law of the jungle with justice and the Law of Allāh. He had to introduce a universal law that commanded the allegiance of these lawless Arabs, and this programme could not be put into action without using the idiom and imagery familiar to the uncouth and rowdy desert dwellers.

George Bernard Shaw, though not a religious man, referred to the Prophet of Islam on many occasions, without ever being scurrilous, and I can find no one more suitable for giving an unbiased assessment of Muḥammad's prophetic career [188, p. 636]:

> Some credulities have their social uses. They have been invented and imposed on us to secure certain lines of behavior as either desirable for the general good or at least convenient to our rulers. I learned this early in life. My nurse induced me to abstain from certain troublesome activities by threatening that if I indulged in them the cock would come down the chimney. This event seemed to me so apocalyptic that I never dared to provoke it nor even to ask myself in what way I should be the worse for it. Without this device my nurse could not have ruled me when her back was turned. It was the first step towards making me rule myself.
>
> Mahomet, one of the greatest of the prophets of God, found himself in the predicament of my nurse in respect of having to rule a body of Arab chieftains whose vision was not co-extensive with his own, and who therefore could not be trusted, when his back was turned, to behave as he himself would have behaved spontaneously. He did not tell them that if they did such and such things the cock would come down the chimney. They did not know what a chimney was. But he threatened them with the most disgusting penances in a future life if they did not live according to his word, and promised them very pleasant times if they did. And as they could not understand his inspiration otherwise than as a spoken communication by a personal messenger he allowed them to believe that the angel Gabriel acted as a celestial postman between him and Allah, the fountain of all inspiration. Except in this way he could not have made them believe in anything but sacred stones and the seven deadly sins.

Stories in which a chimney connects the cosy and intimate world of the child to the unknown world of the ferocious cock, the portly Santa and the kindly stork are like milk teeth, destined to be discarded, but anecdotes in the Scripture, when handed to children as historical events and scientific certitudes, make deep impressions, which are a great deal harder to erase than tattoo marks printed with the so-called indelible pigments.

Most Muslim priests denounced Sir Syed as an apostate; some went a little further and hoped that "God would destroy him", "that he would be severely chastised", and one was so incensed as to recommend that "he should be brought to his senses by beating, imprisonment, and the like" [189, pp. 201–4]. It would have been thoroughly appropriate for Sir Syed to have chosen the title *The Thoughts of One Writing in a Wilderness* for his radical commentary on the Qur'ān; indeed, he must have realized, despite being an indomitable optimist, that only a handful of his coreligionists would have the gumption to abandon their ancient superstitions and part company with angels and jinns, and thereby with their fathers, grandfathers and great-grandfathers and their great-great-grandfathers. Bidding farewell to jinns and angels and walking away like a winged seed loosened from its parent stem is no ordinary parting; repudiating a legacy handed down by the bygone generations and carving out or finding a new path belongs (to use some words from Cecil Day-Lewis's poem *Walking Away*) to life's give-and-take bargains, one of the scorching ordeals which fire one's irresolute clay.

tafsīr: commentary on the Qur'ān

Sir Syed's attitude to the text of the Qur'ān was just too radical to make any real impact on the Muslims of the nineteenth century, who had no choice but to criticize or ignore it; agreeing with him would amount, in their eyes, to calling Allāh and His Messenger blatant liars. His *tafsīr* was quietly buried in the graveyard for stillborn ideas; unaccountably, Iqbal did not mention it in his lectures, and no one presented it to the following generations as a first step towards modernizing Islam. He may be rightly compared to Aristarchus of Samos (ca. 310–230 B.C.), appropriately called the "Copernicus of Antiquity" [190], who proposed a heliocentric model of the solar system without exerting any influence on the course of astronomical tradition. Unlike most other ancient Greeks, whose seemingly rational views were a blend of mysticism and religion [7], Aristarchus stood on the solid pillars of observation and calculation, and was led to his model of the solar system by his finding that the sun is much larger than the earth. His major extant work consists mainly of geometric proofs of this and his other hypotheses, and it describes a spherical moon, much nearer (than the sun) to the earth and illuminated by light from the sun, a fairly veracious world-view for the third century BC, limited only by the accuracy of the measurements available to him. A critical mass of perceptive minds is needed before an idea can germinate and generate a large-scale and enduring change.

In retrospect, Sir Syed's attempt to persuade Indian Muslims to walk away was doomed to miscarry; he might as well have tried to convince the planets to abandon their orbits and rattle off towards a different galaxy. Such a profound change in attitudes needs a century (or more) of widespread liberal education and the creation of an atmosphere where thinkers clamouring for change, modernization and diversity can express their opinions without fear of persecution. Look around the contemporary world, and see where you find free school education, parity (or very nearly so) between the genders, equality (or very nearly so) between the generations, freedom (more than in many other parts of the globe) to express one's political views, liberty to practice one's avowed faith, and subject it to a searching examination and even severe criticism, license to translate foreign books, libraries that acquire, shops that sell, and readers who borrow or buy provocative books, and ask yourself—if you too regard these changes as signs of progress—how such advances came about. These changes, which originated in Western Europe, were driven by a variety of factors: Protestantism, Swedenborgianism (see below), agnosticism, Darwinism, the interplay of economic forces, the two Great Wars. It is very unlikely that anything approaching this level of progress would have been realized if Western Europe had adhered to the doctrines of Catholicism during the last couple of centuries. It was in fact, the candid Cardinal Carlo Maria Martini who stated that the Roman Catholic Church was two hundred years out of date [191–193]. Since Islam does not have a "Church", one can only speak of something nebulous, such as the Muslim world, and if we use adherence to a literal interpretation of the Qur'ān and aversion to scientific enquiry as two indicators, we cannot avoid the conclusion that the present-day Catholic Church is well ahead of contemporary Islam in many important respects. I will return to this issue in Chapter 5 and argue that, if we take religious intolerance and bigotry as an index, the contemporary Muslim world can quite reasonably be compared to seventeenth century Europe.

Who was Emanuel Swedenborg?

We may assume that, though the Reverend Samuel Shaw derided the common Christian perception of heaven, those whose lust for carnal delights were the butt of his disapproval did not think of him as a lunatic or heretic. Emanuel Swedenborg (1688–1772), who was born in Stockholm and died in London, has been called both. His father, Jesper Svedberg, rose from a very humble beginning to become a Bishop; Emanuel's surname was changed to Swedenborg when he was made a nobleman. The adult part of the first five-and-a-half decades of his life were spent in scientific pursuits, and he worked in many fields, ranging from cosmology, structure of matter, and theories of light and colours, to geology and metallurgy [194]. Though highly respected as a serious scientific investigator by his contemporaries, he cannot be counted among the major original scientists.

In 1743/44, Swedenborg experienced the first of several religious crises, and the rest of his life was beset by severe psychological problems, though he and his small band of followers would not agree with this description [195].

As to the exact scope of Swedenborg's mission, I cannot do better than to quote briefly from his book "The True Christian Religion," published shortly before his death. He says [196, pp. 516–7], "Since the Lord cannot manifest Himself in person . . . and yet He has foretold that He would come and establish a New Church, which is the New Jerusalem, it follows that He is to do it by means of a man, who is able not only to receive the doctrines of this church with his understanding, but also to publish them by the press. That the Lord has manifested Himself before me, His servant, and sent me on this office, and that, after this, He opened the sight of my spirit, and thus let me into the spiritual world, and gave me to see the heavens and the hells, and also to speak with angels and spirits, and this now continually for many years, I testify in truth; and also that, from the first day of that call, I have not received anything which pertains to the doctrines of that church from any angel, but from the Lord alone, while I read the Word." In the words of Swedenborg, his writings, being a revelation from the Lord, constitute His second coming.

Swedenborg expounded his religious philosophy in a series

of thirty volumes [197], all written in Latin and published outside Sweden, where Lutheran censorship would not have permitted him to propagate his views. It is hard to find an author who is prolific without being excessively repetitive, and Swedenborg, his readers soon discover, is not among those rare individuals who have something new to say in every new book. I find it miraculous that an author who recounted his revelations endlessly, and with an oppressive dullness of expression, found any adherents at all.

Swedenborg believed in the Word (the Scriptures), but found a literal interpretation of the Word distasteful, and sought therefore to avoid the conflict by giving new meanings to the old and distressing concepts, meanings that were consistent with a benevolent and decent Deity. He devised a way to preserve the Word through a new interpretation, a compromise that kept infidelity at bay, at least in the eyes of some fellow Christians. Had Swedenborg taken the ground that the Bible was not the Word of the Lord, most of his readers would have turned a deaf ear to his musings, for they wanted to hold firm to the dogma of inspiration, and asked not how to discredit the Bible, but how to reconcile it with their knowledge of the world and their changing values. Through their insistence on the necessity of giving new meanings to the draconian legal code of Jehovah, Swedenborg and his followers served to advance, however unconsciously, the cause of intellectual enfranchisement [198]. They attacked the literal text with great zest, taking the ground that if the old way of interpreting the Bible was right, the book was fit only for savages, and they exposed, for defending their view that a new interpretation was sorely needed, the absurdities, contradictions and cruelties in the Word. The inhuman character of Christianity could be changed, they claimed, only by following the path carved out by Swedenborg.

According to Swedenborg, love for the Lord and charity towards the neighbour are the hallmarks of, and lead to, heaven; self-love and a vainglorious pursuit of the world secure the sufferer a place in hell. There are many heavens and many hells, and Swedenborg was given the privilege to sample some of these societies. Anyone who lives a selfless life in this world will become an angel in the Afterlife and will have a heaven as his place of abode, whereas anyone here whose love for himself exceeds that for his neighbour will be sent to a hell and live there as a devil, but—mind you—this is not a cruel punishment, since a devil cannot live happily in a heaven. "Whatever may be the appearance of Infernal Spirits to Angels, amongst themselves they are Men—*and according to their phantasies not without beauty*." Hell-fire is an expression which, however terrible to us, causes little dismay to a devil, for it is merely a synonym for self-love. Devils, whose actions are guided by self-love, are condemned to live in a society where everyone else shares this passion; such a place would indeed be very uncomfortable except for a few alpha devils; escape from a hell is possible only when a devil is prepared to abandon self-love and embrace neighbourly love. Emigration from a hell to a heaven is not possible without a change of heart, and it comports with an angelic nature that no resident of a heaven would ever want to take up residence in a hell.

A fictional character claimed that people are either charming or tedious [199]. For Swedenborg, people fall into two types, God-loving altruists and self-absorbed egotists. He senses that the mortal world is imperfect because individuals of one type must mingle daily with persons of the other type, and is pleased to find that the two groups are kept apart in the Afterlife. Whatever one's opinion of his sanity and whatever credence one is willing to give to his claims of making frequent celestial trips, who can doubt his toleration (especially towards Islam), and who can fail to admire his description of the other world? Muslims and Christians are scrupulously segregated, with separate hells and heavens for the follower of each religion, and Muslims are allowed polygamy, since *their* religion permits it. Without this wise arrangement, which imposes total isolation of the votaries of the two faiths, Christian devils would have vented their spleen, every now and then, through invectives against Islam and its Prophet, and Muslims, whether angelic or devilish, would have gone on a rampage after each provocation. However imperfect, eighteenth-century Europe was a Christian citadel, where Turks no longer posed a real threat, and Christians were free to fight Christians, so unlike present-day Europe, which has become a heterogeneous society with a maddening variety of faiths and sub-faiths and sects and cults, often ill at ease with one another. With segregation out of the question, toleration is the only alternative, and proper education the only means to cultivate it.

Was Swedenborg insane? Ingersoll [200, p. 11] and Denslow [200, p. 34] have no doubt that he was, and both have compared his mental state to that of the Prophet of Islam, but Hitchcock thinks otherwise [201, p. 58]: "Swedenborg was not mad, nor was he under any peculiar hallucination." Such opinions cannot settle the question of the meaning or merit of Swedenborg's musings or of Muḥammad's message. Explain the alleged communications with an unseen world as we will, our explanations neither enhance nor diminish the value of the revelations. As Iqbal wrote in *The Reconstruction of Religious Thought in Islam* [181, p. 189]: "It does not matter in the least if the religious attitude is shaped by some kind of physiological disorder. George Fox may be a neurotic; but who can deny his purifying power in England's religious life of his day? Muḥammad, we are told, was a psychopath. Well, if a psychopath has the power to give a fresh direction to the course of human history, it is a point of the highest psychological interest to search his original experience which has turned slaves into leaders of men, and has inspired the conduct and shaped the career of whole races of mankind. Judging from the various types of activity that emanated from the movement initiated by the Prophet of Islam, his spiritual tension and the kind of behaviour which issued from it, cannot be regarded as a response to a mere fantasy inside his brain."

Two comments will be inserted here before we continue with Swedenborg's contributions. 'Umar, the Caliph who began the Islamic expansion, was no slave; on the contrary, he owned a slave himself. The Umayyads, who consolidated the early gains and established an 'Islamic' Empire with hereditary succession, were also free men; slaves did become kings later, but they owed their promotion, not to Islam's stress on equality, but to court intrigues. The genius of Muḥammad lay in converting an unruly tribal society with primitive idolatrous beliefs into a unified community subservient to a single Almighty Creator, called Allāh. Secondly, if conquest is taken as a criterion of the truth of a message, the followers of Christ can also claim that Jesus, who appeared (to his doubters) to have suffered from delusions, inspired his people to conquer an even larger part of the world.

Swedenborg wrote about a New Church, but he took no steps to start it. In 1787 his many devotees created the Church of the New Jerusalem in London, and his creed also had a small following in North America, but his movement appears to have run out of steam. The reasons for its demise will be discussed later, when I examine the changes in Christianity which have taken place since the middle of the nineteenth century.

Initially, Swedenborg's message was not well received by the average Crosstian clergyman. As one example, I mention an American pamphlet published in 1834 under the title *Swedenborgianism Depicted in its True Colors or A Contrast Between the Holy Scriptures and the Writings of Baron Swedenborg on a Variety of Important Subjects* [202]. To the author of this pamphlet, the contrast between Jesus Christ and Emanuel Swedenborg was as stark as that between Jesus and Muḥammad. He asked: "Is the Lord Jesus Christ or Swedenborg the prophet we should revere, and the Teacher whose religion we should embrace? This shows the important nature of the question, and this is the correct view of it; for the two systems of the Lord Jesus and Swedenborg, are, as will here be manifested, so diametrically opposed, that it is as impossible to adhere to them both, at the same time, as it is at the same time to be a Christian and a Mahometan, or a Christian and a heathen." In the preface to the pamphlet, its publisher complained that under the name of Christianity, Emanuel Swedenborg had presented "a system having scarcely one feature in common with the gospel of the grace of God—a system, in most respects, as wild as the wildest dreams of romance; and what is worse, more largely steeped in obscene sensualities than even Mohammedanism itself". However, even he did not contemplate a violent suppression of Swedenborg's disciples: "Towards Swedenborgians we would ever cherish the kindest feelings—(we are seeking, in this very effort [of publishing the pamphlet], to do them good)—but who can read over the following extracts from the pages of the High Priest and Apostle of their profession, without feelings of deep disgust at their filthy wickedness may, by reading this exposé, have their eyes opened to its abominations, and escape the fatal delusion."

Not every Christian recoiled with horror and disgust at the mention of the New Church. A highly appreciative evaluation was published as an anonymous contribution [203] in the *The Monthly Religious Magazine and Independent Journal* under the title "Claims of the New Church Upon Unitarians". The editor added a footnote containing the following text: "This article is from one of our most respected Unitarian preachers and scholars, and will not fail to interest the readers of the Magazine. It was originally read before an Association of Unitarian Ministers."

I pause here to present the scene to you with as many details as I have been able to gather and as little poetic license as is necessary for making my point: The date is 26 May 1858 and we are in the vestry of the Federal Street Church of Boston (whose entrance is on Berry Street). A Unitarian pastor stands on the platform. He is about to address a gathering of Unitarian ministers, who are attending an annual event that came to be called the Ministerial Conference at Berry Street. He opens his mouth to say, "Gentlemen, the topic of my talk is *Deficiencies of Unitarian Theology*". Did that statement let loose a pandemonium? Was the speaker pelted with rotten eggs or tomatoes? As Ṭabarī would have said, only Allāh knows for sure. In fact, we don't even know the name of the speaker, for sure; he has been tentatively identified as Octavius Brooks Frothingham [204], and the article published anonymously in 'the Magazine' is believed to be the text of his essay. Considering the composition of the audience, it is safe to assume that the speaker (whom I will now call Frothingham) came to no harm.

I prolong my pause to add that it would be so, so refreshing to hear a Wahhābī (or Barelawī or Deobandī or Athnā-ashʿarī or whatever) preacher addressing members of his own sect on the deficiencies of their theology. Sectarian strife in Islam has reached such a fever pitch that most priests find it more natural in their frenzy to deliver condemnatory sermons against the other sects and to extol their own interpretation of Islam, and they sincerely believe that the creeds of all other sects lead to the eternal fire of hell.

To return to the essay: Frothingham begins by pointing to the many similarities between the beliefs of the Unitarian Church and the New Church of Swedenborg. Both assert the undivided unity of God, in opposition to any tripersonality whatever; both put charity before faith, and emphatically renounce the doctrine of justification by faith alone; both believe that man makes his own hell or his own heaven, here and in the afterlife; they equally agree that there is no place of torment created for the purpose of future punishment, still less that there are any beings called devils who were created full of malice and wickedness; both believe that hell and heaven are spiritual states. They both agree that a man's living is the test of his believing. "They strikingly resemble each other in the approval of recreations and amusements and natural cheerfulness, as opposed to the asceticism which has so long been associated with the saintly character. Swedenborg's saints do not wear long faces, or speak in sepulchral tones, or refuse to mix with "worldly" people, or reject all worldly occupations. Far from it."

In the rest of his essay, Frothingham discusses the deficiencies of the Unitarian Church and the remedies offered by the New Church. I will mention here only one element, pneumatology (the study of spiritual beings and phenomena), whose absence in Unitariansim strikes Frothingham as a loss. "Most Unitarians evidently have no definite belief in regard to angels and spirits,—whether clothed in flesh or unclothed,—and therefore no positive ideas concerning the nature of the life after death. What is more remarkable, they do not *care* to have any; they hold it to be only superstition and self-delusion which can pretend to any knowledge of the future world. A self-satisfied ignorance or unbelief I should not seek to invade; but there can be few who are not sometimes visited with longings for a clearer insight into the spiritual world, its laws and modes of existence. Swedenborg professes to unveil those laws. He professes to have "seen and heard" spirits in that world who once were inhabitants of this, and to have had authority from the Lord to declare what was thus heard and seen." Frothingham finds himself more at home in the spiritual world portrayed by Swedenborg than in the Unitarian universe where angels and spirits are hardly in evidence. He was convinced that anyone who would read Swedenborg's "writings without any prejudice or prepossession would be amazed at the self-evident character of the knowledge they impart", and would feel that even where one cannot understand, one must still defer to so wonderful a person.

Stephen Hales: scientist and clergyman

The Reverend Stephen Hales (1677–1761), an English contemporary of Swedenborg, is ranked among the fathers, perhaps the most important one, of plant physiology, but he also made several seminal contributions to other fields, particularly haemodynamics, where he will be remembered as the first person to measure blood pressure. He was ordained in 1709, and earned his living as a professional clergyman. He is mentioned here only to show that even an outstanding scientist is likely to be a product and prisoner of his era. This may be seen by reading his essay "Some Considerations on the Causes of Earthquakes" [205]. The introductory paragraphs assert that the ordinary course of Nature is as much carried on by the Divine agency as the extraordinary and miraculous events. "God sometimes changes the Order of Nature, with design to chastise Man for his Disobedience and Follies; natural Evils being graciously designed by him as Moral goods." When we see this cohabitation of eighteenth century superstition and cutting-edge science in one mind, we realize how daring Swedenborg's departure from the beaten track was, and it also inclines us to take a more kindly view of the contemporary Muslims who have earned degrees in engineering or medicine or a scientific discipline, but remain contaminated by the prevalent superstition, just as Stephen Hales was in his time.

Some of Sir Syed's contemporaries in Christendom

By the end of the nineteenth century, Sir Syed's Christian counterparts in the United States were pleased with the changing attitudes of their enlightened coreligionists; this will become manifest if we look at two essays published in 1882, whose authors were prominent clergymen with liberal views: O. B. Frothingham (1822–1895) [204], who has already been mentioned above, and H. W. Beecher (1813–1887) [206].

Frothingham's essay [198], entitled "Swedenborg", is a useful read for those who would like to learn a little about the Swedish seer's scientific attainments and a little more about his religious thoughts. After a few pages, the author remarks that there is a suspicion "abroad that, whatever our views respecting Swedenborg, Swedenborgianism, as a form of religious institution, has outlived its excuse for being". Why? "And this, for the very reason that it was originally so noble. It is closely associated with some things which have passed away, because their work was done." He admits that (at an earlier time) when all religious institutions in Christendom were perceived as being completely corrupt, utterly devoid of the spirit of its founder, and hostile to rational apprehension of truth, the doctrines of Swedenborg must have shone as if illuminated by light from a different sun. "But in our age they have become religious truisms. We hear them enunciated from all more or less liberal pulpits. They form the burden of popular preaching."

After dealing with the preliminaries, Frothingham pays a lavish tribute to Swedenborg and begins to analyze the message and its presentation: "The doctrine was little short of a new gospel when it was delivered. None but a true prophet could have announced such truths in that generation. I name only the most searching: That there is but one life, and that life from the Lord; that Satan has no substantial being or existence; that there is no principle of evil; that heaven and hell are both from the same source; that no man is born predestinated to hell; that heaven removes hell in man; that true religion consists in love to God and love to man; that the sacraments are signs; that the church is representative. Such are a few of the divine commonplaces which are scattered up and down the pages of Swedenborg's writings, recurring again and again with a colorless monotony that soon becomes tiresome, and with a sober-sidedness of statement which deprives them of effect. It was probably the simple, undemonstrative, prosaic, child-like mode in which they were set forth that prevented their recognition."

Besides being an ardent advocate of the theory of evolution, Frothingham was an anti-slavery campaigner at a time when abolition had not yet gained wide support even in New England; beyond these facts, I know very little about his life. Henry Ward Beecher, a contrasting figure, led a life too eventful to be captured in a few sentences. He was the subject of a recent biography, entitled *The Most Famous Man in America* [207], and there is also an earlier biography [208]. For my purpose, it is enough to state that he was possibly the most prominent American clergyman of his time, a social reformer, an ardent supporter of women's suffrage and Darwin's theory of evolution, and a trenchant opponent of slavery and (what he called) mediaeval theology. Beecher's essay, entitled "Progress of Thought in the Church", expressed joy at the retreat of cold Calvinism, and the advance of a progressive, compassionate and more intellectually honest Christianity [209]:

> It is in this way that the pulpit is changing its methods and material of sermons. No matter what becomes of Decrees of Election and of Reprobation, an audience of fathers and mothers understand what Fatherhood is. No ingenuity or eloquence can persuade them that a God, who for ten thousand years has labored to produce an infinite population of damnable souls, can with decency be called our Father. The common sense, the humanity, the moral sense which have grown out of the Gospel are judging theology. Little by little the pulpit shrinks from mediaeval theology. Ministers first gloss it by new interpretations, then they prudently hold it in suspense, then doubt it, then cast it away.

Sir Syed argued that it is not necessary for a Muslim to turn towards the *K'aba* when praying, and in building his argument, he stated, "Religion is made for man, man is not made for religion". Staying within the Christian narrative, Beecher also stressed the importance of giving back free rein to man:

> Much of what is called infidelity is a revolt from the errors of old theology. The Church, the Bible, the Creed, have been confounded with Religion. Religion is the state of a man's soul, it is disposition and conduct. Neither church, book, nor theology is of value except as an educating instrument. They have no sacredness of their own. They are mere servants. Man alone, as a son of God and an heir of immortality, has an inherent sanctity. But the popular impression has been assiduously cultivated that a man falls into infidelity who no longer accepts the reigning creeds, no matter how just, how pure, how beneficent his life may be. Heresy is dissent from a reigning creed. Courts and councils have again and again decided that heresy is substantial ostracism. Men may be proud, self-seekers, worldly, self-indulgent—thus denying, in practical forms, every principle of Christian life, and yet be orthodox and of relative good standing; but a saintly life, dissenting

> from a barbaric creed, is not worthy of sympathy or a membership in the church.

If I had replaced Christian references (the Church, the Bible, etc) with their Islamic equivalents, I could have easily stated that the preceding paragraph expresses Sir Syed's thoughts in free translation. Unfortunately, an Islamicized version of the next paragraph (and the one after that) could not have come from the pen or the mind of Sir Syed, and much as I would like to to make a similar statement for contemporary Islam, I must not allow my desire to see change run ahead of the course of events:

> Our age is not in rebellion against clear, intellectual statements of religious truth. But there is a rebellion against the tyranny of mediaeval creeds. It is not extravagant to say that a revolution is at hand in regard to the whole philosophy of Christianity, and that this revolution is led on, not from restless impatience of restraint, nor by novelty, nor by a worldly spirit, but by the deepest moral consciousness of men who love truth above all price, and who value a Christian manhood above all measure.

What Beecher writes next is very exhilarating indeed:

> The signs are in the air. *Men no longer preach doctrines to which they swore in their ordination vows—or they give to them new meanings, at variance with historic fact. It is beginning to be permitted men to preach their own view of truth unclipped by creeds.* Sagacious and cautious men are quietly sowing seed which they know will by and by destroy old notions. Other men testify to change, by greater zeal in teaching the old symbols of doctrine. Every age has a race of men who elect themselves to the care of other men's beliefs, who appoint themselves God's sheriffs to hunt and run down heretics. They are very busy. Men are ceasing to employ creeds as lines of separation between sect and sect, and are shaking hands in a higher fellowship over and across them. Creeds have ceased to be employed as conservatories of piety. Orthodoxy confesses that truth can no longer be kept in church or seminary by creeds, but only by living faith. (My italics.)

The change foreseen and passionately advocated by Beecher did take place, but a large portion of American Christians are still not ready to shelve the old symbols of doctrine.

Christ and Muḥammad. Christians and Muslims

The jinns, who can be good as well as evil, are distinct from demons, but the two do share many traits, and if I do not ignore their differences, I will not be able to compare Islam with Christianity, and indeed the other faiths as well. Belief in evil spirits is truly universal; generally a demon brings disease and recovery comes when it is driven away. Sickness as well as recovery was attributed to God's will. Both the Old and the New Testament speak of demons; Christ, for example, cast out demons from two possessed men and made the demons enter swine in such a way that the swine rushed into the lake and were drowned (Matthew 8:28–34).

New England faced, in 1721, an epidemic of smallpox, and in Boston alone almost one thousand people were killed by the disease [210]. Sickness was generally regarded as Divine punishment, and the colonists, who had little understanding of either the nature or transmission of most illnesses, were incapable of taking effective steps to prevent outbreaks. A physician named Zabdiel Boylston, who was an ardent advocate of inoculation (actually variolation, since a live virus was used) started administering the procedure as an alternative to what had been the response of the community in previous outbreaks, namely passive acceptance. This provoked an intense debate, pitting religion against science, priests against medical practitioners. The debate centred round such questions as: "Is inoculation a sin insofar as it amounts to undoing the punishment sent by God?", "Is refusing to be inoculated against God's reason?"

Around the middle of the nineteenth century, educated opinion in the Western world began drifting away from the old, metaphoric language and people started speaking of germs and microbes and mosquitos instead of demons, and of inoculation, antiseptics and vaccination instead of exorcism.

On the whole, a reconciliation has been achieved in the Western world by marking off the domain and methods of scientific investigation and scientific teaching on the one hand, and of religious experience and religious teaching on the other, and, with some restraint on both sides, this tense truce can be maintained if neither party insists on an inherent and *inevitable* contradiction between science and religion. This state of affairs has been reached without any undue depreciation of the tenets of either side. There is a scientific truth, valid irrespective of geography and one's political affiliations, and there is a religious truth, recognized by some and rejected by others. The antibiotic relieves the agony of a Buddhist, a Christian, and an atheist alike. No faith in the Almighty is a prerequisite, nor an appeal for intervention a guarantee, for the efficacy of the the surgical and pharmaceutical miracles wrought by modern science.

In 1941 Rudolph Bultmann (1884–1976), a Lutheran theologian and Professor of New Testament in the University of Marburg, set off a lively debate by publishing an essay with the title "Neues Testament und Mythologie". Twenty years later, the Society for the Promotion of Christian Knowledge (SPCK) made this essay available to the English-speaking world by publishing a monograph, entitled *Kerygma and Myth: A Theological Debate.*

kerygma; proclamation (of religious truth)

The mythological language of the New Testament (NT) had been nagging liberal Christian theologians long before Bultmann. Briefly stated, they supposed that the problem could be solved by simply discarding the mythology—lock, stock, and barrel. But the twentieth century saw the rise of the "kerygmatic" emphasis in the interpretation of the NT faith, which made this solution untenable, since mythological elements are an inseparable aspect of the message. The need for "demythologizing" rather than dropping these elements became, in Bultmann's view, very pressing, especially since the stress on the kerygma threatened the revival of an uncritical biblicism in some quarters. He deserves credit for raising this issue in all its sharpness and offering a proposal which sought to meet the outlook of Christians in modern societies.

Bultmann, who was contemplating pre-1940 Western Europe, a predominantly Christian or Agnostic society, knew that every community has some uncommonly gullible individuals, whom he described as "primitive enough to qualify for an age of mythical thought", but he counted them as nonentities. What matters, he stressed, is the world view which men imbibe from their environment, and it is science which determines that view of the world through the school, the press, the wireless, the cinema, and all the other fruits of technical progress. He thought that it is impossible to use electric light and the wireless and to avail ourselves of modern medical and surgical discoveries, and at the same time to believe in the NT world of spirits and miracles.

Bultmann wrote his essay at a time when science and technology bore the same relationship as is expressed by the saying "The child is father to the man", and the two went hand in hand, each feeding (and feeding on) the other; the fruits of technology were used mainly by those whose forefathers had laid the scientific foundations for the development of technology, and in so doing had paved, albeit unintentionally, the way for discrediting the mythological universe of the NT. Maxwell's inspired unification of electric and magnetic forces and Hertz's generation of electromagnetic waves shortly afterwards; Thomson's deduction of the equation of telegraphy and the laying of the transatlantic cable for sending electrical signals between England and America (the launching of the Victorian "Internet"); Heaviside's "heavification" of the cable to make it suitable for telephony; Röntgen's discovery of X-rays and its almost instantaneous adoption by the medical community; these events were all miracles in the sense that each of these mind-boggling events was unprecedented, but unlike the Biblical miracles, which could not be repeated over and over again to silence every doubting Thomas, each scientific miracle led to further miracles: the radio, the television, the cellular phone, medical imaging and whatnot. The child had not yet turned into a demon (in 1941); the world had not yet woken up to the fact that the beautiful brainchild of a scientist, the equation $E = mc^2$, can turn, when nourished by nuclear technology and satanic politics, into a terrible monster.

The European trinity of science-technology-demythology was a unique phenomenon that is unlikely to be repeated; we have since seen that it is possible to train scientists and technologists without "burdening" them with a liberal education, that it is possible to own a refrigerator without any obligation to venerate, or even know the names of, those who developed the science of thermodynamics. Anyone in Afghanistan can buy a cellular phone and use it for sending a divorce notice to his wife, and a few can even use it for detonating an IED or sending a graphic film of the beheading of an "infidel", if their heads have been filled with enough absurdities and hatred. Seventy years after

Bultmann, "credulous people" can still be found even among Christians, in larger numbers than implied by Bultmann's dismissive and wishful phrase "here and there", but mostly "there" in America, and many of them criticize him, which is indeed their right; it is also right and proper that they do not clamour for burning his followers or even his books.

Who is to blame for the eclipsing of Islam?

Who is to blame for the backwardness of the Muslims? Is it the Prophet himself? Muḥammad is often blamed for sanctioning belief in jinns and angels and many other outlandish notions that were rife in Arabia, but this must be considered too glib an explanation, unless one can show that Christ set a better example. It seems polite to express my opinion indirectly by referring to T. Witton Davies (1851–1923), Baptist minister and Semitic scholar, who admitted that Christ was either "winking at the ignorance or superstition of His contemporaries" or was "Himself the victim of such ignorance or superstition". Christ and Muḥammad, the Bible and the Qur'ān, stand on equal footing, here as in most other matters.

A study of the next chapter will show that through most of its long history the Church has feared and discouraged independent thinking and extolled credulity. The Dark Age of Christianity has been well portrayed by Lecky [211, p. 218]: "[T]he period of Catholic ascendency was on the whole one of the most deplorable in the history of the human mind. The energies of Christendom were diverted from all useful and progressive studies, and were wholly expended on theological disquisitions. A crowd of superstitions, attributed to infallible wisdom, barred the path of knowledge, and the charge of magic, or the charge of heresy, crushed every bold enquiry in the sphere of physical nature or of opinions. Above all, the conditions of true enquiry had been cursed by the Church. A blind unquestioning credulity was inculcated as the first of duties, and the habit of doubt, the impartiality of a suspended judgment, the desire to hear both sides of a disputed question, and to emancipate the judgment from unreasoning prejudice, were all in consequence condemned. The belief in the guilt of error and doubt became universal, and that belief may be confidently pronounced to be the most pernicious superstition that has ever been accredited among mankind. Mistaken facts are rectified by enquiry. Mistaken methods of research, though far more inveterate, are gradually altered; but the spirit that shrinks from enquiry as sinful, and deems a state of doubt a state of guilt, is the most enduring disease that can afflict the mind of man. Not till the education of Europe passed from the monasteries to the universities, not till Mahommedan science, and classical freethought, and industrial independence broke the sceptre of the Church, did the intellectual revival of Europe begin."

In their heyday, Muslims believed that their ascendancy over Christians was a proof of the truth of their faith, but the tables were turned afterwards when the demons who despised rational, open-minded enquiry were exorcised (by Divine will?) from the minds of Christians and driven into the minds of Muslims, who went into a deeper and darker *jāhilliya* than that from which the Arabic Qur'ān, a revolutionary and inspiring book, had extricated them. The second *jāhilliya* turned this Arabic Qur'ān into an Archaic Qur'ān, the *Ṣiḥa Sitta* into Scriptures, and countless commentaries on the Archaic Qur'ān into treasures of infallible wisdom. These books have dissipated the strength of Islamica by diverting its energies from useful and progressive enquiries to regressive theological debates; they have replaced a healthy curiosity by a blind and unquestioning credulity, toleration by a hateful intolerance. The Western world has meanwhile moved along the road to progress, under relentless pressure from heretics, unbelievers and a handful of honest-to-God progressive Christians, some of whom have been mentioned in this chapter.

Ṣiḥa Sitta: the six books of 'correct' Prophetic Traditions

Giving new meanings to the old doctrine

Madame Swetchine (1782–1859) summed up the uniqueness of the relation between a book (or a picture) and one who studies it by saying "No two persons ever read the same book, or saw the same picture" [212, p. 33]. Every man who reads a book, necessarily gets from that book all that he is capable of receiving, just as every man who looks at a picture, or stares at a waterfall, or smells a flower, derives all the intellectual wealth, aesthetic pleasure, sensual delight and spiritual satisfaction he is capable of receiving. What the picture or the flower or the waterfall is to him, depends upon his mind, and upon the stage of development he has reached. The Bible or the Qur'ān must appear a different book to each person who reads it seriously (in a language that he understands); the revelations of nature depend upon the individual to whom they are revealed, or by whom they are discovered. As the extent of the revelation or discovery depends entirely upon the intellectual and moral development of the person to whom, or by whom, the revelation or discovery is made, the Bible or the Bhagavad Gītā or the Qur'ān or the *Four Quartets* or the *Ṣiḥa Sitta* cannot be the same to any two people, but each one must necessarily interpret it for himself.

The moment it is accepted that we can give to the books held to be divine such meanings as are consistent with our highest ideals, that we can regard the original words as purses in which to put our gold and pearls, that no one is obliged to surrender his right to interpret a text to a person who claims to understand God's words better than any other human being, each reader will be on his way to making a new, inspired and individual version of the book. If his mind is narrow, if he has been raised by ignorance, nursed by fear, tamed by doctrinaire parents and teachers, and poisoned by petty prejudices, he will cling to the literal meaning of what he reads. If he has some courage and critical capacity—if he is among those who understand—he will doubt and ask questions, and his search for answers will lead him to new interpretations and adaptations, which will modify the literal text. When this becomes acceptable to the majority of Muslims, the Qur'ān will indeed become a book for people who *do* understand, and Islam will regain its lost glory.

5 Can the Hare Catch Up?

Thanks to caliph Mā'mūn, the irrepressible champion of scholarship, Arabophone science galloped at a delirious pace and took an early lead over its soundly asleep Christian rival, European science. Like the hare in the Æsopian fable, Arabophone science decided (or was obliged) to take a snooze after a while, but its rival, initially even slower than the tortoise of the same fable, became brisker and brisker as time went on, and overtook the recumbent hare some six centuries ago. Unlike the race in the fable, or one on a real track, there is no finishing line in the contest for scientific advancement, and supporters of the hare have been at their wit's end for well over a century, trying to find a pick-me-up for their favourite contestant.

To appreciate just how dejectingly hard it is to establish world-class research activity in a scientifically impoverished society, let us consider an analogy and compare science to football (soccer).

Why are the rich Arab nations so poor at football?

For more than three decades almost every oil-rich country in the Middle East has been spending fabulous sums of money—enough to break the backs of a thousand camels—for the sake of joining the ranks of the top twenty or so footballing nations. Lack of public interest (at the fan/spectator level) is certainly not a reason for this failure; indeed, many clerics, deeply disturbed by the competition between the stadium and the mosque, have issued *fatwās* against football [213–215]. The principal reasons for the poor performance are the emaciated state of the domestic leagues, the lack of penetration of the game within the society, and the small size of the pool of talented and devoted

fatwa (or *fetwa*): religious edict

players dying to represent their country in international competitions. In countries which are power houses of football, the game is played at every conceivable level: the backyard, the neighbourhood, school, work place, small privately organized groups and clubs, five-a-side, eleven-a-side, indoors, outdoors, a multi-tier domestic league, the UEFA Champions League, the UEFA Cup Winners' Cup, the UEFA Cup, competition at the continental and intercontinental level, and who-knows-where-else except the Milky Way Cup and the Intergalactic Cup. Pouring more money and importing foreign players is hardly a feasible remedy for the Amīrs and the Sultāns, because truly gifted players are not likely to leave the UEFA region where prestigious clubs are located. Allowing the best of the local players to hone their skills by accepting offers from reputed foreign clubs can help, but only in the long run and only if those players decide to return to the mother country, resisting the temptation to continue playing at the more elevated level abroad.

All in all, the manager and fans of a football club or a national team in the Middle East cannot have much reason for optimism. Likewise, no minister of science in the Muslim World, no matter how young, should expect success within his lifetime if his goal is to bring full-fledged scientific activity, let alone scientific glory, back to his country.

Plan of the chapter

History, as every serious student of the subject knows, is adulterated with blatant lies and wishful guesses, but the passage of time acts as an open-meshed conveyor belt that sifts and sorts various reports, allowing sheer propaganda to drop out, and solidifying the remaining material into great blocks of facts, more or less trustworthy. When similar patterns are observed in blocks belonging to different eras or different nations, we repeat the cliché *history repeats itself*, most often as a warning (look what happened to those who behaved in this manner) and occasionally as a descriptive device, which is my purpose here.

Sensible and humane people will agree that we should try to learn from history and avoid near repetitions of calamitous collisions. Such agreement notwithstanding, history itself has shown repeatedly that its lessons are lost on humans when they act as mobs. Still, I cannot look ahead without reflecting at the past, for it is time past that has moulded the present, which is another name for the latent future, the time that waits, unnoticed but not unformed, shaped already by what has preceded. David Hume told his readers that if they want to know the sentiments, inclinations, and course of life of the Greeks and Romans, they should study well the temper and actions of the French and English [216, pp. 85–6]. "You cannot be much mistaken in transferring to the former *most* of the observations which you have made with regard to the latter. Mankind are so much the same, in all times and places, that history informs us of nothing new or strange in this particular." I will begin by examining, in the next two sections, the attitude of the early Christian Church and see whether it differed significantly from that of ʿUmar (the second Caliph) or of Ghazālī. However, my main purpose in this chapter is to ask at what point conditions in Europe (as regards inter-sectarian strife and the relation between science and religion) were closest to those obtaining in the Muslim world of today. If the reader will agree with my diagnosis, it will not be difficult to find a consensus about the possible remedies.

Has Christianity been hostile to science?

Two books, both published first in the United States, must be mentioned in any discussion of the relationship between science and Christianity. A reader of this chapter need not know at present anything about these books other than their titles: *History of the Conflict between Religion and Science* (1874) by William Henry Draper [217] and *A History of the Warfare of Science with Theology in Christendom* (1896) by Andrew Dickson White [218]. Each book has had its admirers and detractors, but I can find space here for answering only one critic of each work, namely James Joseph Walsh and Daniel D. Whedon.

Walsh responded to White's book by writing two of his own, *Catholic Churchmen in Science* [219] and *The Popes and Science* [220], published in 1906 and 1908, respectively. The latter, dedicated to

Pope Pius X, argued that the Popes had always supported medical research, a claim that will not be disputed here, since I have discussed its analogue, Islamican rulers' support for medicine. The first chapter of the 1906 book is entitled "The Supposed Opposition of Science and Religion", and I would like to quote one paragraph from this chapter:

> There is no doubt that at times men have been the subject of persecution because of scientific opinions. In all of these cases, without exception, however—and this is particularly true of such men as Galileo, Giordano Bruno, and Michael Servetus—a little investigation of the personal character of the individuals involved in these persecutions will show the victims to have been of that especially irritating class of individuals who so constantly awaken opposition to whatever opinions they may hold by upholding them over-strenuously and inopportunely. They were the kind of men who could say nothing without, to some extent at least, arousing the resentment of those around them who still clung to older ideas. We all know this class of individual very well. In these gentler modern times we may even bewail the fact that there is no such expeditious method of disposing of him as in the olden time. This is not a defence of what was done in their regard, but is a word of explanation . . .

Only someone who bewails the banishing of barbaric penalties would agree with Walsh.[1] Burning to death for the crime of heresy was the "expeditious method" used for dealing with Bruno and Servetus. The murder of Bruno in Catholic Rome (1600) requires no reminder here, but the execution of Servetus in Calvinist Geneva (1553) is not sufficiently known, even to many

[1]A Calvinist, writing in 1909 (four hundredth anniversary of Calvin's birth), criticized Servetus (1509–1553) in savage terms, but even he had the decency to emphasize the sanctity of the freedom of expression [221]: "And yet the darkest shadow falls across his [Calvin's] record at this auspicious moment. Heresy must have martyrs. It is a pity that a better man than Servetus should not head the list. He was a persistent liar, a foul reviler, and at the best a vain dreamer. But it is a greater pity that the man who has unquestionably contributed more than all others in the sixteenth century to establish the religious liberty of the twentieth, did not redeem this magnificent opportunity to rise above his own passions and above the dense darkness of his times, to defend the right of free thought and free speech for his bitterest adversary, and by this one brilliant achievement to make Geneva the very City of God!"

Christians. Details about the life and theological views of this victim of Protestant persecution may be found in Refs. [222–224].

Walsh has yet another argument for exonerating religion: "In this matter it must not be forgotten that persecution has been the very common associate of noteworthy advances in science, quite apart from any question of the relations between science and religion" [219, p. 6]. True, but only if we replace the word *persecution* to *resistance* (or *ridicule* or *reproof*), and recognize that there has never been a period in which scientists were vested with the power to impose, on someone who came forward with a heretic idea, punishments other than indifference, ostracism, professional banishment, whereas religious authorities, whether or not they were competent to pass judgment on the disputed issue, have enjoyed the privilege to persecute the heretic, by incarcerating, pillorying, banishing, beheading, burning, whatever.

In a review of Draper's book, Daniel Whedon asked [225, 226]: "How came it that these "dark ages" were the mother of modern Europe?" My retort to this rhetorical question is that the emergence of modern Europe from such a womb was a veritable miracle, akin, but only in its unlikelihood, to the virgin birth of Jesus. My reading of Whedon's review (many years after reading the book itself) left me with the impression that what Whedon disliked most was Draper's use of the word *martyr*:

> What a glorious army of martyrs this Church of the Scientists is. It sends out a cry of "persecution," "persecution," and you would think by the howl and growl they make that their books were burned, and their persons were obliged to lurk in sheepskins and goat-skins in the fastnesses of the mountains and the dens of the earth. *The ferocious theologians are often after them with a Bible in one hand and a fiery fagot in the other*. And the joke and felicity of it is that they have all the glory of this martyrdom without the slightest inconvenience of martyrdom. When the old Christians suffered martyrdom, it was an awkward endurance. The Roman axe did chop; the beasts of the amphitheater did bite and draw actual blood; the fire of Nero did burn to ashes. But as for these scientific martyrs, their furious theological executioners string them up to the very staple of the gallows without the slightest squeeze of the neck; the pincers and thumb-screws torture them without the slightest pain ... (My italics.)

fagot (US) or faggot: bundle of sticks bound together as fuel

Let us pause a little to download an electronically searchable version of Draper's book so that we may count the number of times he used the word "martyr" (or "martyrs" or "martyrdom") and in what context. I found altogether eleven occurrences, nine of which concerned *Christian* martyrs. Elsewhere, it was applied once to Giordano Bruno, and once in describing Galileo's ordeal [217, p. 171]: "He was ordered to renounce that heresy, on pain of being imprisoned. He was directed to desist from teaching and advocating the Copernican theory, and pledge himself that he would neither publish nor defend it for the future. Knowing well that Truth has no need of martyrs, he assented to the required recantation, and gave the promise demanded."

Whedon finishes his paragraph with a statement that was true at the time it was written but not a century earlier:

> Even after they have been burnt at the stake, and are in the condition of cinders and ashes, they quietly sit as professors in Christian universities, and issue volumes against Christianity; they assemble great congregations in a nominally Christian city, and lecture against what they suppose to be theological dogma, to be applauded to the echo by the public press.

Before closing this section, I must deal with two more points in Whedon's review: a claim he made in support of Christianity, and a challenge that he issued to the scientists.

One of the most persistent claims on behalf of Christianity, made also by Whedon, is that the Christian Church kept learning alive during the Dark and Middle Ages. This is how Whedon puts it: "Now, as we [Christian clergymen] are rather a feeble, unarmed folk, and belong to a class that in past ages has done more for education and science than all the other classes put together ...". As for the first part, it would suffice to say that the clergy were not *always* a feeble and unarmed lot. As for the second, I refer the holder of such an opinion to what Lecky writes after stating a conclusion that I share [211, p. 220]: "It is an undoubted truth that, for a considerable period, almost all the knowledge of Europe was included in the monasteries, and from this it is continually inferred that, had these institutions not existed, knowledge would have been absolutely extinguished. But such a conclusion I conceive to be altogether untrue."

Whedon offers truce if the scientists can demonstrate the truth of their theories and the falsehood of rival theories:

> *Science is bound, when she propounds any claim to a new discovery, to demonstrate it against all previous opposite opinions.* Such previous opposite opinions may be based upon imaginative conceptions; or upon the immediate perceptions of the senses; or upon the teachings of former science; or upon the interpretation of religious records; or upon the dogmas of a false, or partly false, revelation. Now these previous opinions have their rights. They have a right to sit in judgment upon the newly propounded discovery, and to claim that it demonstrates its positive reality before they can be required to surrender their own. They have a right to say to the scientists: "Gentlemen, it is false that we have any 'conflict with science,' or any war with discovery. Go and work with honesty and zeal in your own fields, irrespective of any previous conceptions, and learn the truth as it is. But when you have arrived at a conclusion, do not shirk scrutiny. Do not whine and whimper, and cry 'persecution,' because we put your announcements to the severest tests. Do not turn into fierce martyrs because we refuse you credit until you have given us, what you are bound to give, *demonstration*. When that comes, and not till then, your hypothesis is science; and every opposed opinion accepts its claim, and crowns you, not with the amaranth of martyrdom, but with the laurel of successful discovery." (Emphasis in the original.)

One hopes that while the scientists are scurrying around to collect evidence, the theologians are cudgeling their brains, not lighting their faggots.

I cannot enter into a detailed discussion of how unscientific it is to ask a scientist to produce a proof. One might as well ask him to bring the milk of a male tiger. I will only say that we always seek, and speak of, proofs in mathematics but not in the other sciences. That there is no largest prime, that $\sqrt{2}$ is irrational, that π is transcendental[2] are all propositions which have been proved once and for all; there's no going back now. Once one has acquired—by revelation, by induction, by hook or by crook—a mathematical proposition or a conjecture, its proof must be based

a real number is said to be *irrational* if it cannot be expressed as a ratio of two integers

[2]A number (possibly complex) is *transcendental* if it is not the root of any integer polynomial; every real transcendental number is also irrational.

on deductive (or demonstrative) reasoning; if such a proof can be found, the proposition will remain eternally incontrovertible. On the other hand, when a physicist hits upon a hypothesis, (s)he has no hope of proving it once and for all. In this respect, there is a world of difference between mathematics and other scientific disciplines.

It is wrong to think that a theory or a model may be regarded as basically sound if its predictions are borne out by experiments. This pragmatic view is accepted so widely that most students of science—and indeed many scientists themselves, until they reflect—take it as a logical truth and an essential ingredient of scientific methodology. It is, of course, neither. The logical fallacy is seen easily: If $\mathbb{A}$ implies $\mathbb{B}$, where $\mathbb{A}$ is the set of assumptions on which a particular model is hased and $\mathbb{B}$ is the predicted outcome of an experiment, then a verification of $\mathbb{B}$ does not necessarily imply the truth of $\mathbb{A}$ (because $\mathbb{B}$ may also be a consequence of $\mathbb{X}$ or $\mathbb{Y}$ or $\mathbb{Z}$). What is not readily perceived, and if seen not always fully appreciated, is that the demolition machinery of science (or scientific method) derives its strength from the contrapositive assertion "if $\mathbb{B}$ is false, then $\mathbb{A}$ must also be false," i.e., if the experimental observations do not accord with its predictions, the theory must be discarded. This, in a nutshell, is Popper's message: science does not prove anything at all, but it disproves a great deal.

A scientist is able to acquire new knowledge only by abandoning the holy grail of proof, and seeking instead inductive evidence by making intelligent and informed conjectures, which may be subjected to a process of confirmation or refutation. For those who are not familiar with these ideas, I recommend the preface to *Induction and Analogy in Mathematics*, in which Polya discusses the distinction between *demonstrative reasoning* and *plausible reasoning* and states [227]: Demonstrative reasoning is safe, beyond controversy, and final. Plausible reasoning is hazardous, controversial, and provisional. Demonstrative reasoning penetrates the sciences just as far as mathematics does, but it is in itself (as mathematics is in itself) incapable of yielding essentially new knowledge about the world around us. Anything new that we learn about the world involves plausible reasoning, which is the only kind of reasoning for which we care in everyday affairs.

Early Christian Fathers

Saint Paul, the real founder of the Christian Church, is known for saying that "the wisdom of this world is foolishness in God's sight" (I Corinthians 3:19). As to how the great Apostle became aware of God's opinion about worldly wisdom, or what he meant by the word *wisdom* eludes me. If he meant shameful skulduggery of the type exposed by Edward Snowden, I would agree with him. However, when we read the words of those who came after St. Paul, it begins to look more likely that he meant the wisdom sought by philosophers (the lovers of wisdom).

In a chapter entitled "Science and the Early Church" [228, pp. 19–48], Lindberg expresses his dissatisfaction with the criticism, unreasonable in his opinion, levelled at the Roman Church by Draper and against Christianity by White. Lindberg decides, therefore, to "consider with particular care" the views of Tertullian, the "church father who is generally taken to epitomize the anti-intellectualism of the early church". After quoting two passages authored by Tertullian, Lindberg comments: "There can be no doubt that Tertullian was not an enthusiast for secular learning; but neither was he the uncompromising opponent of reasoned discourse that these passages, if allowed to stand alone, might seem to imply." It is worthwhile therefore to take an even closer look at Tertullian's writings and see where he really stands.

Tertullian, called the Father of Latin Christianity (because he was the first Christian writer to use Latin as his medium of expression), was born around 150 in the ancient city of Carthage in what is now Tunisia. A selection of his writings is available in English; the cluster "philosopher(s)" occurs nearly 110 times in the 220 pages which make up Part I of this selection. What he thought of the philosophers may be gleaned from the remark "Opinions of philosophers all more or less absurd", which is a part of the title of §54 of *A Treatise on the Soul,* the last piece in Part I. It is also easy to see that Tertullian's feelings towards these misguided pagans did not include Christian compassion [229, p. 133]:

> It therefore served Thales of Miletus quite right, when, star-gazing as he walked with all the eyes he had, he had the mortification of

falling into a well, and was unmercifully twitted by an Egyptian, who said to him, "Is it because you found nothing on earth to look at, that you think you ought to confine your gaze to the sky?" His fall, therefore, is a figurative picture of the philosophers; of those, I mean, who persist in applying their studies to a vain purpose, since they indulge a *stupid curiosity on natural objects*, which they ought rather (intelligently to direct) to their Creator and Governor. (My italics.)

Thales of Miletus is considered to be the first philosopher of Greece because he discarded mythical answers to questions involving natural phenomena; indeed, Tertullian calls him 'the first of natural philosophers' [229, p. 51]. "Curiosity on natural objects" has matured into what we now call natural science, and it has no serious rival for acquiring knowledge about the material universe. I am tempted to insert here a story that Kirchhoff liked to relate [230]. When the question as to whether Fraunhofer's lines[3] indicated the presence of gold in the sun was under investigation, Kirchhoff's banker remarked: "What do I care for gold in the sun if I cannot fetch it down here!" Shortly afterwards Kirchhoff received a medal and a prize in gold sovereigns from Queen Victoria. While handing the prize over to his banker, he quipped: "Look here, I have succeeded at last in fetching some gold from the sun."

ante-Nicene: before the first council of Nicaea (325), called by the Emperor Constantine.

Let us look now at Lactantius, another highly esteemed ante-Nicene Father. The third book of his *Divine Institutes* is entitled *Of the False Wisdom of Philosophers*. Anyone who has read this book and also Ghazālī's *Incoherence of Philosophers* would readily agree that Lactantius's soul re-emerged in the body of Ghazālī, for they have both been animated by the same spirit. Lactantius, who thought that the Scriptures indicated a four-cornered earth, was unable to see how anyone could believe in a spherical earth [231, p. 94]:

> [I]s there any one so senseless as to believe that there are men whose footsteps are higher than their heads? or that the things which with us are in a recumbent position, with them hang in an

[3]Dark lines in the spectrum of a star, caused by absorption of the stellar radiation at specific wavelengths by elements in the gaseous atmosphere of the star.

> inverted direction? that the crops and trees grow downwards? that the rains, and snow, and hail fall upwards to the earth? And does any one wonder that hanging gardens are mentioned among the seven wonders of the world, when philosophers make hanging fields, and seas, and cities, and mountains?

I have interrupted Lactantius just before he launches into an explanation of why *they* (the philosophers) are *always* wrong. His words would ring truer if *they* be taken to mean dogmatic theologians like himself, and if one of his clauses (italicized below) is replaced by my words. Inebriated by hubris, Lactantius babbles on:

> The origin of this error must also be set forth by us. For they are always deceived in the same manner. For when they have assumed anything false in the commencement of their investigations, *led by the resemblance of the truth,* they necessarily fall into those things which are its consequences. Thus they fall into many ridiculous things; because those things which are in agreement with false things, must themselves be false. But since they placed confidence in the first, they do not consider the character of those things which follow, but defend them in every way; whereas they ought to judge from those which follow, whether the first are true or false. (My italics.)

I would suggest replacing "led by the resemblance of the truth" by the clause "misled by the assumption that the Bible is an infallible source of scientific knowledge".

Probably the most elaborate work on the connection between science and the Bible which the early Church has bequeathed to us is *Topographia Christiana* [232, 233]. Its author, Cosmas (perhaps not his real name), who had travelled as a merchant over the greater part of the then known world (including India, which accounts for his being called *Cosmas Indicopleustes*), took his abode in a monastery in his latter years, and there, though suffering from a poor eyesight, declining strength and insufficient education, set himself the task of proving, once and for all, that our world was not a sphere but a solid plane. The book has two prologues, the first of which makes an appeal to the reader: "First of all I exhort those who will read this book to peruse it with all attention and diligence ...." I would have complied with his exhortation if the rest of Prologue II had shown some politeness to those who cling to the pagan notion of the rotundity of the earth.

Prologue II opens with a summary of its contents: *The Christian Topography of the whole world demonstrated from divine scripture about which Christians ought not to doubt.* Cosmas is reasonable insofar as he does not expect an infidel to accept a topography derived from a source sacred only to the Christians. After a short preamble, in which Cosmas talks of his motives for writing the book and of the encouragement accorded by a certain Pamphilus, he continues: "And let no one condemn me as overbold, because I conduct the exposition of my subject in a style homely and unmethodical, since it is not fine phrases the Christian requires but right notions [and, I might add, some milk of human kindness and a little humility]. For while many be the darts and helmets and shields and wars set in motion against the Church, some supposed to be Christians, holding divine scripture of no account but despising and looking down upon it, assume like the Pagan philosophers, that the form of the heavens is spherical, being led into this error by the solar and lunar eclipses." The rest of Prologue II lays out the structure of the book, much as a modern scientific tract would do, but the authorities cited include "Moses and the prophets" and "the Holy Ghost".

I have not found any remark attributed to ʿUmar that shows him to be more antagonistic to profane learning, or more misogynistic, than the great Apostle Paul, to whom he has been compared by some [234]; nor does any of the Ghazālī books scrutinized here contain something sillier than what I have quoted from Tertullian or Lactantius. These parallels vouch for the truth of Hume's claim that the chief use of history "is only to discover the constant and universal principles of human nature, by showing men in all varieties of circumstances and situations, and furnishing us with materials from which we may form our observations and become acquainted with the regular springs of human action and behaviour" [216, p. 86].

Let us move our gaze from the early Fathers and look instead at the period where the halcyon centuries of Arabophone science (the hare) have already slipped so far into the past that only the tortoise is visible. Let us begin at the opening of the seventeenth century.

Seventeenth century Europe. I: Banishment of Vorstius

A large part of Europe went through a series of conflicts known as the Thirty Years War (1618–1648), which embraced, after 1621, the last phase of the Eighty Years War of the Low Countries (see below). The former, triggered by the Reformation, had many offshoots, and was brought on by the Roman Catholics in attempting to suppress the Reformation, to exterminate Protestantism, and to stifle freedom of thought, and freedom of religion. Philip II of Spain thought that he could best please God and earn a well-deserved place in heaven by redeeming mankind, even if this meant taking the reigns of the empire of the world in his hands, and using his authority and might to extirpate Protestantism in all its forms, to behead, torture, roast or bury alive whosoever opposed him or the Holy Church. The key to the political climate of the time is the fact that, though diversity had become an undeniable fact, all men still hankered after the blissful state of doctrinal uniformity, and the word *toleration* was not a part of everyday vocabulary. One's own views were to be respected not because religious diversity was enshrined in the constitution, but because all other beliefs were necessarily false and pernicious. Diversity in an age of uniformity cannot but lead to persecution, and the craving for uniformity as a sacred principle meant that each party fought mercilessly for the supremacy of its own doctrines.

The Low Countries had endured a longer conflict, known also as the Dutch War of Independence (1568–1648), but had earned a twelve years pause (1609–21) by entering into a truce with Spain. You would be wrong to think that the only religious disputes were those between the Protestants and the Catholics. This part of Europe was ablaze with the flames of controversies involving different factions of the Calvinist variant of Protestantism, and the disputes revolved around predestination and Arianism.[4]

---

[4]Arianism, the doctrine which precipitated the first major controversy within the Christian Church, is named after Arius of Alexandria (d. 336), who denied the divinity of Christ (also called *the Son* and *the Word*); in his view God (the Father) alone was without beginning, uncreated; the Son was created, and once had not existed. Though at first influential, the doctrine was condemned at the Council of Nicaea, at which Arius was opposed by Athanasius, also of Alexandria, who maintained the now orthodox view that the Son is of one

This was an uncanny replication (but the Christian version) of the theological dispute that flared up during the reign of Mā'mūn.

Jacobus Arminius (1560-1609) and Franciscus Gomarus (1563–1641), two professors of theology in the university of Leyden, became embroiled in a dispute, the former supporting the doctrine of free-will in opposition to the latter who held fast to the strict predestinarianism of Calvin. The whole country became divided into two hostile factions, arguing about issues which no prophet and no thinker has been able to settle, even to this day, to the satisfaction of all parties. The Arminians were also called Remonstrants, from the remonstrance of Arminius against Calvinism. Jan van Olden Barneveldt, the patriot, took the side of the Arminians, while Prince Maurice of Nassau backed the Gomarists (or the anti-remonstrants). On the death of Arminius, his position was offered to Vorstius, who published a treatise in defence of his predecessor's opinions. This treatise was put into the hands of James I of England (who was also James VI of Scotland).

James was a monarch who divided his time between drinking, hunting, writing, tending his kingdom, and reminding everyone that he was, above all else, the ever vigilant current holder of the title *Defender of the Faith*. His zeal reached a peak in 1611, and he explains why [235, pp. 349–50]:[5]

> In Autumn last, about the end of August, being in our hunting progress, there came to our hands two books of the said Vorstius, the one entitled *Tractatus Theologicus de Deo*, dedicated to Landgrave of Hesse, imprinted in the year 1610; the other his *Exegesis Apologetica* upon that book, dedicated to the States, and printed in the year 1611. Which books, as soon as we had received, and (not without much horror and detestation) cast our eye only upon some of the principal Articles of his disputations contained in the first book, and his commentary thereupon in the second, God is our witness, that the zeal of his glory did so transport us, as (to say with St. Paul) we stayed not one hour, but dispatched a letter presently to our Ambassador resident with the States [Ralph Winwood], to this purpose following.

substance with the Father. Arius was banished and the heresy expired before the end of the fourth century, but disbelief in the divinity of Christ has formed part of the doctrine of many minor sects since, notably in Unitarianism.

[5]I have modernized the spellings in James's text.

The Dutch were not particularly pleased with this foreign interference in their affairs, and politely communicated their resentment to James. But the meddlesome monarch wrote back in his own hand that he was not going to take "Leave it to us" for an answer; that "if peradventure this wretched Vorstius should deny or equivocate upon those blasphemous points of heresy and atheism, which already he hath broached, that perhaps may move you to spare his person, and not cause him to be burned (which never any heretic better deserved, and wherein we will leave him to your own Christian wisdom)". That he was not only the king of England but also the *Defender of the Faith*, and that if they would not disown the heretic, he would distance himself from them, in which case he would "exhort all other reformed Churches to join with us in a common Council, how to extinguish and remand to hell these abominable heresies".

The States still obstinately ignoring James's interference, he published *A Declaration against Vorstius* [235]. The Dutch theologian is described in this abusive tirade as "a wretched heretic or rather atheist" (p. 349), "monster" (350, 357) "viper," (351) "wretched and wicked atheist," (363) and the like, while Arminius himself is called "that enemie of God" (355). James attacks these and their likes as "pestilent heretics to nestle among you, who dare to take upon them that licentious liberty, to fetch again from hell the ancient heresies long since condemned, or else to invent new of their own brain, contrary to the belief of the true Catholic Church." (356) His views of the danger of heresy are in no respect different from those of the Holy Office. "It is furthermore to be noted, that the spiritual infection of heresy, is so much more dangerous, then the bodily infection of the plague; by how much the soul is more noble than the body." (366) Such doctrines are less dangerous in a commonwealth among a thousand laymen than in "one Doctor that may poison the youth." (366) "For Christian liberty is never meant in the holy Scripture, but only in matters indifferent." (371) The King's refers to the book of Vorstius, *De Filiatione Christi* in vicious words (378): "for which title only, an author, so suspected as he, is worthy of the faggot."

Though James did not succeed in getting Vorstius burnt at the stake, his efforts were not completely in vain. He would have suffered total defeat only if the Dutch had not been divided as to what was orthodoxy and what heterodoxy. A powerful sect and party, called the Gomarists, hated Vorstius as much as did James, Winwood and Abbot (Archbishop of Canturbury) and, eventually, poor Vorstius was not only dismissed from his professorship but also expelled from Leyden.

For about seven years Vorstius concealed himself from his bigoted enemies in Tergau, but James would not let him rest there; he sent a number of English and Scotch divines to the Synod of Dort,[6] who loudly demanded the further proscription of Vorstius. They succeeded, and the unfortunate advocate of Arminianism was expelled from Holland. After wandering about in penury and obscurity, hiding from the face of his enemies, who would well have liked to kill him, the duke of Holstein, in 1622, offered him an asylum in his states, with seven hundred families of his adherents, who had been exiled with him. But the persecuted man was now sinking fast under his miseries, and died in the autumn of that year.

Describing what happens to Barneveldt is not a part of my plan, but I must mention that this decent man, a national hero for most of his illustrious life, was beheaded at the age of seventy two, due to the manipulations of the ambitious and unscrupulous Prince Maurice, who knew how to fan the flames of sectarian passion to his advantage. For a succinct recent account of the Arminian controversy, I recommend Christoph Thüly's biography of David Gorlæus. He begins with the remark [237, p. 104]: "The Arminian controversy and the violent tones it quickly assumed are nowadays hard to understand and to explain." I will only add that these controversies are re-enactments (in different theatres) of the controversies that took place in Mā'mūn's time and also of the disputes that are convulsing the Islamic world of today. Indeed, someone who has an intimate knowledge of the contemporary Muslim world would have no difficulty un-

---

[6]The Synod of Dort (1618–1619): The Arminians had wanted their articles of faith to be adopted by the Churches in Holland, and so had petitioned the Dutch Parliament with a Remonstrance containing five points. The parliament called for the Synod, which met at Dort (in full Dordrecht); voting representatives from the Reformed churches in eight foreign countries were also invited to participate. In all 81 theologians (56 Dutch and 25 foreign) met for 154 sessions, and reached the conclusion that all five points of the Remonstrance were contrary to Scripture and heretical [236].

derstanding the Arminian controversy of the seventeenth century; conversely, anyone who wishes to acquire a proper understanding of the religious strife raging through the Muslim world without observing it at first hand would do well to begin with the relevant pages in Thüly's book [237] and other sources.

Seventeenth century Europe. II: Burning of heretics

Thomas Fuller (1608–1661), an English divine, wrote *The Church History of Britain*, which covered the years 1–1648. He describes, in glowing terms and in considerable detail, James's zealous campaign against the unfortunate Vorstius. Fuller brings his report to a close with the following words [238, p. 251]: "Once I intended to present the reader with a brief of his majesty's *Declaration*, till deterred with this consideration,—that although great masses of lead, tin, and meaner metals, may by the extraction of chymists be epitomized and abridged into a smaller quantity of silver, yet what is altogether gold already cannot, without extraordinary damage, be reduced into a smaller proportion. And seeing each word in his majesty's Declaration is so pure and precious, that it cannot be lessened without loss, we remit the reader to the same in his majesty's Works; and so take our leave of Vorstius for the present; whose books, by the king's command, were publicly burned at St. Paul's Cross in London, and in both universities [Oxford and Cambridge]."

After praising James for his valiant effort to give Vorstius a foretaste of hell, Fuller has this to say [238, p. 252]:

> But leaving this outlandish—let us come to our English—Vorstius, though of far less learning, of more obstinacy and dangerous opinions: I mean, that Arian,[7] who this year suffered in Smithfield. His name, Bartholomew Legate; native county, Essex; person, comely; complexion, black; age, about forty years; of a bold spirit, confident carriage, fluent tongue, excellently skilled in the Scriptures: and well had it been for him if he had known them less, or understood them better; whose ignorance abused the word of God, therewith to oppose "God the Word." His conversation, for aught I can learn to the contrary, very unblamable; and the poison

outlandish meant *foreign* in Fuller's time

[7] See footnote 4 on p. 149.

> of heretical doctrine is never more dangerous then when served up in clean cups and washed dishes.
>
> King James caused this Legate often to be brought to him, and seriously dealt with him to endeavour his conversion. One time the king had a design to surprise him into a confession of Christ's Deity, (as his majesty afterwards declared to a right reverend prelate,[8]) by asking him whether or no he did not daily pray to Jesus Christ? Which had he acknowledged, the king would have infallibly inferred, that Legate tacitly consented to Christ's Divinity, as a "Searcher of the hearts." But herein his majesty failed of his expectation, Legate returning, that indeed he had prayed to Christ in the days of his ignorance, but not for these last seven years. Hereupon *the king in choler spurned at him with his foot*. "Away, base fellow!" saith he, "it shall never be said, that one stayeth in my presence, that hath never prayed to our Saviour for seven years together." (My italics.)

In plain modern English, the italicized text means that the king, in anger, kicked Legate. It stands to reason that Legate, after he became an Arian, could not continue praying to Christ. Fuller would have us believe that it was Legate's incurable depravity that made the king lose his temper, but the "Defender of the Faith" had been aware of the offender's views all along. No, the king became choleric because he had underestimated the resolve and perspicuity of Legate, and well it would have been for the latter to behave like a base fellow and tell his majesty what he wanted to hear.

Shortly afterwards, Edward Wightman, accused of multiform heresy, suffered the same fate as Legate. I will merely quote the title of the relevant section in Fuller's book [238, p. 255]: *Wightman worse than Legate. The Success of this Severity.*

Misdeeds and ignoble thoughts, conceived by infected minds and perceived as noble feelings and responses, become undeniable when the miscreant himself proudly preserves them for posterity. Reverend Fuller has left us a permanent record of defamatory evidence against himself. He makes no attempt to conceal his satisfaction at the suffering of those who were subjected to a

---

[8]Fuller's footnote: James archbishop of Armagh; from whose mouth I had the relation.

barbarous treatment in the name of Christ, worthy of the faggot and expects his Christian brethren to join him in drawing a pious satisfaction from the persecution of those who are and in thanking the king for his severe handling of heretics. Fuller's shameful expression of glee and his approval of severe punishments may be taken as a typical example, applicable to similar people in the Muslim world of today, of the pernicious influence of sectarian hatred in a society where one is raised to believe that one's own party is the only one in possession of the absolute and divine truth.

Seventeenth century Europe. III: Galileo, Harriot and Kepler

I find it pretty hard to believe that, in the midst of so much bigotry and such devilish cruelty, science was not totally suffocated, and it continued to attract people with penetrating minds and insatiable curiosities. Let us recall first that three of the greatest masterpieces of science created during the Renaissance appeared in print almost simultaneously: *De revolutionibus orbium coelestium* (On the Revolutions of the Heavenly Spheres) of Nicolaus Copernicus in 1543; *De fabrica humani corporis* (On the Fabric of the Human Body) of Andreas Vesalius in 1543; *Artis magnae sive de regulis algebraicis* (The Great Art, or The Rules of Algebra) of Girolamo Cardano in 1545. The *Ars Magna*, highly praised as a milestone in the history of mathematics, carried algebra to a point well beyond the reach of an Islamican algebraist, alive then or in an earlier epoch, and likewise for *De Revolutionibus*.

A daring thinker had to surmount more obstacles than belief in an inerrant Bible; the shadows of the ancient scholars like Aristotle and Galen were just as menacing as the manacles and fetters maintained in working order by the ecclesiastical authorities. In Oxford, a scholar who held an opinion different from Aristotle was penalized by a heavy fine. The first serious blow to Aristotle's towering status was struck by Tycho Brahe (1546–1601), one among many who observed a highly luminous object in the sky in 1572 that had not been seen before. Many explanations were offered by learned men of the time to reconcile the appearance of the new object with the dogma of Aristotle,[9] but Tycho was able to demonstrate that it was, in fact, a new star. The appearance of the 1572 star showed the world how little it knew about the heavens. The efforts of Copernicus and Tycho became the foundation on which Kepler built his glorious laws of planetary motion, and set astronomical science on the brilliant career which it has pursued ever since.

Though a devoted Lutheran, Kepler was no blind follower, and he showed the same intellectual independence in science. He writes in the Introduction to his epoch making 1609 book:[10] "In Theology we balance authorities, in Philosophy we weigh reasons. A holy man was Lactantius who denied that the earth was round; a holy man was Augustine, who granted the rotundity, but denied the antipodes; a holy thing to me is the Inquisition, which allows the smallness of the earth, but denies its motion; but more holy to me is Truth; and hence I prove, from philosophy, that the earth is round, and inhabited on every side, of small size, and in motion among the stars,—and this I do with no disrespect to the Doctors." The book bears the appropriately confident and challenging title *Astronomia nova* (The New Astronomy); he adopts the heliocentric picture but jettisons everything else from the past by announcing his first law of *elliptical* orbits as well as the second law according to which planets move with nonuniform speeds (the radius vector drawn from the sun's center to the planet sweeping over equal areas in equal times). His third law, that the squares of the times of the revolution of any two planets around the sun are to each other as the cubes of the mean distances from the sun, was discovered much later, in 1618, and was published in his *Harmonices mundi* (Harmony of the Worlds), 1619. Kepler suffered from religious persecution at the hands of both Protestants and Catholics.

Thomas Harriot (or Hariot or Harriott; 1560–1621), a versatile and virtuoso English scientist who deserves to be placed at

[9]Aristotelian science made a distinction between the superlunary sphere (above the moon) which was immutable and perfect, and the sublunary sphere (containing the earth, the moon and meteors) which was subject to change.

[10]This translation is due to Whewell [239, Vol. 2, pp. 151–2], who assures the reader that Kepler's tone is sincere, not ironic.

the same level as Galileo and Kepler, deduced the sine law of refraction in the summer of 1602 [240, 241]. Harriot was among the foremost mathematicians of his time, and his astronomical interests and achievements covered an exceedingly wide range. Despite all his achievements, he is not a household name for a variety of reasons, the chief among them being his reluctance to publish his scientific findings.

The birth of modern science

How came it, one is bound to ask, that (what many consider to be) the first genuine scientific revolution took place in Europe just when the sixteenth century was drawing to a close? How could it happen amid all the heat and dust of dogma, the awful din of wrangling sects, each telling a tale full of nonsense and folly, making promises of salvation and threats of damnation. However improbable it may sound, this is when modern science was born, these were the decades during which the sine law of refraction became known to more than one person, the years during which Kepler formulated his laws of planetary motion, and Galileo his law of inertia; the time for the invention of telescope, seen by most as a toy or an appliance that might yield military or mercantile benefits, and by a few as a tool for bringing themselves closer to some heavenly bodies, those who revolutionized astronomy by turning their telescopes towards the heavens out of sheer curiosity. Among the possible causes for the sudden march of intellect, there are a few which would appear in every list—the Reformation, translations of the Bible, and the discovery of the New World—and there must be a host of incidental and fortuitous causes, for which there can be no accounting.

It is important to note that, in the period under discussion, men of science joined forces with commercial and colonial entrepreneurs. In an interesting article entitled "Thomas Harriot's reputation for impiety", we find the following comment [242]: "Ralegh [the first of Harriot's two generous patrons] was moved by intellectual curiosity, but also by the desire to improve the arts of war and navigation, and to succeed in his colonial enterprises." Harriot took part in the second expedition to Virginia, and published (1585) what may be seen both as a contribution to scholarship and a brochure for attracting prospective investors, a well documented report entitled *A Briefe and True Report of the New Found Land of Virginia*, detailing the residents and resources of the country [178]. More recently, Stephen Clucas has made two interesting observations concerning the voyages of discovery [243]. First, the late sixteenth century surge for maritime trade and colonial settlement spawned a large volume of printed material, culminating in Richard Hakluyt's series of books issued under the general title *The Principal Navigations, Voyages, Traffiques, and Discoveries of the English Nation*. Secondly, the commercial ventures of Elizabethan traders and investors gave birth to a 'knowledge economy', which expanded vigorously over the next two centuries; his phrase is appropriate because the production of knowledge went hand in hand with the generation of capital, and science found a new partner/patron. Clucas mentions in particular the Roanoke voyage and the above mentioned report of Thomas Harriot, an excerpt from which appears on p. 107.

Science used for refuting atheism

Before the end of the seventeenth century, Christian scholars had begun to present science as an ally of religion, not an ally with an independent mind, but a fawning, corroborative lickspittle. John Ray (1627–1705), an English divine and one of the leading naturalists of his time, published (1691) *The Wisdom of God Manifested in the Works of the Creation* [244]. There are plenty of snide remarks about atheists and references to sacred writings, but there is also enough science to show the author's mastery of contemporary state. William Derham, another English divine and naturalist, published a similar book in 1712 [245], and in 1718 appeared the English translation of a Dutch book, with the title *The Religious Philosopher: Or, the Right Use of Contemplating the Works of the Creator* [246], and the title page stated that it was "Designed for the conviction of atheists and infidels". Getting the right mixture of Science and Scripture is never easy, and the translator, not pleased with the Author's composition, is forced to take matters into his own hands, as we find on reading the dedication:

> My Lord, I beg leave to call the Learned Physician, who is my Author, the Dutch Ray or Derham, because, like those two English Philosophers, he has so well prov'd the Wisdom, Power, and Goodness of God by the strongest Arguments, Observations on Facts, and Demonstrations drawn from Experiments. It were to be wish'd, that he had apply'd the Texts of Scripture, which he quotes, as properly as he has done his Philosophical Considerations; but since he has not so well succeeded in what may be call'd his Divinity, I have left several of the Texts out of this Translation; but have retrench'd none of his Glosses upon the particular Texts by him quoted, nor any of his Glorious Tautologies, in which he does so often call upon Atheists and Infidels; excepting where his Comment is wrong, or the Repetitions are too tedious and, I hope, unnecessary, even for convincing of those unhappy Men to whom he addresses himself; of whom it may be pronounc'd, that if they still persist in the Denial of a God, after so many irrefragable Arguments, drawn from the wonderful Structure of Humane Bodies, and all the other Glorious Works in the Universe, God will then harden their Hearts, and, like the Pharisess, they will not be perswaded tho one rose from the Dead.

The creation of the earth and the universal deluge was a topic that fascinated many Christian scientists. In his highly influential book "Principles of Geology", Sir Charles Lyell has given an excellent summary of their conclusions and, in addition, a brief account, borrowed from Karl Ernst Adolf von Hoff [247, p. 406], of 'Umar al-'Ālim ('Umar, the learned), a tenth century Arabophone scientist, whose views were "declared contradictory to certain passages in the Koran". Unfortunately, I have not been able to find out more about 'Umar al-'Ālim, but I was struck by how much Lyell had learnt about Mā'mūn's contribution to secular scholarship and his troubles with "orthodox doctors". Lyell has quoted only one source, namely the second volume of *Modern Universal History*, and it is rather impressive to see how well the authors of the volume have integrated the reports of Arabophone and other historians. Of all the authors considered by Lyell, I will single out Whiston for a closer look.

William Whiston (1667–1752), both a mathematician and a priest, and one of the first converts to Newtonian mechanics, wrote a highly acclaimed book (1696) with the title *A New Theory of the Earth, wherein the Creation of the World in Six Days, the Universal Deluge, and the General Conflagration, as laid down in the Holy Scriptures, are shewn to be perfectly agreeable to Reason and Philosophy*. This work explained the deluge as a consequence of the near approach of a comet to the earth. The book received wide acclaim, winning words of praise even from John Locke, who wrote [248, p. 534]: "You desire to know what the opinion of the ingenious is concerning Mr Whiston' book. I have not heard any one of my acquaintance speak of it but with great commendations, and, as I think, it deserves: and, truly, it is more to be admired that he has laid down an hypothesis whereby he has explained so many wonderful and before inexplicable things, in the great changes of this globe, than that some of them should not easily go down with some men, when the whole was entirely new to all. He is one of those sort of writers, that I always fancy should be most esteemed and encouraged: I am always for the builders who bring some addition to our knowledge, or, at least, some new things to our thoughts." William Thomas Brande (Professor of Chemistry at the Royal Institution) came to a different conclusion in 1825 [249]: "But Locke's opinion upon such a subject, is not entitled to any especial weight. I have perused Whiston's book, without being able to find any particular merit in his speculations, and am rather inclined to side with his opponents, in forming an estimate of its value." Five years later, the geologist Lyell was even more scathing [250, p. 39]: "Like all who introduced purely hypothetical causes to account for natural phenomena, Whiston retarded the progress of truth, diverting men from the investigation of the laws of sublunary nature, and inducing them to waste time in speculations on the power of comets to drag the waters of the ocean over the land—on the condensation of the vapours of their tails into water, and other matters equally edifying."

Newton, who was Lucasian Professor of mathematics at Cambridge, took leave of absence to become Master of the Mint and moved to London in the spring of 1696. In 1701, he delegated his teaching duties to Whiston. When Newton finally resigned his professorship two years later, he saw to it that the vacancy was filled by Whiston. It is clear that the two exchanged views about matters other than Newtonian mechanics.

"Let me tell you," says Dr Stockmann at the end of Ibsen's *An Enemy of the People*, "the strongest man in the world is he who stands most alone". Newton, the most innovative scientist of his age, was happy to have a mind full of ideas that belonged to him alone, but even he felt the urge to share his faith and opinion with a few others. It seems that he confided his anti-Trinitarian beliefs to Whiston and possibly infected the latter's mind. It is clear, at any rate that, like Newton, Whiston could not accept the doctrine of the Trinity, but unlike his mentor Newton, he was not afraid to stand alone and announce that he was an enemy of the people who had been duped by the Athanasian conspiracy against the pristine (or primitive, in his terminology) Christianity of the early centuries. It is hardly surprising that Whiston was dismissed by the university authorities on grounds of heresy (in 1710). Only expelled, no other punishment! What a difference from the fate he would have suffered just a hundred years earlier, or a century or two later but in another part of the world!

Whiston moved to London and managed to eke out a living by dint of hard work and his considerable talents as a teacher and a popularizer of science [251, Ch. 1]. To convince you that he made no attempt to conceal his religious affiliation requires no proof other than quoting the title of a book he published in 1717 [252]. Titles used to be rather long in those leisurely days, and the front page often contained what might justifiably be called a short abstract. I reproduce below the title and part of the text that comes immediately below the title [252]:

AN HUMBLE AND SERIOUS ADDRESS TO THE PRINCES AND STATES OF EUROPE, FOR THE ADMISSION, OR AT LEAST OPEN TOLERATION OF THE CHRISTIAN RELIGION IN THEIR DOMINIONS

Containing

1. A demonstration, that none of them do, properly speaking, admit or openly tolerate the Christian religion in their dominions at this day.
2. The true occasions, why it is not admitted, or openly tolerated by them.
3. Some reasons, why they ought to admit, or at least openly tolerate this religion.

4. An earnest address to the several European Princes and States, grounded on the premises for the admission, or at least the open toleration of the same Christian religion in their dominions.

Humble and Serious Address begins by explaining that the term *Christian religion* is used in the book to mean "primitive Christianity", what Christ and his Holy Apostles taught and as it stands in *all the original records of Christianity*; that "it is to be distinguished from bare natural religion, Jewish or Mahometan institutions" and that "also it is different from, or contrary to those particular sects and parties which are called *Greeks* or *Latins*, *Papists* or *Protestants*, *Lutherans* or *Calvinists*, *Presbyterians* or *Independents*, *Baptists* or *Quakers*, or any other professing the same religion among us". It says much for the forbearance of the Princes and States of Europe that they did not dispatch hitmen in answer to Whiston's address.

Whiston also published (1717) *Astronomical Principles of Religion, Natural and Reval'd*, into which he poured his knowledge of the Scriptures, Newtonian mechanics and astronomical observations, and put his synthetic skills at work to show that the two sources of information concur with each other. What is more, he has left us with an example of the fulfilment of the middle part of Matthew 7:7:[11] He solved the great riddle of where hell is located [252, pp. 155–6]:

> I observe, that the Sacred Accounts of Hell, or of the Place and State of Punishment for wicked Men after the general Resurrection, is agreeable not only to the Remains of ancient profane Tradition, but to the true System of the World also. This sad State is in Scripture describ'd as a State of Darkness, of outward Darkness, of blackness of Darkness, of Torment and Punishment for Ages, or for Ages of Ages, by Flame, or by Fire, or by Fire and Brimstone, with Weeping and Gnashing of Teeth; where the Smoak of the Ungodly's Torment ascends up for ever and ever; where they are Tormented in the Presence of the Holy Angels, and in the Presence of the Lamb; when the Holy Angels shall have separated the Wicked from among the Just, and have cast them into a Furnace of Fire. Now this Description does in every Circumstance, so ex-

[11] Ask, and it shall be given you; *seek, and you shall find*; knock, and it shall be opened unto you. (My italics.)

> actly agree with the Nature of a Comet, ascending from the Hot Regions near the Sun, and going into the Cold Regions beyond Saturn, with its long smoaking Tail arising up from it, through its several Ages or Periods of revolving, and this in the Sight of all the Inhabitants of our Air, and of the rest of the System; that I cannot but think the Surface or Atmosphere of such a Comet to be that Place of Torment so terribly described in Scripture, into which the Devil and his Angels, with wicked Men their Companions, when delivered out of their Prison in the Heart of the Earth, shall be cast for their utter Perdition or second Death; which will be indeed a terrible but a most useful spectacle ot the rest of God's rational Creatures; and all will admonish them above all Things to preserve their Innocence and Obedience; and to fear him who is thus able to destroy both Soul and Body in Hell.

Whiston *sought* and he *found* where hell was, and we may assume that he did not *knock*. As for the first part of the verse, Whiston asked the Almighty to get him the Lucasian chair in mathematics, which he was given, and the Fellowship of the Royal Society, which he was denied, the mighty Newton pushing his candidature in the first case and blocking it in the second. Though both Whiston and his mentor Newton were anti-Trinitarians, the latter chose to be reticent about his religion, whereas the former was a reckless propagandist. Though Newton had very few endearing qualities, one can see why he began to look askance at his former protegé. Those who are curious to know more about the two decades long relationship between Newton and Whiston will find the details in Snobelen's article [253].

The article on Willaim Whiston in *Encyclopedia Britannica* (1911 edition) describes him as "a striking example of the association of an entirely paradoxical bent of mind with proficiency in the exact sciences", a person who "also illustrates the possibility of arriving at rationalistic conclusions in theology without the slightest tincture of the rationalistic temper", "paradoxical to the verge of craziness".

Millenarianism (also millennialism or chiliasm) refers to the belief that Christ will return to the earth (a thousand years before its end), overthrow the existing order, and replace it with just rule; determining the start of this period has occupied more than a thousand minds. The emergence of science and its acceptance by Christian clergymen could hardly fail to give birth to "scientific millenarianism", and a man like Whiston could hardly fail to become one of the major figures of this movement. Whiston is all but forgotten, but Millenarianism did not become extinct, and is making a comeback, though it can no longer count respectable scientists or theologian among its supporters. The late R. H. Popkin concluded his foreword to James Force's *William Whiston: Honest Newtonian* [254] with some remarks on the resurgence of millenarianism in politics, and warned that those who think that, with the triumphant march of modern science, the millenarian view met with the same fate as befell Humpty Dumpty are struck by surprise when they find the Whistonian conception of the end of history "popping up in statements by U.S. cabinet ministers, a President of Guatemala, and various Jewish and Christian spokesmen in America and Israel", and even in "the latest pronouncements of the Rev. Jerry Falwell". Who is/was Rev. Falwell and what did he pronounce? I would rather leave it to you to find out.

Nearly thirty years have elapsed since Popkin wrote those words, but they still ring true; indeed, their domain of validity extends to a larger part of the world. It may not seem surprising now that so much attention has been paid to someone who will be considered today as a fringe figure in the history of Western science; all that I need to add is that Whiston displays, more than anyone else I have studied, the characteristics which appear, in different proportions and often without his bonhomie, among many learned members of Muslim societies.

Bishop Berkeley lashes out at mathematicians

My last example is an attack on mathematicians by the famous theologian George Berkeley (1685–1753), Bishop of Cloyne, in Ireland. In 1732, he published a book [255] bearing the title *Alciphron: or the Minute Philosopher* and the subtitle *Containing an Apology for the Christian Religion, against those who are called Freethinkers*. Two years later, a sequel followed, in which he carried his war against materialism to the camp of its champions, the mathematicians of his time. The sequel [256], which made a huge splash, is called *The Analyst; or a Discourse Addressed to an Infidel Mathematician. Wherein it is examined whether the Object, Principles and Inferences of the modern Analysis are more distinctly conceived, or more evidently deduced, than Religious Mysteries and Points of Faith.* I like to think that Bishop Berkeley must have been (or at least approximated well to) a reincarnation of Ghazālī, since this is the only way I can explain why *Alciphron* and the non-mathematical parts of *The Analyst* read like updated versions of *Tahāfut* and *Munqidh*, respectively.

Before going into the contents of *The Analyst* I would like to quote Berkeley's friend Edmund Gibson (Bishop of London), who summed up the tension between scientists and theologians by confiding in Berkeley in a letter written on 9 July 1735 [257, pp. 238–9]: "What your Lordship observes is very true, and appears to be so in experience here, that the men of science (a conceited generation) are the greatest sticklers against revealed religion, and have been very open in their attacks upon it. And we are much obliged to your lordship for retorting their arguments upon them, and finding them work in their own quarters, and must depend upon you to go on to humble them, if they do not yet find themselves sufficiently humbled."

The Analyst opens with a passage that echoes Ghazālī's grudge against mathematicians (see pp. 45–46). Although the butt of the Bishop's attack is a single infidel mathematician, it soon becomes obvious that he has a bone to pick with 'too many more of the like character' (see below), who may be called, using his own words in *Alciphron*, members of the Sect of Free-thinkers [256, p. 17–8]:

> 1. Though I am a stranger to your person, yet I am not, Sir, a stranger to the reputation you have acquired in that branch of learning which hath been your peculiar study; nor to the authority that you therefore assume in things foreign to your profession; nor to the abuse that you, and too many more of the like character, are known to make of such undue authority, to the misleading of unwary persons in matters of the highest concernment, and whereof your mathematical knowledge can by no means qualify you to be a competent judge. Equity indeed and good sense would incline one to disregard the judgment of men, in points which they have not considered or examined. But several who make the loudest claim to those qualities do nevertheless the very thing they would

> seem to despise, clothing themselves in the livery of other men's opinions, and putting on a general deference for the judgment of you, Gentlemen, who are presumed to be of all men the greatest masters of reason, to be most conversant about distinct ideas, and never to take things upon trust, but always clearly to see your way, as men whose constant employment is the deducing truth by the justest inference from the most evident principles. With this bias on their minds, they submit to your decisions where you have no right to decide. And that this is one short way of making Infidels, I am credibly informed.
>
> 2. Whereas then it is supposed that you apprehend more distinctly, consider more closely, infer more justly, and conclude more accurately than other men, and that you are therefore less religious because more judicious, I shall claim the privilege of a Freethinker; and take the liberty to inquire into the object, principles, and method of demonstration admitted by the mathematicians of the present age, with the same freedom that you presume to treat the principles and mysteries of Religion; to the end that all men may see what right you have to lead, or what encouragement others have to follow you. It hath been an old remark, that Geometry is an excellent Logic. And it must be owned that when the definitions are clear; when the postulata cannot be refused, nor the axioms denied; when from the distinct contemplation and comparison of figures, their properties arc derived, by a perpetual well-connected chain of consequences, the objects being still kept in view, and the attention ever fixed upon them; there is acquired a habit of reasoning, close and exact and methodical which habit strengthens and sharpens the mind, and being transferred to other subjects is of general use in the inquiry after truth. But how far this is the case of our geometrical analysts, it may be worth while to consider.

Whom did Berkeley brand as *an infidel mathematician*? The general feeling at the time has been described in the following words [258]: "When Dr. Garth[12] was on his death-bed, Mr. Addison endeavoured to direct his attention towards the preparation for a future life, but received for answer, that he had good reason not to believe in the doctrines held out to him, because

[12] For a biographical account of Dr Samuel Garth, poet and physician, see [259].

his friend Dr. Halley, who had dealt so much in demonstration, had assured him that the doctrines of Christianity are incomprehensible, and religion itself an imposture. To Dr. Halley, therefore, it was universally understood that Dr. Berkeley addressed his "Analyst," in the title, under the denomination of *An Infidel Mathematician.*" This might well have been so, but—as the book challenges an entire sect—I agree with Cantor [260] that Berkeley was not "concerned with confuting Halley or any other individual". There is no *clear* evidence of religious scepticism in Halley's published writings, and his 'infidelity' rests, like that of Thomas Harriot, upon rumours and private expressions of opinion in, for example, Whiston's memoirs, or in a letter to Abraham Sharp in which the astronomer Flamsteed wrote [261, p. 6]: "Mr Wallace is dead. Mr. Halley expects his place. He now talks, swears and drinks brandy like a sea captain, so that I much fear his own ill-behaviour will deprive him of the vacancy". It is a reflection of the times that almost a hundred years after Halley's death, the unproven charge of atheism was considered, by the Rev. S. J. Rigaud, to be a smear serious enough to require a refutation in a document entitled *Defence of Halley against the charge of Religious Infidelity* [262].

As may be judged from the subtitle of *The Analyst*, Berkeley's aim is to argue that mathematics is like religion insofar as it too is a belief system. Certain mathematicians reject religion, on the ground of its ultimate incomprehensibility, though their own science is ultimately incomprehensible, and indeed some of its doctrines rest on reasonings which seem (to Berkeley) incoherent, if not contradictory. Mathematics, like all other human knowledge, lacks omniscience, and is sustained only by faith or trust. Religion, which has its own share of incomprehensibility, is thus no worse than mathematics, the most demonstrable portion of human knowledge. In the words of Fraser, an editor of Berkeley's works [256, p. 6]: "At the root of all human knowledge, there are working principles which cannot be reduced to our ideas: it is unreasonable to insist on so resolving them. In this respect science and religion are upon the same footing. *Force* is as incomprehensible as *grace*. Both have a practical meaning; but neither of the meanings can be fully exhibited in our ideas of sense or imagination. So, too, with the 'infidel mathematician.' He objects to religion because God cannot be fully represented in a sensuous image: he ought equally to reject mathematics because it too is rooted in like mystery."

To support his claim, Berkeley examines the foundations of differential calculus (Newton's version, phrased in terms of *fluxions*, as well as that developed by Leibnitz). To quote Fraser again [256, p. 6]: "Fluxions are unrepresentable in imagination: we cannot realise them in ideas of sense; and the demonstrations which support them, useful in the results, are humanly incomprehensible at last [in the final analysis]. Yet mathematical 'freethinkers' are found ready to accept within their own science what they reject in religion: fluxions, like religion, when resolved into ultimate principles, involve incompleted or mysterious conceptions which transcend human understanding; and 'infidel mathematicians' receive them, trusting to the authority of incompletely comprehended principles, some infidels on the personal authority of Sir Isaac Newton."

I am willing to accept that science (including mathematics) is in itself a belief system,[13] but it differs from religion in one crucial aspect: nothing can prevent one from believing in physics (or mathematics, or biology, or any other science) and, at the same time, in a given religion, but I can't for the life of me see how anyone can subscribe to disparate religious systems at the same time. No one would raise his eyebrows on hearing of Hindu mathematicians, Muslim mathematicians, Christian mathematicians, infidel mathematicians. But a Hindu Christian or a Trinitarian Muslim is more, much more, than a strange wonder: it is, to coin a new term, a paradoxymoron as inconceivable to me as a true and fair woman was to the despondent poet who wrote the following verses [264, p. 4]:

> If thou be'st born to strange sights,
> Things invisible to see,
> Ride ten thousand days and nights,
> Till age snow white hairs on thee,
> Thou, when thou return'st, wilt tell me,
> All strange wonders that befell thee,

---

[13]Thomas Kuhn was probably stating consensus opinion when he wrote [263, p. 80]: "But science students accept theories on the authority of the teacher and the text, not because of evidence."

And swear,
No where
Lives a woman true, and fair.

Religion and science also differ in many other respects, which I have discussed at length in *MoB* [7].

Summing up

In an interview published shortly after his death, Cardinal Carlo Maria Martini (1927–2012) had described the Catholic Church as being "200 years behind" the times [191–193]. The algorithm that led to this estimate was not revealed in the published accounts of the interview (and perhaps not to the interviewer either), and it is very likely that the forthright Cardinal meant it to be no more than a figure of speech. I have been led to conclude, on the basis of the evidence that has been presented above and in *MoB* [7], that, so far as religious toleration is concerned, attitudes in the Muslim world are no more enlightened than those which blighted Europe at the close of the sixteenth century and the first few decades of the next. Religious bigotry and denominational divides determine the inner concerns and outward behaviour, the unconscious responses and the conscious choices of contemporary Muslims in a manner that evokes the horrid events which afflicted the lives of European Christians four centuries ago; sectarian strife tears the tranquility and peace of Muslim societies with the same brutality as it did during the Thirty Years War; men and women of any age, Muslims as well as non-Muslims, are beheaded, burnt alive, tortured, blown into pieces, robbed and evicted from their homes, because they worship a different God, or follow a different *Imām*, even if they worship the same God and revere the same prophet; young men (and even women) go to death as to a bridal bed, sacrificing themselves and blowing up others with a passion fed by centuries of simmering prejudices and accumulated superstitions.

We have seen that scientific giants like Galileo, Kepler and Harriot sprouted from the soil of early seventeenth century Europe, while it was being scorched by the flames of religious hatred. Would it be right, then, to argue that science can return to the Muslim world of today, even if it is ablaze with a fire equally ferocious. I hardly think so. Scientists go where circumstances seem congenial to them, where consequences of nonconformity are likely to be less perilous. Harriot had two extremely generous and enlightened patrons, who became acquainted with each other when they were both prisoners in the Tower of London [265, 266]; Harriot must have known that, with his reputation for impiety, he had to tread very carefully and keep a low profile. Many others—Tycho Brahe, Kepler, and Galileo, for example—had to move around, not always voluntarily. The Muslim world loses potential scientists because it has no attraction for most of them. Science will come to Islam only if good scientists, gainfully employed in scientific institutions of premier rank will be willing to give up their positions and laboratories in order to take up residence in Muslim states, and this would require much more than a mere injection of capital.

It is my firm belief that, if science is to take root in an Islamic state, a revolution is indispensable, and that this revolution need not be a bloody affair; whatever the nature of the revolution, it must involve a change of paradigm, a transition, gradual rather than abrupt, from a closed society to an open one, a society where criticism is not confused with betrayal and disloyalty, where demand for change is not equated with sedition, where censorship is not seen as the best way to preserve the old way of life and the outdated cosmology that goes with it, where clichés and aphorisms, supposedly genuine sayings of saints and prophets no longer feed and sustain superstitions. Science can come back to Islam but only if the forces which suffocate free thought in the contemporary Muslim world are subdued, and freedom of expression established as an inalienable human right.

What are the forces opposing the advancement of liberal attitudes and respect for rational thought in the Muslim world? Mass illiteracy, the power of priests (most of whom are hostile to science), sectarian slaughter, malfeasant public servants and politicians—in brief, anything that is both the cause and the effect of the curse commonly called *underdevelopment*. In a society that has become accustomed to the barbarous tyranny of tradition, the threat of religious persecution becomes an instrument for enforcing uniformity and acquiescence; one can settle any score by accusing the adversary of *blasphemy*, silence any opponent by calling him an *apostate*, stifle any unpalatable proposal for change by denouncing it as a *heresy*.[14]

May we expect some worthwhile scientific activity in the Muslim world during the coming decades? Hardly any. Of course, academics, mostly pedestrians, will publish papers, mostly trite, in journals that can only be called the bane of the scholarly world, but this output will not have much impact on the global stage, nor will it lead to a noticeable improvement in the quality of life of the local folk by providing them employment, or better and cheaper education, or low-priced effective medicines, or by bringing some light to the minds which have been kept for so long in total darkness. Mediocre and submediocre scientists will spend their time, as did Whiston, on writing books and articles, giving talks and sermons, eulogizing the scientific attainments of the great "Muslim" scholars of the bygone ages and claiming that all the secrets of nature are locked into the pages of the Scriptures, waiting to be uncovered by diligent unlockers. There will be many seekers and as many finders, but their findings will retard (not further) progress towards the three objects of intellect: the *true*, the *beautiful* and the *beneficial*.

Can anything be done to reverse the trend described above? As a preamble, consider another analogy: the outbreak (in 2014) of the ebola virus disease (EVD) in West Africa, rated as "unquestionably the most severe acute public health emergency in modern times" [273] by the Director-General of the World Health Organisation (WHO). The UN Security Council Resolution 2177 (2014) declared "that the unprecedented extent of the Ebola outbreak in Africa constitutes a threat to international peace and security" [274].

Why were there no vaccines or other remedies for a virus that

[14]Mature readers will not accept an assertion unattested by sound evidence, sceptics least of all. A reader who doubts the statement concerning the recurrent abuse of religious accusations will be able to verify it by following the daily news from the Muslim world for six months or so. I will mention two incidents that occurred in late 2014, one in Bangladesh (BD), the other in Pakistan. A federal BD minister was dismissed and arrested for making some unflattering remarks on the custom of Hajj [267–269], one of the five *pillars* of Islam; a Christian couple in Pakistan were beaten to death and their bodies were burnt in a kiln for allegedly desecrating the Qur'ān [270–272].

was discovered as far back as 1976? What does the latest outbreak reveal about the state of the world at large? What lessons should the citizens of the Western world and their elected leaders draw from it? A WHO document [273] raised these questions, and provided detailed and frank answers. I present a synopsis below in my own words.

Until quite recently, there was no vaccine nor an effective antidote because EVD was traditionally confined to poor African countries, and a profit-driven pharmaceutical industry had no incentive to make products for altruistic purposes. The outbreak brings to the fore the dangers of the growing social and economic inequalities of our world. The prosperous get the best care, and the poor are left to perish. When a deadly virus hits a poverty-stricken people and, left unchecked, spirals outward beyond control, the outbreak threatens the whole world as never before, because it can be exported, inadvertently and unnoticed, to distant regions, thanks to the modern high-speed means of transport. A country suffering from chronic neglect of its health-care system and other public services collapses when it is jolted by, for example, an extreme weather event, an epidemic, civil unrest or a prolonged armed conflict.

At the time of writing these words, none disputes that Guinea, Liberia, and Sierra Leone—the countries most infected—cannot contain the virus without outside help, and it is thought that a concerted international effort will achieve success within a year, a reasonable conclusion, because the problem is well identified, the virus is confined to a sufficiently small geographical region and, furthermore, there are no conflicts of interest between the sufferers and the outsiders, who are committed to the containment and eventual eradication of the ebola virus, and—crucially—are themselves not contaminated by a different deadly virus. Thankfully no columnist or cartoonist has (as yet) come up with what might be termed the contagion-cleansing final solution, namely: bomb out and incinerate the populations acting as hosts to the ebola virus.

The Muslim world, debilitated by a pernicious affliction, that can only be called *jāhilliya*, stands likewise in need of outside help, but here ends the analogy. The Qur'ānic term *jāhilliya* is usually taken to mean the *time, or state, of ignorance, or paganism*

[89], but it may be interpreted more widely; for example, Karen Armstrong [275, pp. 19–20] has argued that the term refers not to a particular era 'but to a state of mind that caused violence and terror in seventh century Arabia'. *Jahilliya*, she observed, 'is also much in evidence in the West today as well as in the Muslim world'. I, for one, agree with Armstrong. Indeed, I would go a step further by calling *jāhilliya* a mental virus (or *mirus*) and claiming that it has several strains, of which only two concern us at present: *jāhilliya-M*, which is prevalent in the Muslim world, and *jāhilliya-W*, which thrives in the West. Infection by either strain creates the delusion that the best way to extirpate the other strain is to explode the infected brains by dropping bombs indiscriminately, or to remove them by simply severing the head from the body.

I do not share the shallow optimism of those who believe that only one strain of the mirus can be eradicated. One strain is the mother of the other. Some suggestion for eliminating both strains are discussed in *MoB* [7]. But *this* book is about Islam, and its purpose is to answer the question *Can Science Come Back to Islam*?

The answer to the above question is "Yes, science can come back to Islam, but only if the Muslim world succeeds in confining the *jāhilliya-M* virus to a small section of the community". No magic squares, no talismans, no amulets, no burning of frankincense and myrrh, no incantations and no sermons can exorcise this stubborn germ, which is ensconced in over a billion brains, and is both the source and the product of monstrous ignorance and subterranean darkness. The only antidote to this malady is the slow percolation of the glorious germicidal rays of enlightenment, which requires decades of proper education.

I must end here, but exhort you, dear reader, to ponder the far more incisive question, taken up in *MoB* [7]:

How can Western voters help in this important project?

Appendices

A More on Transliteration

Apart from introducing an extra symbol ($\ddot{h}$ for ة), I have followed the transliteration scheme used by Ziadeh and Winder [276, Ch. 1]. For the sake of completeness, I have listed all the symbols in Table A.1. *The New Encyclopaedia of Islam* [277], a title abbreviated in this book as *EoI*, uses *ḳ* instead of *q* and uses a ligature (an underline) to indicate that the digraphs <u>dh</u>, <u>gh</u>, <u>kh</u>, <u>sh</u> and <u>th</u> stand for a single Arabic letter. If a construction like the English word *mishap* arises, I will write it as *mis|hap*, using a vertical line before *h* to signify that the two consonants on either side of the vertical line are to be pronounced separately. **EoI**

The concept of two cases (upper and lower) is alien to Arabic, but transliterators customarily begin a proper name with an upper case letter. Accordingly, the names of the fifth ʿAbbāsid caliph will be spelt as *Hārūn al-Rashīd* and the official name of his capital city as *Madīna$\ddot{h}$ al-Salām*. Those who know Arabic pronounce these names as *Hārūn ar-Rashīd* and *Madīnat as-Salām*, but they will pronounce the name of his son, the seventh caliph of the dynasty, as *al-Māʾmūn* not as *am-Māʾmūn*. A good analogy would have been available, if English orthography had to obey the commandment "Thou shalt not commit adulteration in using the negating prefix *in*", forcing people to write *inlegal, inpossible,* and *inrelevant* but permitting them to pronounce these words as *illegal, impossible,* and *irrelevant*.

The Arabic letter ة (called *tāʾmarbūtah*), which occurs only as the terminal letter, is a combination of two letters, namely ه and ت. When vocalized, it is pronounced like ت (*t*); otherwise, it is pronounced like ه (*h*). To deal with this duality, $\ddot{h}$ will be replaced by *t* or *h* according as it is vocalized or not vocalized. This means that a word like *jannaḧ* (meaning *paradise*) will be written as *jannah*, but *Jannaḧ al-Baqī‘* (the name of a cemetery) will be written as *Jannat al-Baqī‘*. The word محنة, transliterated here as *miḥnah* (not as *miḥnaḧ*), appears in *EoI* as *miḥna*. The policy used by *EoI* amounts to dispensing with the entire terminal symbol (standing for ة), which is acceptable, since the letter is almost silent.

The Arabic alphabet consists of twenty-eight characters, written from right to left, and each character represents a consonant. The stand-alone form of the consonants are shown in Table A.1. Frequently *alif* is shown as the first letter, but strictly speaking it is only a "chair" on top (or at the bottom) of which the *hamzah* "sits".

Table A.1: Table showing the transliteration of Arabic letters

ض	ص	ش	س	ز	ر	ذ	د	خ	ح	ج	ث	ت	ب	ء
ḍ	ṣ	sh	s	z	r	dh	d	kh	ḥ	j	th	t	b	’
ا	ة	ي	ه	و	ن	م	ل	ك	ق	ف	غ	ع	ظ	ط
	ḧ	y	h	w	n	m	l	k	q	f	gh	‘	ẓ	ṭ

Almost a quarter of the surāhs (sections) in the Qur’ān begin with a cluster of two to five letters without any intervening diacritical marks. They are always recited as letters of the alphabet; hence the label *al-ḥurūf al-muqaṭṭa‘ah* (الحروف المقطعة), meaning *disjointed letters*. Two examples occur in this book: *alif-lām-rā’* (pp. 18, 99) and *ḥā-mīm* (p. 99). No Muslim knows the true significance of these clusters, which is why European authors have usually referred to them as mysterious letters [278].

disjointed letters

mysterious letters

B — *The Ḥadīth of the Fly*

The intelligent Muslim's guide to flies and antibiotics

Dear Hoshiyar Mufakkir,

Several weeks have elapsed since you resurfaced, after holding yourself incommunicado for almost four decades, and referred me to a news item entitled "The new buzz on antibiotics" [279], which, you told me, has made a big splash, and you were curious to know if I agree with the millions of Muslims who claim that the study covered by the above news item from the Australian Broadcasting Commission provides incontrovertible evidence in support of a *ḥadīth* which had earlier been a source of much embarrassment to those Muslims who believe that the *ḥadīthes* recorded by the venerable Imām Bukhārī are all true sayings of the Prophet of Islam, but admit, under the scorching flame of their Western schooling, that the house fly is a carrier of many serious diseases. Where, you asked me, lies the truth? It will be convenient, from now on, to refer to the hadīth in question as the hadīth of the fly (for short, *HotFLY*), and the above news item as *BuzzABC*.

Although I feel that life is too short to be wasted in the investigation and correction of mass delusions and aberrations, that a *jihād* against the merchants of mental miasma is best left to the likes of Richard Dawkins, I found your faith in my ability to sort out truth from falsehood (in this matter) and to explain it in simple terms to the intelligent lay person so flattering, your ploy for persuading me to provide an answer so endearing, that I decided to take the plunge and drop everything else. You have always known how to coax me into undertaking a challenge. You wrote that it was my wont to say "I will give the problem the full force of the Razi Naqvi brain, and there are few problems capable of standing that treatment for long", and then dared me to solve the problem or eat my youthful braggadocio. I have no recollection of this unbecoming display of immodesty, but I will not doubt your word, and will attribute my selective amnesia to belated maturity, a consequence of having to eat my words on countless occasions.

This is a task that cannot be undertaken by an anonymous writer. On a matter so contentious, a reader cannot be expected to receive evidence from a witness whose qualifications and antecedents are unknown. The five decades I have spent in the pursuit of science on a rather broad front proved, it goes without saying, to be of immense help in overcoming my lack of familiarity with the morphology, anatomy and the disgusting life style of a house fly. Having assessed the situation, I venture to present my deductions to the intelligent Muslims who have allowed themselves, because their grasp of science is as superficial as my understanding of the stock market, to be seduced by the specious arguments and hasty conclusions of their more zealous brothers in faith, namely those who claim that *HotFLY* "is confirmed by Science", where by "Science" they mean the contents of *BuzzABC*. It is my aim to put these Muslims in possession of certain facts concerning the mode in which the house fly carries diseases, its ability to produce antibacterial compounds, and the (ir)relevance of the results reported in *BuzzABC*. I authorize you, my old friend, to circulate this memorandum to whomsoever you deem an intelligent Muslim.

For such among my readers as think that the concluding part of a thesis is the best starting point, let me summarize my findings with no further ado. A drowning man will clutch at a straw, but the "scientific evidence" adduced by the defenders of *HotFLY* is flimsier than a straw, flimsier even than the wing of a house fly, and clutch as desperately as they might to *BuzzABC*, drown they will.

I will be using the bilingual edition of *Ṣaḥīḥ Bukhārī*, which spans nine volumes [32]; your knowledge of the world of Islam will not be enhanced when I mention, for the benefit of other readers, that the translator, Muḥammad Muḥsin Khan (MMK), a medical doctor by training, is rather well known among Muslims, for he has also translated the Qur'ān, and this translation happens to be freely available.

Let us now read the text of *HotFLY* (*ḥadīth* number 1397 in MMK's compilation): "If a housefly falls in the drink of anyone of you, he should dip it (in the drink), for one of its wings has a disease and the other has the cure for the disease."

The translation cannot be faulted, but I would like to point out that the English text has put healing and disease in reverse order, and an even more faithful translation is the following: "If a fly falls in the vessel of any of you, let him dip all of it (into the vessel) and then throw it away, for in one of its wings is (the) cure and in the other (the) malady." I will assume that the *ḥadīth* refers to a vessel containing water, milk, soup, or some other non-alcoholic beverage.

MMK, acutely aware that some soothing words are needed to assuage a reader who may feel as uncomfortable as a fly that has fallen into a body of water, looks for a plausible scientific justification, is relieved to find one, and delighted to share it with his readers by adding an explanatory footnote:

> Medically it is well-known now that a fly carries some pathogens on some parts of its body as mentioned by the Prophet (before 1400 years approx. when the humans knew very little of modern medicine). Similarly Allah created organisms and other mechanisms which kill these pathogens, e.g., Penicillin Fungus [*sic* a *Penicillium* fungus] kills pathogenic organisms like Staphylococci [*sic* staphylococci] and others etc. Recently experiments have been done under supervision which indicate that a fly carries the disease (pathogens) plus the antidote for those pathogenic organisms. Ordinarily when a fly touches a liquid food it infects the liquid with its pathogens, so it must be dipped in order to release also the antidote for those pathogens to act as a counter balance to the pathogens. Regarding this subject I also wrote through a friend of mine to Dr. Muhammad M. El-Samahy chief of *Hadith* Dept. in Al-Azhar University, Cairo (Egypt), who has written an article upon this *Hadith*, and as regards medical aspects, he has mentioned that the microbiologists have proved that there are longitudinal yeast cells living as parasites inside the belly of the fly and these yeast cells, in order to repeat their lifecycle, protrude through respiratory tubules of the fly and if the fly is dipped in a liquid, these cells burst in the

> fluid and the content of those cells is an antidote for the pathogens which the fly carries.

One does not have to be a lawyer or a logician to notice that the existence of "some pathogens on some parts" of a fly is not consistent with the text of *HotFLY*, according to which the malady is localized on one wing. The reader is not told who "the microbiologists" are, nor where the results of their investigations, and those of other "recent" experiments "done under supervision", were published. Even if we suppose, for the sake of the argument, that the microbiologists were competent scientists, their finding undermines *HotFLY*, since we are told that the protruding parasitic yeast cells burst, once the fly is dipped into a liquid, and release the antidote, not on the pathogen-free wing, but directly into the fluid. Other objections to this footnote can only be presented after I have examined the evidence mentioned in *BuzzABC*.

The author of *BuzzABC* began his news report with the following words: "The surface of flies is the last place you would expect to find antibiotics, yet that is exactly where a team of Australian researchers is concentrating their efforts. Working on the theory that flies must have remarkable antimicrobial defences to survive rotting dung, meat and fruit, the team at the Department of Biological Sciences, Macquarie University, set out to identify those antibacterial properties manifesting at different stages of a fly's development."

BuzzABC described, in two sentences, the experimental procedure employed by the Australian scientists and their principal findings. These investigators [Clarke, Gidding and Beattie; hereafter CG&B] extracted the chemicals adhering to the surface "by drowning the flies in ethanol, then running the mixture through a filter to obtain the crude extract", which was found to have antibacterial properties. CG&B published a short popular account of their work in a *Microbiology Australia*, but one would look in vain here for more details. To the best of my knowledge, the results of this study were not published in a scientific journal or in the patent literature, but two short notes (authored by Gilling, Beattie and others) describe similar studies with other insects (bees and thrips), in which the solvent was removed by vacuum evaporation at room temperature [280, 281]. I do not know what precautions, if any, the investigators took to dissuade the insects from defecating and vomiting when they faced death by drowning.

Does the research reported in *BuzzABC* support the statements made in *HotFLY*? Not in the least bit, I am afraid, since *HotFLY* considers a vessel containing water, not ethanol or some other organic solvent. The solubility of a chemical compound in water is not the same as that in ethanol, the solvent used by CG&B. In fact, most antibiotics are insoluble in water, which explains why they did not use water for extracting the cuticular antimicrobial secretions.

Note, my dear Hoshiyar, that the title of the short note published by CG&B was "Hypothesis driven drug discovery". As to why the details of this work were not published, or how thorough the study was, I will not speculate, but I will not hesitate to say that their project satisfied the canons of scientific investigation. Someone who still wants to believe in the veracity, science and prescience of *HotFLY* might retort by putting forward the following hypothesis: among the antidotes secreted by a house fly, at least one is highly water-soluble, it is this antidote to which the word *shifā'* (meaning cure) in *HotFLY* applies. In science, such a suggestion is called an *ad hoc* hypothesis, and it is easy to expose the fallacy in this approach.

ad hoc: arranged for this purpose, special

I know from our school days, my delicate friend, how queasy you are, and how studiously you avoided visiting the slums of the huge city where we grew up. I wish I could spare you the disgusting details, but I know that your love of truth would prevail over your abhorrence of scatology and your distaste for descriptions of insanitary conditions. A house fly, a foul and filthy creature down to its last micrometers, is attracted to dung, manure and faeces, to heaps of garbage and rotting food, to sputum, to anything whose smell and sight would make us sick, and it flits from one place to another at great speed. It carries pathogens mainly in its gut and on the hairy and bristly parts of its body, namely its legs (which it uses for smelling) and proboscis (the insectal counterpart of an elephant's trunk), which it uses for sucking liquid food. We use our jaws or a blender for turning solid food into a fluid blob, but when a fly, not naturally endowed with a blender, lands on dry food (which may be a crystal of sugar or a

scatology: study of faecal excrement

sputum: saliva, spittle

piece of filth), it exudes a droplet of saliva from the end of its proboscis, fluidizes the food material and then proceeds to siphon it up.

Let us grant now that the house fly does indeed secrete a water-soluble antibacterial compound. Consider two flies identical in every respect when they take off from the same rubbish heap, and suppose that each falls, a short while later, into a glass of water. We will suppose that one flew directly from the departure point to the glass into which it fell, whereas the other, the greedier, made a stopover at the stool of a child inflicted with typhoid before it fell into a different glass. Will the exterior of both flies have the same amount of filth (pathogens) and the same amount of cure (water-soluble antibacterial compounds)? The reasonable among my readers will surely agree that this would not be the case. Someone who wants to defend *HotFLY* can still dodge the objection by putting forward another ad hoc hypothesis. Can you guess what this person would say? The fly with the bigger payload of germs secreted on the second leg of its flight enough antidote to nullify the perils of the extra cargo. Mention Occam to him, if you think he is intelligent and reflective, but don't paraphrase Voltaire by saying "I disapprove of your hypotheses, but I will defend to the death your right to frame them".

For *Occam* and his razor, see p. 1

The phrase "breeding like rabbits", coined before the dawn of modern bacteriology, is too firmly entrenched to be replaced with "breeding like bacteria", but this does not mean that we should overlook the fact that bacteria multiply at a phenomenal rate, and this they do by dividing, but molecules, whether inorganic or otherwise, are incapable of such mathematical manipulations. Now, the growth rate of a bacterial population depends on the medium, which means, first, that considerably more bacteria will be generated by the immersion of a single fly in a dish of lukewarm nutritious soup than in a glass of cold water, and secondly, that even if one accepts the simple equality of cure and disease, a zillion times more bacteria might enter the stomach of the believer in *HotFLY* without a proportionate increase in the antidote. Chemists have shown great ingenuity, during the last two decades, in synthesizing self-replicating molecules [282], but such replication, since it only takes place under controlled conditions, does not invalidate what I have written above.

It has been known for some yeas that bacterial infection induces antimicrobial activity in the hemolymph (the equivalent of blood) of the fruit fly [283]; various kinds of antimicrobial protein (AmP) are among the molecules produced by the fat body (the equivalent of liver) in response to infection. Natori [284] made the serendipitous discovery that merely pricking the body wall of flesh fly larvae with a needle activated the immune system of this insect and led to the formation of various immune molecules, including different AmP's. It does not follow from this, but one cannot exclude the possibility, that the antibacterial compounds secreted by the house fly are also similar proteins. No one can claim, without undertaking a painstaking investigation, that what is good for the house fly is beneficial also for human beings. Even if we assume that the house fly has been created to make antidotes that protect *it* as well as humans, a defender of *HotFLY* will have to show that spasmodic injestion of such antibiotics at arbitrary concentrations is beneficial rather than harmful. Taking a prescribed course of antibiotics is not to be equated with swallowing tiny bits of penicillin (or chewing blue cheese) now and then.

As I ploughed my way through the Internet to acquaint myself of the arguments employed by the defenders of *HotFLY*, I was struck by their garrulity and gullibility, and realized how easy it is to propagate error. Someone, after chancing upon a report that seems to offer the community a way out of an imbroglio, posts it on the Internet, and it spreads like avian influenza, before you can say "Falsehood has come and truth has vanished", infecting everyone who has been waiting for the (false but) good news. I understand this aberration even if I do not sympathize with it, but I feel uncomfortable when I come across blatant distortion and deception. In one YouTube video, an Arab "scientist" claims that a German pharmaceutical giant was inspired by *HotFLY* to develop a cure for AIDS [285]. *BuzzABC* has been posted, reposted, and swallowed as the last scientific word on flies-and-antibiotics. One never finds, in this campaign for defending *HotFLY*, references to scholarly works and peer-reviewed scientific journals—what scientists call *the literature.* I have therefore coined a word to describe the text and videos on the Internet: I will call it *interature*, and emphasize that it is not the proper forum for settling scientific controversies.

Your question has been answered, but I shall encroach a little further on your precious time so that I may present to you some other thoughts that entered my mind as I pondered the issues discussed above. I have coined another phrase, "dogma-driven science", and would like to compare it with "hypothesis-driven science". Scientists, too, are human, and every scientist does her/his best to protect her/his favourite hypothesis, but no one can succeed as a scientist, or deserves to be called one, if she/he is not prepared to abandon a hypothesis that is belied by experimental data. Defenders of *HotFLY* are anti-science because they already *know* the answer, but in a scientific investigation the answer is not known beforehand.

C — *Ghazālī's Views on Science*

The purpose of this Appendix is to let Ghazālī speak for himself and let the reader decide whether the summary presented in Chapter 2 gives a fair picture of his thoughts.

Organization of *Iḥyā'*

We begin by taking a closer look at *Iḥyā'*, his magnum opus, which was compiled between 1096 and 1105 [286]. The book was written in Arabic, and several editions (and translations in other languages) are available online [287]; I have used the two-volume 1982 Beirut edition [288, 289].

In the preface to *Iḥyā'*, Ghazālī explains his motive for writing the book, and this can be inferred from the title itself: he felt that proper knowledge and guidance, as revealed by the Almighty Allah in the Qur'ān, had vanished and been replaced by the sermons and writings of self-seeking scholars and jurisprudents. One can understand why *Iḥyā'* did not become the favourite book of every Muslim priest, and why copies of the book were burnt in Muslim Spain at the command of the jurisprudents [290, p. 720]. Put simply, the purpose of *Iḥyā'* is to provide directions for the path to the Hereafter.

Ghazālī divides *'ilm* into *'ilm al-mukāshafa* (the 'science' of revelation and vision), and *'ilm al-mu'āmala* (the 'science' of behavior and relationship), and he declares that only the latter falls within the scope of *Iḥyā'*. Notwithstanding this declaration, he returns to the former on several occasions.

Iḥyā' is a quartet, in which each of the four volumes (or parts) has ten books. The first volume deals with *'ibādāt*, or the acts of worship; the second, with the *'ādāt*, or the religious dictates concerning interpersonal and social relations and their meanings; the third, with *muhlikāt*, meaning those blameworthy characteristics of the heart which destroy a person; the fourth and final part, with *munjiyāt*, meaning those praiseworthy qualities which bring a believer closer to Allah, and save him from the fire of Hell. I will focus almost entirely on the first book of the first volume, entitled *Kitāb al-'Ilm*, which is easily rendered in English as *The Book of Knowledge*, and from now on I will refer to both the original and one of its English translations as *BoK*. One finds in *BoK* the very core of Ghazālī's thoughts on knowledge, which is why it has been called the flagship book of *Iḥyā'* [84]. Fortunately, the flagship book has been rendered into English by two diligent translators, McCall [94] and Faris [60]. In what follows, translations unaccompanied by a specific citation are to be attributed to the present author.

I remind the reader that confusion can arise if one translates *'ilm* as *science*, and that, on most occasions, it is far more appropriate to use the word *knowledge*. In this Appendix, I will continue using, when translating Ghazālī, the Arabic word itself (*'ilm* or *'ulūm*).

Branches of philosophy

In *Munqidh*, philosophy is said to embrace six fields: *al-riyāḍiah* (mathematics), *al-manṭiqiyāt* (logic), *al-ṭabī'īyāt* (natural science), *al-ilāhīyāt* (metaphysics), *al-siāsīyāt* (politics), and *al-ikhlāqiīyāt* (ethics). However, in *Tahāfut* and *Iḥyā'* he mentioned only the first four. He did not write much about *al-ṭabī'īyāt* in *Iḥyā'* or *Munqidh*, but went into great detail in *Tahāfut*. Apart from some minor changes and additions (references to Aristotle's works), the following passage is from Kamali's English translation of *Tahāfut* [113, p. 180–1]:

> The sciences called by them [the philosophers] 'physical' are many. We will mention some of them, so that it may be seen that the Sacred Law does not require a dispute over them, except on a few points which we have mentioned.
>
> These sciences are divided into principal and subsidiary sciences. The principal sciences are eight: (i) The discussion of all

that relates to body, *qua* body (i.e., division, motion, and change); and all that appertains to movement, or follows from it (i.e., Time, Space, and the Void). This is the subject-matter of the book called *samʿa al-kiyān* (*Physics*). (ii) The inquiry concerning the various kinds of the component parts of the world (e.g., the heavens, and all that is in the hollow of the sphere of the Moon—viz., the four elements); the nature of these things, and the cause of the location of each one of these in a definite place. This is discussed in the book called *al-samāʾwa al-ʿālam* (*De cælo et mundo* = On the Heavens and Earth). (iii) The inquiry concerning the laws of generation and corruption: development and reproduction and growth and decay; transformations; and the manner of the preservation of species, in spite of the corruption which overtakes individuals because of the two—i.e., Eastward and Westward—celestial movements. This is discussed in the book called *al-kaun wa al-fasād* (*De generatione et corruptione* = On coming-to-be and passing-away). (iv) The inquiry concerning the accidental conditions of the four elements whose mixture results in meteorological phenomena—e.g., clouds, rain, thunder, lightning, the halo, the rainbow, thunderbolts, winds, and earthquakes. (v) The study of the mineral substances. (vi) The science of botany. (vii) The study of animals. It forms the subject of the book called *ṭabʿā al-ḥaiwānāt* (*Historia animalium*). (viii) The study of the animal soul, and the faculties of perception, showing that the soul of man does not die because of the death of the body, but that it is a spiritual substance whose annihilation is impossible.

The subsidiary sciences are seven: (i) Medicine. It aims at discovering the principles governing the human body; its various conditions (e.g., health and disease); the causes of these conditions, and their symptoms—so that disease may be prevented, and health may be preserved. (ii) Astrology. It is an estimate, based on the figures and constellations of stars, as to what will happen to the world and to people; how new-born babes will fare, and how the years will progress. (iii) Physiognomy. It infers moral character from physical appearance. (iv) Interpretation of dreams, which is an elucidation, derived from dream-images, of what the soul has observed of the Hidden World, and the imaginative faculty has represented through a different symbol. (v) The talismanic art, which combines celestial forces with those of some terrestrial bodies, so as to produce from the combination another force which will work wonders in the world. (vi) The art of magic, which combines earthly substances to produce strange things from them. (vii) Alchemy, which aims at changing the properties of mineral substances, so that finally gold and silver may be produced through some controlled device.

We can now move on to *Iḥyā'*, and become better acquainted with Ghazālī's views on knowledge.

First chapter of *BoK*

Chapter 1 of *BoK*, a panegyric on knowledge and those who acquire it, is peppered with words said to have been uttered by the Prophet. For example: "The passing away of an entire tribe is more bearable than the death of a scholar", and "On the Day of Judgment the ink of scholars will have the same weight (that is, worth) as the blood of martyrs" [288, p. 6]. A hint that the death of Khayyām or Ṭūsī would not be mourned with a heavy heart and tearful eyes can be gleaned already in Chapter I, if one reads a few more sayings, but anyone who wants Ghazālī's opinion in his own ink will find it more rewarding to move on to Chapter 2.

Second chapter of *BoK*

The divinely ordained obligatory duties placed on a Muslim are divided into two categories: those which are placed on every individual and those which are placed collectively on the community. The former are termed *fardh 'ayn*; the latter, termed *fardh kifāyāh*, can be discharged for the community by the action of some, and is thus not necessarily binding for each individual member of the community.

Chapter 2 begins with two sayings of the Prophet, both of which have, in fact, already been quoted in Chapter I; according to the first "acquiring *'ilm* is the bounden duty of every Muslim", while the second commands a Muslim to "Seek *'ilm* even [if that takes him] as far as China" [288, p. 14]. Ghazālī informs his readers that Muslims disagreed as to what was meant by knowledge, and splintered into over twenty factions, each group insisting that its own specialty was the most meritorious. Among the groups listed by him, one would search in vain for astronomers, mathematicians or chemists; those who are mentioned include scholastic theologians, jurisprudents, exegetes, and the Sufīs. Ghazālī, a jurisprudent himself, concludes that jurisprudence is above all other *'ulūm*, and he leaves the reader in no doubt as to the meaning of the word *'ilm* in the first saying quoted above: *'ilm* is to be interpreted as 'the knowledge of practical religion'.

Ghazālī announces that the scope of *Iḥyā'* is confined to the "*'ilm* of practical religion". One may infer, from what he writes next, that this term means the nuts and bolts of Islam, the nitty-gritty of being a Muslim. For those whom Ghazālī calls [288, p. 14] *ajlāf al-'arab*—the common Ḥejāzī at the time of the Prophet (thus—by implication—for the illiterate masses of our times), it was (and is) enough to believe in the words of *al-shahādah*, the two clauses of affirmation, namely 'There is no God but Allah and Muḥammad is His Prophet'. Illiterate Muslims are not required to fully grasp the significance of these words through discussion and disquisition, but only to believe and confess them unequivocally without the least hesitation or doubt.

ajlāf: plural of *jilf* meaning boorish, uncouth

Present-day duplicates of Ghazālī

Concerned more with the present and the future, I pause to see if contemporary Muslims are being offered better advice. 'Islam Q&A' is a web site that 'aims to provide intelligent, authoritative responses to anyone's question about Islam, whether it be from a Muslim or a non-Muslim, and to help solve general and personal social problems'. A Muslim woman submitted the following enquiry [291]:

> I study in USA. When I go to my University I cover myself with loose clothes and wear hijab. But, still that University is coeducation. I try to avoid talking to Non Mahram but sometimes I have to talk to them. I want to complete my education here and then want to live in some Islamic country. Is it right for me to study in USA? Does this hadith "Even if u have to go to China to earn knowledge, go" applies to woman too?

The reply is reproduced below:

> Praise be to Allaah.
>
> With regard to girls studying in these mixed societies and in this corrupt environment, please see the answer to Question # 5384.
>
> With regard to the hadeeth mentioned, "Seek knowledge even if you have to go as far as China, for seeking knowledge is a duty on every Muslim," Shaykh al-Albaani said in Da'eef al-Jaami': "(It is) fabricated." (no. 906).
>
> The proven hadeeth is that which was narrated by Ibn Maajah from the hadeeth of Anas ibn Maalik, who said: "The Messenger of Allaah (peace and blessings of Allaah be upon him) said: 'Seeking knowledge is obligatory upon every Muslim.' " (220. Classed as saheeh by al-Albaani in Saheeh Sunan Ibn Maajah. What is meant by knowledge here is knowledge of sharee'ah (Islamic knowledge). Al-Thawri said: "It is the knowledge for which no person has any excuse for not knowing." And Allaah knows best.

I think even Ghazālī, who spent dozens of pages arguing that *'ilm* means the knowledge revealed to the Prophet of Islam, ought to have suspected that the go-to-China *ḥadīth*, which he quoted twice [288, pp. 9,14], must be a fabrication. One does not say "You must learn to swim even if you have to go to the Sahara".

As stated earlier (p. 4), Ghazālī quoted the following words as a ḥadīth: *Talk to people about what they know and leave what they do not know. Do you want to give the impression that Allāh and His Messenger lie?* The remark occurs in the Bukhārī collection [32, Vol. 1, p. 130], but its source is stated to be 'Alī bin Abū Ṭālib, not the Prophet; indeed several online versions [292–294] have omitted the text of this particular 'saying' (Vol. 1, Book 3, Nr. 128). I leave it to the reader to verify that the accompanying remark (about swine and pearls) attributed by Ghazālī to Jesus can hardly be called a rendering of Matthew 7:6 and the following verses.

fatwa (or *fetwa*): religious edict

The cleric who issued the above *fatwa* (almost 900 years after Ghazālī's death) followed the same approach as would have been used by Ghazālī, thus providing us with a vivid example of how stagnant Muslim jurisprudence has remained all these years. Let us go back to Ghazālī again.

Back to Ghazālī's *BoK*

When he discusses the communal obligations placed on Muslims, Ghazālī classifies the different *'ulūm* into sacred (*sharīah*) and profane (*ghayr sharīah*). Sacred *'ulūm* are "those which have been acquired from the prophets and are not arrived at either by means of ratiocination, like arithmetic [he writes *al-ḥisāb*], or by experimentation, like medicine, or through hearing, like language." [The modern world 'osmosis' might serve better than 'hearing']. He further divides profane *'ulūm* into praiseworthy, blameworthy, and permissible; in the first category fall those *'ulūm*—medicine and arithmetic, for instance—on whose knowledge the activities of this life depend. He grants that

> Medicine is necessary for the perpetuation of bodily existence; arithmetic, for daily transactions, the division of legacies and inheritances and such like. A lack of practitioners of these *'ulūm* in a city would place the community in dire straits. But should there already be such practitioners, the other members of the community are absolved from the duty to acquire these *'ulūm*. No one should be surprised that medicine and arithmetic [he writes *al-ḥisāb*] are included among the communal obligations; for the [arts and] crafts—such as agriculture, weaving, politics, even cupping and tailoring—also fall under communal obligations. Indeed if a town were void of cuppers, its people would soon face extinction.

Ghazālī returns later to put medicine into its place:

> It might be asked, "Why have you placed medicine on par with jurisprudence, given that the former pertains to the affairs of this world, namely the welfare of the body, while the latter pertains to the welfare of religion; does not this parity conflict with the general consensus among Muslims?" Then know that it is not necessary to treat the two on equal terms, and in fact there is a difference between them. Jurisprudence is superior to medicine on three counts; first because it is sacred knowledge, derived from prophecy, but medicine is not sacred knowledge; second, it is superior to medicine because no one, sick or healthy, who is treading the road to the hereafter can do without it, while only the sick, who are a minority, need medicine; third, because jurisprudence is close to the *'ilm* of the road of the hereafter. ...No matter how the two are com-

> pared, the superiority of jurisprudence over medicine is obvious, just as when jurisprudence is compared to the science of the way to hereafter, the superiority of the latter is evident.

One does not expect, even in the midst of a massive economic meltdown, a votary of venture capitalism to express his dismay at the popularity of vocations like banking and finance, and the attendant neglect of more altruistic and less remunerative professions. Ghazālī wrote *Iḥyā'* because Islamic learning looked, to him, like a dying body in need of a kiss of life. And what had sapped the vitality of this body? A surfeit of self-seeking jurisprudents, according to Ghazālī, the patron saint of jurisprudence. The same Ghazālī who has declared jurisprudence to be the most prized branch of learning now complains that in many Muslim cities

> there is no physician except one who is a *dhimmī* (follower of the protected religions), whose testimony about medical matters is not admissible. Yet we find no Muslim practising medicine, although plenty of people are engaged in polemics and controversy. Furthermore, the town is teeming with jurisprudents occupied with issuing *fatāwa* and defending cases. Now, why are people flocking to (the communal obligation) jurisprudence, whose experts are already plentiful, but no one turns to medicine, the communal obligation which is not being pursued by any Muslim? Can there be any other cause than the fact that the practice of medicine does not lead to the management of religious endowments, execution of wills, guardianship of funds for orphans, to judicial and official appointments through which one exalts oneself over others and gains dominance over one's enemies?

It is time to examine his attitude to what we may call secular knowledge, which he categorized as a branch of philosophy. I quote now from McCall [94, p. 87]:

> As for philosophy, it is not a science by itself, but is composed of four parts, one of which is geometry and arithmetic [Ghazālī writes *al-handasa wa al-ḥisāb*]. These two are permissible as we have seen, and no one is withheld from them except one who fears that he will go beyond them into the blameworthy sciences, for most of those practicing them have departed from them into innovations. The weak are guarded from them not on account of (any harm they

> have in) themselves but as a boy is barred from the edge of a river for fear that he may fall into it, and as a novice in Islam is guarded from association with unbelievers because of fear for him, although (even) the person who is well-grounded in his Islam is not recommended to associate with them.

The term 'innovation' has a specific meaning in Islam, roughly equivalent to heresy, but we need not delve into it now, for even those who are not aware of the background will be able to figure out that Ghazālī suffers, like most of his kind, from a morbid fear of innovations, and wants to keep Islam as close as possible to what he perceived as its original form. Presumably, he is not objecting to novelties in mathematics, and is concerned only with the fact that the pursuit of mathematical investigations suits those who have enquiring minds, and some of them—the feeble-minded, in his opinion—might be emboldened by their mathematical advances to ask awkward questions and begin to advocate 'innovations' in Islam as well. We skip over his comments on the second and third parts of philosophy (logic and metaphysics) to see what he thinks of *al-ṭabī'īyāt*, the fourth part of philosophy [288, p. 32]:

> The fourth is natural science, some parts of which conflict with religious law and true religion, and these should rather be called *jahl*, not *'ilm*, and thus cannot be classified among the *'ulūm*. Some of these discussions treat the qualities and special properties of bodies and their manner of change and transformations. To this extent, it resembles physicians' studies except that they consider the sickness or health of man's body, while the others observe all bodies from the point of view of change and movement; however, medicine is superior since it fulfils a need, whereas *al-ṭabī'īyāt* is unnecessary.[1]

jahl: ignorance (antonym of *'ilm*)

I am tempted to mimic Ghazālī's own opening words in the concluding section of *Tahāfut* [113, p. 249] and say, "Now that I have exposed Ghazālī's antipathy to natural sciences, do you not think that he and his followers should be banished from a society that wishes to cultivate scientific activity?".

[1] This is my translation. For other versions, see Faris [60, p. 47] and McCall [94, p. 88]

Ghazālī's critique of *'ilm al-nujūm*

Ghazālī's critique of nujūmology [60, pp. 69–70] is presented below, but the reader is reminded that whenever the word "astrology" appears below, it should be interpreted as "nujūmology":

> Umar ibn-al-Khattab said, "Acquire of the science of the stars enough to lead you on land and on sea but no more." He warned against it for three reasons: First, because it is harmful to most people, since if they were told that these results would ensue consequent upon the course of that [*sic* the] stars, they might think that it is the stars which influence the course of events and are also the gods who direct the world. Furthermore, in view of the fact that the stars are glorious celestial bodies and awe-inspiring to the hearts, man's heart would naturally become focussed upon them and would see both good and evil required or forbidden by the stars with the result that the name of Allah would be erased from the heart. The feeble-minded one does not look beyond the means, and only the learned man who is well-grounded in knowledge would understand that the sun, moon, and stars are subject to the will of Allah. Thus the parable of the feeble-minded person who thinks that the light of the sun is the result of its rising, is like the parable of an ant which as it happened upon the surface of a sheet of paper, was endowed with reason and thereupon watched the movement in the process of writing, only to think that it was the work of the pen, but would not go beyond that to see the fingers, and behind the fingers the hand, and behind the hand the will which moves it, and behind the will a deliberate and an able scribe, and behind all, the Creator of the hand, and the ability, and the will. Most people do not look beyond the nearby and earthly causes and never arrive at the Cause of all causes. This, therefore, is one of the reasons why the science of the stars has been forbidden.
>
> A second reason is that astrology is purely guesswork and in the opinion of the average man, the influence of the stars is not determined either with certainty or even with probability. Pronouncements in connection with it are the result of ignorance. Consequently, astrology has been pronounced blameworthy because of this ignorance, not because it is knowledge. Furthermore, this knowledge, it is said, was of a miraculous nature possessed by Prophet ldris,[2] but has now vanished and is no more. The rare cases

[2]Footnote due to Faris:—The Muslim equivalent to Enoch. See *Surahs*

in which the astrologer happens to be correct are coincidences. He may happen upon some of the causes, but the effect will not result therefrom unless several other conditions, the comprehension of whose realities are beyond the reach of human beings, should prevail. If, however, Allah should grant to him the knowledge of the remaining causes, the astrologer's prediction would come true; but if that is not granted to him, he would err and his prediction would be not unlike the guess of a man who is moved to say whenever he sees the clouds gathering and rising from the mountain tops, that there will be rain this day. Rain may actually fall though it is also possible that a hot sun should rise and disperse the clouds. The mere presence of clouds in the skies is not sufficient for bringing down rain; there are other conditions which cannot be determined. Similarly, the sailor's guess that the ship will have a safe sailing is based upon the usual behaviour of the winds with which he is familiar. But there are unknown factors which control the movements of the winds and which the sailor would never know. Consequently, he would sometimes guess correctly and sometimes he would err. For this reason, even the strong minded person has been forbidden to practise astrology.

A third reason why man has been warned against the science of the stars is because it is of no use at all. The most which could be said on its behalf is that it is, at its best, an intrusion into useless things and a waste of time and life which is man's most precious belonging. Such a thing is the most serious loss.

The science of the stars (nujūmology) may have been forbidden, but it has not been abandoned by the majority of Muslims, whose minds have still not been illuminated by proper education. They followed the Imām and abandoned astronomy, but they could not resist retaining astrology; they kept the filthy bath water and threw out the baby, whereas the Imām wanted them to get rid of both.

There are still societies, Muslim as well as others, where the birth of a baby with a cleft palate is attributed to the pregnant mother's handling of a knife during an eclipse [163]. Faith in astrological predictions and the notion that celestial bodies influence human affairs lost ground only with the ascendancy of the alternative approach of appealing to reason and experimenta-

XIX:57, XXI:58; *cf.* Gen. 4:17, 5:18–24; Heb 11:5. *For other identifications,* see Ref. [295]

tion, of respecting science and questioning authority. One cannot vanquish astrology merely by issuing edicts.

Ghazālī, the superstitious mystic

It is noteworthy, but hardly surprising, that Ghazālī, who dismissed nujūmology, did believe, like most of his contemporaries, in the *'ilm al-sahr wa al-ṭalismāt* (the *science* of magic and talisman), and thought that its successful implementation required a knowledge of the movement of stars [60, pp. 67–8]:

> The Apostle of Allah himself was the victim of magic which caused him to become sick until Gabriel made it known to him and exorcized the evil spirit from underneath a stone in the bottom of a well. Magic is something obtained through the knowledge of the properties of the precious stones and mathematical calculations relative to the places and times of the rising of the stars. A skeleton resembling the person to be charmed is made out of these precious stones, which is gazed into, to the accompaniment of constant repetition of words of unbelief and obscenity which are contrary to law, until a special time in the rising of the stars arrives. Through it the aid of the devils is secured with the result that, in accordance with the established order Allah has ordained, strange states befall the charmed person.

In *Munqidh* Ghazālī mocks a form of specious reasoning in which a fact was supposed to be established by an astounding illustration of something else, and he put it in startling words, which may be summarized as follows: "If a conjurer should say to me, 'Three is larger than ten, and to prove this, I will change this stick into a serpent', I might be surprised at his legerdemain, but I would not concede the argument, since I *know* that the converse is true." Within a few years of the publication of the French translation of *Munqidh*, two American authors [217, 296] quoted this remark with approval, but I refuse to be seduced by this glib demolition of a silly straw man created by Ghazālī himself, for no one, really no one, in his right mind will claim that three is greater than ten, except as a ploy to wrong-foot the opponent, or as a clever piece of pedagogy to introduce the idea of negative integers (unknown in Ghazālī's time), in which case three is indeed greater than ten. Worse still, we will now see that Ghazālī himself falls into the same trap when he shows us a talisman (based on a magic square) in order to prove his point.

At the end of *Munqidh* Ghazālī presents a long argument and tries to convince the reader by dazzling him with numerology:

> If our opponent does not admit this, well, we have given a demonstration that a suprarational sphere is possible, indeed that it actually exists. If, however, he admits our contention, he has affirmed the existence of things called properties with which the operations of reason are not concerned at all; indeed, reason almost denies them and judges them absurd. For instance, the weight of a *dāniq* (about eight grains) of opium is a deadly poison, freezing the blood in the veins through its excess of cold. The man who claims a knowledge of physics considers that when a composite substance becomes cold it always does so through the two elements of water and earth, since these are the cold elements. It is well-known, however, that many pounds of water and earth are not productive of cold in the interior of the body to the same extent as this weight of opium. If a physicist were informed of this fact, and had not discovered it by experiment, he would say, 'This is impossible; the proof of its impossibility is that the opium contains the elements of fire and air, and these elements do not increase cold; even supposing it was entirely composed of water and earth, that would not necessitate this extreme freezing action, much less does it do so when the two hot elements are joined with them. He supposes that this is a proof!
>
> Most of the philosophers' proofs in natural science and theology are constructed in this fashion. They conceive of things according to the measure of their observations and reasonings. What they are unfamiliar with they suppose impossible. If it were not that veridical vision in sleep is familiar, then, when someone claimed to gain knowledge of the unseen while his senses were at rest, men with such intellects would deny it. If you said to one, 'Is it possible for there to be in the world a thing, the size of a grain, which, if placed in a town, will consume that town in its entirety and then consume itself, so that nothing is left of the town and what it contained nor of the thing itself'?; he would say, 'This is absurd; it is an old wives' tale'. Yet this is the case with fire, although, when he heard it, someone who had no acquaintance with fire would reject it. The rejection of the strange features of the world to come usually belongs to this class. To the physicist we reply: 'You are

veridical: truthful [*verum* (true) +*dicere* (to say)]. A veridical dream is one that accords with real events (past, present or future) unknown to the dreamer.

compelled to admit that in opium there is a property which leads to freezing, although this is not consonant with nature as rationally conceived; why then is it not possible that there should be in the positive precepts of the Divine law properties leading to the healing and purifying of hearts, which are not apprehended by intellectual wisdom but are perceived only by the eye of prophecy? Indeed in various pronouncements in their writings they have actually recognized properties more surprising than these, such as the wonderful properties observed when the following figure was employed in treating cases of childbirth where delivery was difficult:—

4	9	2
3	5	7
8	1	6

or

د	ط	ب
ج	ه	ز
ح	ا	و

The figure is inscribed on two pieces of cloth untouched by water. The woman looks at them with her eye and places them under her feet, and at once the child quickly emerges.Ghazālī The physicists acknowledge the possibility of that, and describe it in the book entitled *The Marvels of Properties*.

We have only Ghazālī's claim that his amulet facilitates child birth, whereas turning a staff into a snake, if it were to take place, would be a palpable transformation.

This magic 3 × 3 square[3] became a precious gift from Ghazālī to the Arab masses, who named it after the Imām, though he was not the first to introduce it to the Arab world, let alone invent it. According to one tradition, Ghazālī is said to have developed the formula, under divine inspiration (*ilhām*), from the combinations of the mysterious letters which begin Surāhs 19 and 42 of the Qur'ān, while others trace the formula to Adam [297], who passed it on to Ghazālī. This attribution was in keeping with Ghazālī's established reputation as a custodian of mystical knowledge and particularly of *Kitāb al-jafr*, a book, once in the possession of Ja'far al-Ṣādiq,[4] that was believed to contain information

[3]It is called a *magic* square because the sum of the numbers lying along a row or a column or a diagonal is always fifteen.

[4]The sixth Imām of Shī'ah Muslims (see p. 208)

as to what would happen to the family of Muḥammad in general and to certain members of it in particular.

The table of numbers is used as an amulet, and you can find items of jewelry where it is inscribed [298]. This particular square is called *budūḥ*, in the Arabic world, because of the letters at its corners (ب د و ح) and as the magic square of *Ḥawwā* (Eve حوا), because the three letters in her name (ح وا) (ḥā'/wāw/alif) which occur in one row.

According to a book (published in 1832), which provides a detailed account of the construction and applications of magic squares and talismans, one can solve any problem, or create one for someone else, by using these devices [149, Ch. 32]. Zwemer, writing almost a century later, described the popularity of the "Square of al-Ghazālī" or *al-Budūḥ* [76, pp. 165–6]:

> For the popular mind *Budūḥ* has become a Jinn whose services can be secured by writing his name either in letters or numbers. The uses of the word are most varied to invoke both good and bad fortune. It is used against menorrhagia, against pains in the stomach, to render oneself invisible, against temporary impotence, etc. ... We find the same in magical treatises. It is also engraved upon jewels and metal plates or rings which are carried as permanent talismans, and it is inscribed at the beginning of books as a preservative. But by far the most common use is to ensure the arrival of letters and packages. No letter from one pious Moslem to another is ever posted in the Near East without putting the figure 8642 in Arabic on the outside of the envelope where it is sealed. And one may see thousands of children in Egypt who have never heard of Al-Ghazali and cannot read the letters of his name wearing his magic square on lead or silver amulet to protect them from the hideous power of the Child-Witch (*Um al-Subyān*). In the Azhar University men study his creed but [why *but*?] in the villages they follow his credulity and to all the *fellahin* of Egypt *Budūḥ* has become a guardian Angel!

The *but* above should be replaced by *and*, since the *Budūḥ*, one can hardly deny, *is* a part of Ghazālī's creed.

D — *Clerics and Their Titles*

Formal priesthood with a well defined hierarchy of ranks is not a feature of the manner in which the majority Sunnī sect conducts its religious affairs at present, but it is perfectly legitimate to speak of someone as a Muslim priest if he regularly performs various religious duties and roles (like leading the prayer, delivering sermons, conducting marriage ceremonies and funeral formalities) and commands the allegiance of a group of Muslims, which may be as small as a Muslim "parish" or spread world wide. It is important therefore to gain some familiarity with the titles attached to various religious scholars.

The word *'ulamā'* (or *'ulemā'*) is the plural of the Arabic word *'ālim*, which means a learned man, a scholar, someone who is believed to have acquired *'ilm* (learning); although the title could be given to a secular scholar, it is usually reserved, as already explained on p. 23, for a religious scholar.

A Muslim who is reputed to possess an extraordinary Qur'ānic knowledge is usually addressed, by other Muslims, as an *'allāma*, a *maulānā*, or a *maulvi* (alternatively *maulavi* or *maulevi*). The titles have been mentioned here in descending order of prestige, but the best clue to the significance of a particular form of address is a list of persons to whom the term is applied, or was applied in the recent past. The term *allāma*, which literally means "Highly Learned" (*Super-'Ālim* or *'Ālim extraordinaire*) and is used rather sparingly, connotes a congruence of secular and religious learning commensurate with the highest values of Muslim scholarship. Perhaps the best known bearer of this title was *'Allāma* Iqbāl (d. 1938), who became (informally and consensually) the eternal poet laureate of Pakistan. The term *maulānā*, which literally means "our master (or lord or friend, etc.)", signifies a high **'Allāma Iqbāl** level of attainment in religious knowledge, much higher than that reached by a *maulvi*. A celebrated example is that of Maulānā Abul-ʻAla Maudūdī, an Indo-Pāk scholar who has a very large following throughout the Islamic world. A *muftī* is an Islamic scholar who has the authority to issue a decree, a legal opinion known as a *fatwā* (or *fetwā*). The source of the authority may be an Islamic government or the reputation of the scholar issuing the decree, and a well-respected *maulānā* is entitled, in view of his standing in the community, to issue a fatwā.

In the Indo-Pāk subcontinent, the term *mullā* (usually transcribed as *mullah*) carries a distinctly pejorative connotation, since it bears the same relation to *ʻĀlim* as *scienticulist* (see below) does to *scientist;* there a mullā is a person with little knowledge and a disproportionately large influence (or nuisance value). Outside the subcontinent, *mullā* remains a coveted title (in which case it precedes the given name of the person): the Ṭālibān, who addressed their chief as Mullā ʻUmar, did not mean to belittle him, and it is worth noting that the highly respected Shīʻah theologian Ṣadr-ud-Dīn Muḥammad Shīrāzī, born in the sixteenth century, is popularly called Mullā Ṣadrā. I will use *mullā* as a generic term only when I am quoting someone else.

Oliver Heaviside coined the word *scienticulist* [299, p. 166] when he wanted to ridicule William Preece, a senior electrical engineer in the British Post Office, for Preece's uninformed and obstinate opposition to Oliver's ideas and for not approving the publication of a paper jointly written by Oliver and his brother Arthur, who, as an employee of the Post Office, was obliged to obtain his chief's permission before submitting the paper for publication [300]. I suppose that Oliver's choice was motivated by words ending in *cule*, a suffix for making a diminutive.

The word *imām* has also more than one connotation. It could simply mean someone who is leading a session of worship, in which case he is an *imām* for the duration of the session; it could mean someone who is employed by a community to lead worshipers regularly in a mosque, or one of the founders of the four branches of Sunnī jurisprudence, or a towering figure like Imām Ghazālī; among Shīʻahs the title *Imām* was generally used for ʻAlī and his eleven successors, but after the Islamic revolution in Iran, it became customary to speak of Imām Khomeini.

The word *shaikh* (or *shaykh*) means an elderly, venerable gentleman. The title *Shaikh ul-Islam*, now sparingly used, means (in the literal sense) an *Elder of Islam*, but in the Ottoman days it signified an official appointment to the most prestigious priestly position. Lane-Pool summed up the prestige [301, pp. 333–4]: "At the head of the third great class of State functionaries, that of the Ulema, or Doctors of the Law, stood the Sheykh-ul-Islam—or Elder of Islam, the most important of whose duties was to interpret the sacred Law by declaring whether any proposed action was in accordance with the precepts of the Koran. No war could be begun, no peace could be concluded, no public matter of any kind could be gone on with until the Sheykh-ul-Islam had been consulted and had pronounced the projected undertaking lawful." Those interested in finding out more are referred to the article on *Shaykh al-Islam* in a recent encyclopedia [302].

To illustrate the informal and unfastidious manner in which such titles are often bestowed, I quote a passage in which the author applies three titles to one person [303, Vol. 4, p. 29]:

> Shaikh-ul-Islam, Maulana Shabbir Ahmad Usmani was a great religious scholar and Jurist. I happened to see him at a time when there was none equal to him in learning and accomplishment, not only in Pakistan but in the entire world. In recognition of his deep knowledge and piety some called him "Shaikh-ul-Islam" and some others called him "Allamah". The Allamah sometimes called at our house.

E — *A Bird's-Eye View*

A wit—evidently a fiction writer—has said, "In fiction everything is true except names and dates; in history nothing is true except names and dates." If someone were to classify this book, a non-fiction work, as a chronicle of events, I would not be able to claim that all the dates are correct, or to guarantee that the alias of the author of *Tahāfut al-Falāsifa* was al-Ghazālī, not al-Ghazzālī.[1] Some readers may be tempted, after finding the surfeit of unfamiliar names and calendric data a little overwhelming, or the thread of thought running through a chapter too circuitous, to exchange the book for a work of fiction; the chronological table and accompanying text in this appendix are meant to act as an antidote to such impulses of desertion. Some of the dates given below are subject to an uncertainty that may be as large as five years. I have not always been able to follow the flow of time chronologically because flashbacks are almost inevitable in recounting a long story, and this book is essentially the story of how two great religions which have much in common, Christianity and Islam, have dealt with the slow (but not always steady) rise of science, and what caused its fall in Islam. In one case dogma was defeated by rational thought; in the other, dogma triumphed over rational thought.

No references are cited in this synopsis.

---

[1]In Arabic, a repeated consonant is pronounced twice, which means that Ghazzālī is to be pronounced as Ghaz|zālī.

570 Birth of Muḥammad

632 Death of Muḥammad

632–634 Caliphate of Abū Bakr (father of 'Ā'ishah, the favourite wife of Muḥammad)

634–644 Caliphate of 'Umar. Major conquests

'Umar's role in Islam has been compared by some to that of St. Paul in Christianity. Earlier Muslim writers—for example, Ibn Khaldūn (1332–1406) and Kātib Chelebi (1609–1657)—reported that 'Umar ordered the destruction of the books of the conquered people on the ground that if what they contain is in the Qur'ān, they are unnecessary, and if they do not, they deserve to be destroyed anyway.

One can understand 'Umar's wariness about alien literature, and it also stands to reason that he forbade seafaring to his people, not willing to endanger the lives of his soldiers, most of whom were desert dwellers. 'Umar's successor, who must have understood that a sensible precaution of today can easily become a silly superstition of tomorrow, annulled the ban.

annul: abolish

644–656 Caliphate of 'Uthmān

The second half of Uthman's rule was marred by discontent among many Muslims, who were chagrined by his nepotism and the malfeasance of the kinsmen he had appointed to key posts. He was assassinated by a band of Muslims (which included Muḥammad bin Abū Bakr).

656–661 Caliphate of 'Alī bin Abū Ṭālib (Muḥammad's cousin and son-in-law). The first civil war

According to the Shī'ah belief, a new institution, namely Imāmate (*Imāmah*), filled the vacancy created by the demise of the Prophet, and that 'Alī, the first Imām, was *de jure* the first Caliph. The second and third in the line are 'Alī's sons (and Prophet's grandsons): Ḥasan and Ḥusayn. The next four Imāms are descendents of the latter in the following order: 'Alī bin Ḥusayn, Muḥammad al-Bāqir, Ja'far al-Ṣādiq (epomym of the Ja'farī school of jurisprudence). The first major schism started after the death of Ja'far al-Ṣādiq. Members of one branch, the so-called Athnā-ash'arī (meaning *Twelvers*), believe that the next (seventh) Imām

de jure: by right

Twelvers

was Mūsā al-Kāẓim; a different branch (called Ismā'īlī, currently a minority) regards Ismā'īl bin Ja'far as the rightful successor to his father. Why the 'Abbāsī caliph Mā'mūn designated Mūsā's son 'Alī al-Raḍa (the eighth Imām of the Twelvers) as his successor is a disputed issue. 'Alī al-Raḍa died during Mā'mūn's lifetime (probably as a result of poisoning). The Ismā'īlīs are sometimes called *Seveners*. **Seveners**

'Alī's Caliphate was a time of strife, insubordination and civil unrest. The entire period was plagued by what has come to be called the first civil war of Islam. Two of the major battles during these years are listed next.

656 Battle of the Camel ('Alī opposed by 'Ā'ishah)

657 Battle of Ṣiffīn ('Alī against Mu'āwiyah)

Mu'āwiyah's general, sensing certain defeat, ordered his soldiers to attach pages of the Qur'ān to their lances, and won a temporary, but fateful, truce. 'Alī is reported to have said in desperation, "But this Qur'ān, a writing inscribed between two covers, is inarticulate, and only men can speak through it." The remark is used as a recurring motif in **Chapter 4**.

661–680 Reign of the first Umayyad Caliph (Mu'āwiyah) His son Yazīd succeeds him and dynastic rule enters Islam

661–750 Umayyad Caliphate

750–754 Umayyads are routed. Caliphate of 'Abbāsī I (Saffāḥ)

754–775 Caliphate of 'Abbāsī II (Mansūr). Patronage of secular scholarship starts

762 Founding of the *City of Peace*, now known as Baghdad. The city (or its academic quarters) came to be called the *House of Wisdom*.

786–809 Caliphate of 'Abbāsī V (Hārūn al-Rashīd)

813–833 Caliphate of 'Abbāsī VII (Mā'mūn), the 'Super Patron' of secular knowledge

Mā'mūn, a heterodox Muslim, embraces Mu'tazilism[2] du-

[2]The Mu'tazilah (or Mu'tazilites) accepted the broad outlines of Islamic dogma and were the first to discuss it in terms of Greek philosophical notions. They focussed on the ethical aspects of the conception of God; rejected predes-

ring the last decade of his life, and declares his support for the belief that only *Allāh* is uncreated (and the creator of everything else), and that the Qur'ān, accordingly, is *created*. (To say that the Qur'ān is *uncreated* is to assert that the Qur'ān has always existed and is coeternal with *Allāh*.)

833 Māmūn launches *miḥnah* (inquisition) four months before his sudden death

Religious scholars, among them **Aḥmad bin Ḥanbal** (780–855), who continue to insist that the Qur'ān is (also) uncreated are imprisoned, flogged or executed during the next sixteen years.

Since the Qur'ān does not provide for all the contingencies of daily life, orthodox Sunnī Muslims follow one of the four legal schools (*madhāhib*; singular *madhab*). The head (the founding father and the eponym) of each *madhab* is a revered figure, treated as a saint, and addressed as *Imām*. **Aḥmad bin Ḥanbal**, the head of one of these legal schools, is widely regarded as more conservative than the heads of the other three schools. *Wahhābism and the Saudi interpretation of Islam may be traced to his lasting influence.*

849 'Abbāsī X ends *miḥnah*. Sunnī Islam becomes the state religion

Mu'taizilism retreats, and (from now on) it is the *'ulamā'* (religious doctors), not the caliphs, who are seen as the custodians of Muḥammad's legacy. The Arabic word *'ilm* (meaning *knowledge*) is applied henceforth almost exclusively to religious knowledge.

850– Patronage of profane scholarship continues

850–1150 The first half of **Chapter 2** deals with this and the next period

The terms *Islamica* (meaning the Muslim world) and *Arabophone* are introduced because not every knowledge seeker was a Muslim and only a handful of them were native Arabs. Only a few scholars of this era are named below.

---

tination; denied, in order to oppose anthropomorphic conceptions of God, the independent existence of the divine attributes, including speech, as a corollary of which they held the Qur'ān to have been created, not uncreated (eternal).

Ab'ul Ḥasan al-**Ash'arī** (873–935), Aḥmad bin Ḥanbal, and **Ghazālī** (1058–1111) are generally regarded as the trio that trounced Mu'tazilism and made philosophy disreputable in orthodox Islam. In *The Incoherence of the Philosophers*, Ghazālī wrote: "Now that you have analysed the theories of the philosophers, will you conclude by saying that one who believes in them ought to be branded with infidelity and punished with death?" In his denunciation, Ghazālī specifically named Abū Naṣr al-**Fārābī** (872–950) and **Ibn Sīnā** (980–1037), known to the West as Avicenna.

Ghazālī's attitude to mathematics and the natural sciences, examined in Chapter 2 and Appendix C, is found to be implacably hostile, but no more than that of Tertullian, the Father of Latin Christianity.

1150–1450 Why science and philosophy continued to flourish for centuries after Ghazālī

Many scholars are of the opinion that Ghazālī's role in the degradation and demise of Islamican science has been exaggerated, that blaming Ghazālī diverts attention from what still requires an explanation, namely the fact that science and philosophy continued to exist and develop in Islam for many centuries, despite unrelenting opposition from the '*ulamā*' (also written as '*ulemā*').

Ibn Khaldūn (1332–1406) was perhaps the last luminary on the intellectual firmament of Islamica. One of the longest sections in his highly acclaimed *Muqaddimah* is that dealing with forecasting the future of dynasties and other predictions of this nature. Though astrology is condemned in Islam (and Ghazālī vilified those who believe in it), rich and poor alike have been smitten by it in many societies, but only the rich could afford to employ competent astronomers and mathematicians, and their money could also procure them the services of the most learned practitioners of medicine (who were often experts in astronomy and astrology also). That mathematicians, astronomers and curers of ills continued to enjoy the patronage of Muslim potentates should not be a matter of surprise.

potentate: a ruler or monarch, especially an autocratic one

How come Islamican astronomy reached its zenith near the end of the thirteenth century?

The Mongols ransacked Baghdad in 1258 and killed the

last ʻAbbāsī caliph. Many lost their lives but not the great astronomer Naṣīr al-Dīn Ṭūsī (1202–74), who had won the respect of Īl-Khān Hülegü before the invasion of Baghdad. Hülegü established for Ṭūsī the observatory of Marāgha in Adharbaijān, equipping it with the very best instruments and an immense library. The continuation of the astronomical tradition of Islamica was the result of this extraordinary conjunction of a worldly-wise scientific genius and a heathen despot who, in his eagerness to procure sound astrological advice, was willing to provide unstinting support for the collection of more reliable astronomical data.

The last great Islamican astronomer Ibn al-Shāṭir (1304–1375) should be mentioned here, if only to mark off the start of the eclipsing of Islamican scholarship.

As interest in genuine scientific learning waned, an obsession with pseudo-scholarship and the occult filled the vacuum. In Ibn Khaldūn's discussion of "various kinds of intellectual sciences", fewer than fifty pages deal with agriculture, mathematics, medicine, metaphysics and physics, but some seventy pages are devoted to the occult sciences, described under sections on "the science of sorcery and talismans" and "the science of the secret of letters", the first of which discusses the evil eye, and the second provides a detailed description of magic squares. In fact, Ghazālī offered a magic square for facilitating child birth.

To say that Ghazālī's role in the decline of Islamican science has been exaggerated is to miss the point. Ghazālī is merely the most successful exponent of a cluster of regressive and divisive ideas, the most-listened-to performer in a long line of pipers, who, by playing the same tenebrous tune, have led successive generations of Muslims into the abyss where superstition and ignorance pass for faith and learning. The stagnation and putrefaction of the Muslim world should be imputed to all these pipers, every one of whom is a reincarnated Ghazālī.

tenebrous: dark, gloomy, shadowy

1517–1648 Protestant reformation

1543–1545 Copernicus and his contemporaries

Three of the most momentous scientific books written during the Renaissance were printed at approximately the same time: *De revolutionibus orbium coelestium* of Nicolaus

Copernicus appeared in (1543), *De fabrica humani corporis* of Andreas Vesalius in the same year, and *Artis magnae sive de regulis algebraicis* of Girolamo Cardano two years later. The last, highly praised as a milestone in the history of mathematics, carried algebra to a point well beyond the reach of an Arabophone algebraist, alive then or in an earlier epoch, and likewise for *De revolutionibus*.

1553 Servetus burnt for heresy

Michael Servetus (1511–1553), condemned for heresy by Catholics as well as Protestants, was burnt in Geneva by Calvinists. A brilliant physician and theologian (and much else), he rejected predestination, the immortality of the soul, infant baptism, the Trinity of *persons* (but not the Trinity of Divine Essentials), and ridiculed those who maintain that Jesus Christ existed before his conception.

1572–1577 The nova of 1572 and the great comet of 1577

Aristotle and his followers had demonstrated, by means of ratiocination (the only course they regarded as dependable), that no change could occur in the heavens, that decay and regeneration were limited to the lower, terrestrial spheres. All the same, a new star arose in Cassopeia in 1572. To those steeped in Aristotelian teachings, it was evident that they were witnessing a sublunar event, but Tycho Brahe (1546–1601) proved that it must be above the moon. Frederick II of Denmark rewarded Tycho with more than a ton of gold and the island of Hven, where he built an observatory and collected a large body of precise data, which led Kepler to his concept of elliptic orbits. In 1577, Tycho observed a comet whose oval path delivered another blow to Aristotelian cosmology.

1580 The last nail in the coffin of Islamican science?

Perhaps the last nail to be knocked into the coffin of Islamican science was the destruction, with the blessing of the Shaykh al-Islam, of the Istanbul observatory, built in 1575 and put under the charge of Taqī al-Dīn (1526–1585), who had previously worked in Cairo and Damascus.

The body of Islamican science had already been emaciated because of the outdated curricula followed in the madrasas. Those in charge of these antiquated institutions did not realize how far ahead European science and mathematics had gone since the days of Ṭūsī. The need of the hour was a new wave of translation, but aversion to alien books had re-entered Islam, and the kings and the *'ulemā'*, who lacked the knowledge to grasp the gravity of the situation, took refuge in their invincible ignorance and contemptuous indifference to "heathen knowledge".

The greatest impediment to progress is the insistence of the vast majority of Muslims on a literal interpretation of the Qurā'n, and blind acceptance of the pronouncements made by priests who are altogether unqualified to judge the underlying technical issues. **Chapter 3** discusses some examples of the untold difficulties resulting from the antipathy of the priests towards science.

Chapter 4 is also concerned with the contentious issue of interpreting the Qur'ān. It begins by returning to the period 656–661, and recalling 'Alī's comment "only men can speak through the Qur'ān". Whether the Qur'ān is literally the word of Allāh or a book inspired by Him, matters naught, since only the Prophet had the capacity to grasp Allāh's message. So far as giving guidance is concerned, a divine book is no different from one written by a human author who is no longer in this world. The main purpose of the chapter is to trace the evolution of Christian theology in the last two centuries; to identify the forces which have humanized Christianity and created a new image of the God of the New Testament; to suggest that similar changes are needed in the world of Islam, and to argue that this transformation can only be brought about by adopting the same attitude towards the Qur'ān as enlightened Christians have developed towards the Bible. The chapter ends by applying to the reading of the Qur'ān Mme Swetchine's aphorism "No two persons ever read the same book, or saw the same picture".

1560–1650 Galileo, Harriot, and Kepler

Galileo (154–1642) and Kepler (1571–1630) require no introduction in this summary. Thomas Harriot (or Hariot or Harriott; 1560–1621), a versatile and virtuoso English scientist who deserves to be placed at the same level as Galileo and Kepler, deduced the sine law of refraction in the summer of 1602, and made telescopic observations of the moon. Harriot was among the foremost mathematicians of his time, and his astronomical interests and achievements covered an exceedingly wide range.

In this period men of science joined forces with commercial and colonial entrepreneurs. Harriot took part in the second expedition to Virginia, and published (1585) what may be seen both as a contribution to scholarship and a brochure for attracting prospective investors, a well documented report detailing the inhabitants and resources of the country. The late sixteenth century surge for maritime trade and colonial settlement gave birth to a 'knowledge economy', which flourished and expanded vastly over the next two centuries.

1618–1648 Thirty Years War. Eighty Years War

Anyone who does not have an intimate knowledge of the impulses which are rocking the present-day Muslim world would do well to study in detail the conflict known as Thirty Years War, which plunged Europe into some of its most devastating decades; it embraced the last phase (after 1821) of the Dutch Revolts, also known as the Eighty Years War. Though the battle ground was mainly modern-day Germany, almost all other nations of Western Europe were also involved in it. Since great wars are those which are fought for defending great ideas, this war had also its root in politics and religion—or in the hypocrisy and greed of the manipulators and in the suggestibility, gullibility and greed (but on a lower scale) of the manipulated. From the religious perspective, this war was the Catholic attempt to crush Protestantism; from the political perspective, the determination of the Habsburg (also Hapsburg) dynasty to retain control of the countries under their dominion and repel rival aspirants.

The Eighty Years War (1568–1648) was the revolt of the Netherlands against Spain. Some important events are described in Chapter 5; here it would be sufficient to note that, during the last three decades of the strife, Protestants in the Low Countries were persecuting fellow Protestants in addition to fighting Catholics. Jan van Olden Barneveldt (1547–1619), a great patriot, was executed because of his opposition to Prince Maurice and for defending the theologian Conrad Vorstius, whose appointment at Leyden became a symbolic cause in a struggle involving two powerful political groups.

1603–1625 Reign of James I, the heretic hunter

James I of England (also James VI of Scotland), keen to show that he was not only the King of England but also the Defender of the Faith, did his best (but failed) to have the aforementioned Vorstius burnt as a heretic. He soon found an English heretic, Bartholomew Legate (1575–1612), who had been found guilty of blasphemous heresy. James tried unsuccessfully to bring Legate back to the fold, but the latter refused to renounce his views, and was burnt at the stake.

1550–1650 The birth of modern science

However improbable it may sound, this is when modern science began to sprout. The possible causes for the growth of scientific activity in Europe during this period are discussed in **Chapter 5**.

150–1999 From the early Church Fathers to the 'New Theology'

The early Church Fathers, for example Tertullian (160–220) and Lactantius (240–320), were so vehemently opposed to philosophy and rational enquiry that their proclamations are hard to distinguish from the vituperations of Muslim theologians of later centuries. The harsh criticism, levelled by Bishop Berkeley (1685–1753) against "an infidel mathematician", sounds like an echo of Ghazālī's diatribe.

Neither the early Christians nor the early Muslims had any reason to feel embarrassed by the cosmology or the biology in their Scriptures. Earth, air, fire and water retained their elemental status until a thousand years after the revelation of the Qurā'n, and the only strata people knew were the earth, and what was above (or below). During the last few centuries, most Christians in the Western world have been gradually shedding their belief in the literal truth of the Bible, and this readjustment was over before the end of the twentieth century. However, most Muslims continue to believe that the Qurā'n, being the holy word of Allāh, is not only a source of moral teachings but also a record of history and a scientific text.

Interestingly, voices—which fell on deaf ears—against

a literal interpretation of the Qurā'n have been raised before in the recent past, most notably in the Indian subcontinent, by Sir Syed Aḥmed Khān (1817–1898) and the poet Sir Muḥammad Iqbāl (d. 1938), also called *'Allāma* Iqbāl. Both reformers accepted the theory of evolution and understood that a clash between contemporary science and the Qurā'n can be averted only by giving up the literalist approach, and both clearly stated that Adam is a symbol, not a specific individual, that the story of his fall is a legend, that concepts like hell and paradise are states not places. They failed because a critical mass of perceptive minds is needed before an idea can germinate and generate a large-scale and enduring change.

2000– **Chapter 5**: *Can the hare catch up?*

To appreciate just how hard it is to establish world-class research activity in a scientifically impoverished society, let us consider an analogy and compare science to football (soccer), and ask: Why are the rich Arab nations so poor at football? Chapter 5 begins by explaining why the manager and fans of a football club or a national team in the Middle East cannot have much reason for optimism, and points out that, likewise, no minister of science in the Muslim World, no matter how young, should expect success within his lifetime if his goal is to bring back full-fledged scientific activity, let alone scientific glory, to his land.

Science emerged in Europe after centuries of darkness imposed by the Roman Church. The main purpose of Chapter 5 is to ask at what point conditions in Europe (as regards inter-sectarian strife and the relation between science and religion) were closest to those obtaining in the Muslim world of today.

I have been led to conclude (on the basis of the evidence presented in Chapter 5) that, so far as religious toleration is concerned, attitudes in the Muslim world are no more enlightened than those which blighted Europe at the close of the sixteenth century and the first few decades of the next. Religious bigotry and intolerance convulse contemporary Muslim societies in a manner that evokes the horrid events which afflicted the lives of European Christians four centuries ago.

Early seventeenth century Europe produced, while it

was being scorched by the flames of religious hatred, scientific giants like Galileo, Kepler and Harriot. Would it be right, then, to argue that science can return to the Muslim world of today, even if it is ablaze with a fire equally ferocious. I hardly think so. Scientists go where circumstances seem congenial to them, where consequences of nonconformity are likely to be less perilous.

Tycho Brahe, Kepler, and Galileo had to move around, not always voluntarily. Kepler was persecuted by Protestants and Catholics alike. Though a devoted Lutheran, he was no blind follower. In the Introduction to his epoch making 1609 book, Kepler wrote: "In Theology we balance authorities, in Philosophy we weigh reasons. A holy man was Lactantius who denied that the earth was round; a holy man was Augustine, who granted the rotundity, but denied the antipodes; a holy thing to me is the Inquisition, which allows the smallness of the earth, but denies its motion; but more holy to me is Truth; and hence I prove, from philosophy, that the earth is round, and inhabited on every side, of small size, and in motion among the stars,—and this I do with no disrespect to the Doctors."

antipodes: either or both of the poles

Kepler had to endure persecution, but he was not burnt at the stake. Four centuries later, a Muslim author might meet a fate far worse than Kepler's if he were to write "A holy man was Bukhārī who devoted his life to collating the sayings of the Prophet; a holy man was Aḥmad bin Ḥanbal, who denied, at the risk of his life, the createdness of the Qur'ān; but more holy to me is evidence; and hence I provisionally believe, on the basis of the current corpus of science, that the fly is a source of disease, that in regions close to the poles, a believer would perish if (s)he interpreted the Qur'ān literally, that species are mutable,—and this I do with no disrespect to the holy men of the past.

Since the concluding section of Chapter 5 defies synopsis, I suggest that you read the unabridged version itself, which should not ruin your pleasure, because the last page of a book is often as good a place to start as the first.

Bibliography

[1] Stephen W. Hawking. *A brief history of* a brief history. *Popular Science*, 235(2):70–72, 1989.

[2] Michael White and John Gribbin. *Stephen Hawking: A Life in Science*. The John Henry Press, Washington, DC, 2002.

[3] Jordan Ellenberg. The Summer's Most Unread Book Is .... http://www.wsj.com/articles/the-summers-most-unread-book-is-1404417569. **[N.B. All online resources (including this item) were last accessed on 9-January-2015]**.

[4] R. F. Burton. *The Book of the Thousand Nights and a Night: a Plain and Literal Translation of the Arabian Nights' Entertainments*. Burton Club (https://archive.org/details.php?identifier=bookofthousandni1900burt), London?, Year unknown.

[5] C. E. Raven. *John Ray, Naturalist: His Life and Works*. Cambridge University Press, Cambridge, 1986.

[6] Thomas Love Peacock. *The Works of Thomas Love Peacock*. Richard Bentley and Son, London, 1875.

[7] K. Razi Naqvi. *Enemies of an Open Society: Muslim Pulpits and Western Parliaments*. (Unpublished).

[8] K. Razi Naqvi. The status of science in Muslim nations. *Nature*, 453(7191):27, 2008.

[9] Abu Hamid al-Ghazali. http://www.yanabi.com/index.php?/topic/29547-abu-hamid-al-ghazali/.

[10] Julius Wellhausen. *The Arab Kingdom and Its Fall*. University of Calcutta, Calcutta, 1927. [Chap. 9].

[11] Bernard Lewis. *The Arabs in History*. Arrow Books, London, 1958 [p. 80].

[12] Ab'ul Faraj al Nadīm (author) and Gustav Flügel (translator). *Kitāb al-Fihrist*. F. C. W. Vogel, Leipzig, 1872.

[13] Guy Le Strange. *Baghdad During the Abbasid Caliphate*. Clarendon Press, Oxford, 1900.

[14] Guy Le Strange. Ref. [13, p. 10].

[15] Bernard Lewis. "'Abbāsids". In Vol. 1 of *Encyclopaedia of Islam* (H. A. R. Gibbs, J. H. Kramers, H. Lévi-Provençal, J. Schacht, B. Lewis and Ch. Pellat, editors), pages 34–42. E. J. Brill, Leiden, 1986.

[16] John Laird. The law of parsimony. *The Monist*, 29(3):321–344, 1919.

[17] Isaac Newton (author) and Andrew Motte (translator). *Sir Isaac Newton's Mathematical Principles of Natural Philosophy and His System of the World*. University of California Press, Berkeley and Los Angeles, 1934.

[18] Nabia Abbott. *Two Queens of Baghdad*. The University of Chicago Press, Chicago, 1946.

[19] Ewen MacAskill, Suzanne Goldenberg, and Elana Schor. Barack Obama to be America's first black president. http://www.theguardian.com/world/2008/nov/05/uselections20084.

[20] Anonymous. Obama wins historic US election. http://news.bbc.co.uk/2/hi/americas/us_elections_2008/7709978.stm.

[21] Graham Noble. Barack Obama clearly not the first black president. http://guardianlv.com/2013/06/barack-obama-clearly-not-the-first-black-president.

[22] James Fallows. The impossibility of being Barack Obama. http://www.theatlantic.com/politics/archive/2013/05/the-impossibility-of-being-barack-obama/276065/.

[23] C. E. Bosworth. *The History of al-Ṭabarī Vol. 32: The Reunification of the ʻAbbāsid Caliphate: The Caliphate of al-Māʼmūn A.D. 813-833/A.H. 198-218*. Bibliotheca Persica. State University of New York Press, 1987.

[24] Shiblī Nuʻmānī. *Al-Māʼmūn* (in Urdu). Dār ul-Muṣannefīn Shiblī Academy, Āʻzamgarh, U.P., India, 1889? (The year of publication is not given, but the foreword to the second edition, written by Sir Syed Aḥmad Khān, is dated 12.10.1889).

[25] S. Ameer Ali. *A Short History of the Saracens*. Macmillan, London, 1899.

[26] Robert Payne. *The Holy Sword: The Story of Islam from Muhammad to the Present*. Harper & Brothers, New York, 1959.

[27] Michael Cooperson. *Al-Ma'mun*. Makers of the Muslim World. Oneworld Publications, Oxford, 2012.

[28] Alfred Guillaume. *Traditions of Islam: An Introduction to the Study of the Hadith Literature*. Oxford University Press, London, 1924.

[29] Ignáz Goldziher. *Muhammedanische Studien*. Max Niemeyer, Halle, 1890.

[30] Ignáz Goldziher (author), C. R. Barber, and S. M. Stern (translators). *Muslim Studies* (Vol. 2). Allen & Unwin, London, 1971.

[31] M. G. S. Hodgson. *The Venture of Islam: Conscience and History in a World Civilization* (Vol. 1). University of Chicago Press, Chicago, 1974.

[32] Bukhari (compiler) and M. Muhsin Khan (translator). *Sahih Al-Bukhari: The Translation of the Meanings* (9 Vol. Set). Darussalam, Riyadh, 1997 (https://archive.org/details/SahihAl-bukhariarabicAndEnglish-9VolumeSet.).

[33] H. Laoust. "Aḥmed b. Ḥanbal". In Vol. 1 of *Encyclopaedia of Islam* (H. A. R. Gibbs, J. H. Kramers, H. Lévi-Provençal, J. Schacht, B. Lewis and Ch. Pellat, editors), pages 272–277. E. J. Brill, Leiden, 1986.

[34] W. M. Patton. *Aḥmed Ibn Ḥanbal and the Miḥna*. Brill, Leiden, 1897.

[35] Ibn Khaldūn. *The Muqaddimah.* https://archive.org/details/MuqaddimahIbnKhaldun.

[36] Ibn Khaldūn. *The Muqaddimah.* http://www.scribd.com/doc/60030982/The-Muqaddimah.

[37] Ibn Khaldūn. *The Muqaddimah.* http://www.muslimphilosophy.com/ik/Muqaddimah/.

[38] Rom Landau. *Islam and the Arabs.* Macmillan, New York, 1959.

[39] A. J. Toynbee. *A Study of History* (Volume X. Oxford University Press, London, 1954.

[40] William Muir. *The Caliphate: Its Rise, Decline and Fall, from Original Sources.* John Grant, Edinburgh, 1915.

[41] Ibn Khaldūn (author) and Franz Rosenthal (translator). *The Muqaddimah: An Introduction to History; in Three Volumes.* Routledge & Kegan Paul, London, 1958.

[42] A. M. Fahmy. *Muslim Sea-Power in the Eastern Mediterranean from the Seventh to the Tenth Century A.D.* National Publication & Printing House, Cairo, 1966.

[43] G. F. Hourani and J. Carswell. *Arab Seafaring in the Indian Ocean in Ancient and Early Medieval Times.* Princeton University Press, Princeton, 1995.

[44] Nabia Abbott. Book Reviw: Arab Seafaring in the Indian Ocean in Ancient and Early Medieval Times by George Fadlo Hourani. *Journal of Near Eastern Studies*, 12(2):140–142, 1895.

[45] Nabia Abbott. *Studies in Arabic Literary Papyri. II. Qur'ānic Commentary and Tradition.* University of Chicago Press, Chicago, 1967.

[46] Jalāl al-Dīn al Suyūṭī. *The History of the Khalifahs Who Took the Right Way: A Translation of the Chapters on al-Khulafa ar-Rashidun from Tarikh al-Khulafa.* Ta-Ha Publishers Ltd, London, 1995.

[47] A. J. Butler. *The Arabic Conquest of Egypt.* Clarendon Press, Oxford, 1902.

[48] Isya Joseph. Bar Hebraeus and the Alexandrian Library. *The American Journal of Semitic Languages and Literatures*, 27(4):335–338, 1911.

[49] Luciano Canfora. *The Vanished Library*. University of California Press, Berkeley and Los Angeles, 1990.

[50] Bernard Lewis. The Vanished Library. http://www.nybooks.com/articles/archives/1990/sep/27/the-vanished-library-2/.

[51] Kātib Chelebi. *Balance of Truth* (translated by G. L. Lewis). Allen and Unwin, London, 1957.

[52] Ibn Khaldūn and Franz Rosenthal. *The Muqaddimah: an introduction to history; in three volumes*. Bolingen Series, XLIII. Princeton University Press, Princeton, 1958.

[53] Nasiruddin al Khattab (translator). *English Translation of Sahih Muslim*. Vol. 1. Maktaba Dar-us-Salam, Riyadh, 2007 (Available online at: http://islam114.com/main/wp-content/uploads/2013/07/sahih-muslim-volume-1-ahadith-0001-1160.pdf).

[54] Rahman Baba (author) and Jens Enevoldsen. *Selections from Rahman Baba*. Poul Kristensen, Hellebk, 1977.

[55] D. Gimaret. "Muʿtazila". In Vol. 7 of *Encyclopaedia of Islam* (C. E. Bosworth, E. van Donzel, W. P. Heinrichs and Ch. Pellat, editors), pages 783–793. E. J. Brill, Leiden, 1993.

[56] W. Montgomery Watt. *Islamic Philosophy and Theology*. Edinburgh University Press, Edinburgh, 1962.

[57] Dimitri Gutas. *Greek Thought, Arabic Culture: The Graeco-Arabic Translation Movement in Baghdad and Early 'Abbāsid Society (2nd-4th/8th-10th centuries)*. Taylor & Francis, 1999.

[58] M. Hinds. "Miḥna". In Vol. 7 of *Encyclopaedia of Islam* (C. E. Bosworth, E. van Donzel, W. P. Heinrichs and Ch. Pellat, editors), pages 2–6. E. J. Brill, Leiden, 1993.

[59] F. Rosen. *The Algebra of Mohammed Ben Musa*. Murray, London, 1831.

[60] N. A. Faris (translator). *The Book of Knowledge*. Islamic Book Service, New Delhi (online version available at: http://www.ghazali.org/books/knowledge.pdf), 1962.

[61] K. J. Ahmad. *Hundred Great Muslims*. Library of Islam, Des Plaines, IL, 1987.

[62] Henry VIII (King of England). *Assertio Septem Sacramentorum.* Benziger Brothers, New York, 1908.

[63] E. G. Duff. The Assertio Septem Sacramentorum. *The Library. New Series*, 9(33):1–16, 1908.

[64] J. Ames, W. Herbert, and T. F. Dibdin. *Typographical Antiquities, Or, The History of Printing in England, Scotland, and Ireland: Containing Memoirs of Our Ancient Printers, and a Register of the Books Printed by Them.* William Miller, 1812.

[65] W. R. Riddell. *God Save the King.* Empire Club, Toronto, 1910.

[66] W. Cantwell Smith. *Modern Islām in India.* Minerva Bookshop, Lahore, 1943.

[67] R. S. Mackensen. Four greatl libraries of medieval Baghdad. *The Library Quarterly*, 2(3):279–299, 1932.

[68] H. H. Wellisch. The first Arab bibliography: Fihrist al-ʿUlūm. *Occasional Papers. Graduate School of Library and Information Science* (online version available at: https://www.ideals.illinois.edu/bitstream/handle/2142/3825/gslisoccasionalpv00000i00175.pdf?sequence=1), 1986.

[69] Robert Briffault. *The Making of Humnity.* Allen & Unwin, London, 1919.

[70] W. C. Klein. *Al-Ibānah ʿan Uṣūl ad-Diyānah.* American Oriental Society, New Haven, CT, 1940.

[71] D. B. Macdonald. The faith of al-Islam. *The American Journal of Semitic Languages and Literatures*, 12(1/2):93–117, 1895.

[72] Claire Wilde. "Is There Room for Corruption in the 'Books' of God?". In *The Bible in Arab Christianity* (D. R. Thomas (editor), pages 225–240. Cambridge University Press, Cambridge, 2007.

[73] C. E. Sachau (translator). *The Chronology of Ancient Nations (An English Version of the Arabic Text of the Āthār-ul-Bāqiya of Al-Bīrūnī, or "Vestiges of the Past").* Allen, London, 1879.

[74] D. B. Macdonald. The Life of al-Ghazzālī. *J. Am. Orient. Soc.*, 20(1):70–132, 1899.

[75] D. B. Macdonald. *Development of Muslim Theology, Jurisprudence and Constitutional Theory*. Scribner, New York, 1903.

[76] S. M. Zwemer. *A Muslim Seeker After God*. Revell, New York, 1920.

[77] F. Griffel. *Al-Ghazali's Philosophical Theology*. Oxford University Press, London, 2009.

[78] E. G. Browne. *A Literary History of Persia from Firdawsī to S'adī*. T. Fisher Unwin, London, 1906.

[79] A. Schmölders. *Essai sur les ecoles philosophiques chez les Arabes et notamment sur la doctrine d'Algazzali*. L'Institut de France, Paris, 1842.

[80] W. Montgomery Watt. *The Faith and Practice of Al-Ghazālī*. Allen and Unwin, London, 1952.

[81] A. A. Zidan. *Al-Ghazali's Ihya' Ulum al-Din:* Revitalization of the Sciences of Religion (Vol. 1). Islamic Inc., Cairo, 1997.

[82] S. M. Zwemer. *The Disintegration of Islam*. Revell, New York, 1916.

[83] M. Farah. *Marriage and Sexuality in Islam: a Translation of Al-Ghazali's Book on the Etiquette of Marriage from the Ihya*. University of Utah Press, Utah, 1984.

[84] T. J. Gianotti. Beyond both law and theology: an introduction to al-Ghazālī's "Science of the Way of the Afterlife" in *Reviving Religious Knowledge (Iḥyā' 'Ulūm al-Dīn)*. *The Muslim World*, 101:597–613, 2007.

[85] Shiblī Nu'mānī. *Al-Ghāzālī* (in Urdu). Dār al-Muṣannefīn Shiblī Academy, Ā'zamgarh, U.P., India, 1928 (First published in 1902).

[86] G. H. Lewes. *The History of Western Philosophy*. Longmans, Green, and Co., London, 1871 (Fourth Edition).

[87] G. H. Lewes. Essai sur les Ecoles Philosophiques chez les Arabes. *Par Auguste Schmölders. 8vo. Paris: 1842. Edinburgh Review*, 35(January–April):340–359, 1847.

[88] Rene Descartes (author) and John Veitch. *A Discourse on Method*. Everyman's library, ed. by Ernest Rhys. Philosophy and theology. J.M. Dent & Sons, London, 1912.

[89] E. W. Lane. *An Enlgish-Arabic Lexicon*. Williams & Norgate, London, 1874.

[90] F. Rosenthal. *Knowledge Triumphant: The Concept of Knowledge in Medieval Islam*. Brill, Leiden, 1970.

[91] S. P. Thompson. *Life of William Thomson, Baron Kelvin of Largs*. Macmillan, London, 1910.

[92] W. Thomson and P. G. Tait. *Treatise on Natural Philosophy* (Vol. 1, Part 1). Cambridge University Press, Cambridge, 1879.

[93] J. K. Galbraith. *The Liberal Hour*. Hamish Hamilton, London, 1960.

[94] W. A. McCall (translator). *The Book of Knowledge*. PhD thesis, Hartford Seminary, Princeton, NJ (online version available at: http://www.ghazali.org/books/McCall-1940.pdf), 1940.

[95] Nadīm al-Wājidī (translator). *Iḥyā'ʻUlūm al-Dīn* (Vol. 1). Dar al-Ishāʻat (online version available at: http://www.ghazali.org/books/ihya-urdu-v1.pdf), Karachi, 199?

[96] J. L. E. Dreyer. *Tycho Brahe: A Picture of Scientific Life and Work in the Sixteenth Century*. Adam and Charles Black, Edinburgh, 1890.

[97] L. Thorndike. *The Place of Magic in the Intellectual History of Europe*. Columbia University Press, New York, 1905.

[98] V. E. Thoren. *The Lord of Uraniborg: A Biography of Tycho Brahe*. Cambridge University Press, Cambridge, 1990.

[99] E. Watts. Justinian, Malalas, and the end of the Athenian philosophical teaching in A.D. 529. *The Journal of Roman Studies*, 94:168–182, 2004.

[100] Edward Watts. Where to live the philosophical life in the sixth century? Damascius, Simplicius, and the return from Persia. *Greek, Roman and Byzantine Studies*, 45(3):285–315, 2005.

[101] Larry Hoehn. The Pythagorean theorem: an infinite number of proofs? *Mathematics Teacher*, 90(6):438–441, 1997.

[102] Anonymous. Society for the Diffusion of Useful Knowledge (SDUK). http://www.ucl.ac.uk/bloomsbury-project/institutions/sduk.htm.

[103] Alan Rauch. *Useful Knowledge: the Victorians, Morality, and the March of Intellect*. Duke University Press, Durham, NC, 2001.

[104] H. R. Deese and G. R. Woodall. A calendar of lectures presented by the Boston Society for the Diffusion of Useful Knowledge (1829–1847). *Studies in the American Renaissance*, 10:17–67, 1986.

[105] Robert Doares. A field spacious and untrodden: the Virginian Society for the Promotion of Usefull Knowledge. http://www.history.org/foundation/journal/autumn03/society.cfm.

[106] Jonathan Lyons. *The Society for Useful Knowledge: How Benjamin Franklin and Friends Brought the Enlightenment to America*. Bloomsbury USA, 2013.

[107] Jeremy Bentham (author) and T. Southwell Smith (editor). *The Works of Jeremy Bentham*. Number v. 8 in The Works of Jeremy Bentham. William Tait, Edinburgh, 1843.

[108] G.H. Lewes. *Dr Southwood Smith: A Retrospect*. William Blackwood and Sons, Edinburgh, 1898.

[109] F. N. L. Poynter. Thomas Southwood Smith—the Man (1788-1861). *Proc. Royal Soc. Med.*, 55(5):381–392, 2011.

[110] E. Trattner. ʻUmar Khayyām—Poet. III. Against Al-Ghazālī. *The Muslim World*, 53(2):120–126, 1963.

[111] P. Avery and J. Heath-Stubbs. *The Rubaʻiyat of Omar Khayyam*. Penguin, Hammondsworth, Middlesex, England, 1981.

[112] Ghazālī (author) and S. A. Jackson (translator). *On the Boundaries of Theological Tolerance in Islam* (Annotated translation of *Fayṣal al-Tafriqa Bayna al-Islām wa al-Zandaqa*). Oxford University Press, Karachi, 2002.

[113] S. A. Kamali (translator). *Al-Ghazali's Tahafut al-Falasifa*. Pakistan Philosophical Congress, Lahore (online version available at: http://www.ghazali.org/works/taf-eng.pdf), 1963.

[114] Anonymous. Ibn Rushd Al-Qurtubi. http://www.muslimphilosophy.com/ir/.

[115] Darul Uloom Deoband, India. http://www.darululoom-deoband.com/english/index.htm.

[116] F. Hooper and M. Schwartz. *Roman Letters: History from a Personal Point of View*. Wayne State University Press, Detroit, MI, 1991.

[117] Mumtāz ʿAlī (translator). *Khair al-Maqāl fi Tarjum al-Munqidh al-Ḍalāl)*. (online version available at: http://www.ghazali.org/books/mun-urdu.pdf), 1890.

[118] S. E. Hussain. *Terrorism in Pakistan: Incident Patterns, Terrorists' Characteristics, and the Impact of Terrorist Arrests on Terrorism*. PhD thesis, University of Pennsylvania, (Publicly accessible Penn Dissertations. Paper 136. http://repository.upenn.edu/edissertations/136), 2010.

[119] M. F. Ashley Montagu. *Man's Most Dangerous Myth: The Fallacy of Race*. Columbia University Press, New York, 1945.

[120] Ghazzālī and M. E. Marmura (translator). *The Incoherence of the Philosophers*. Brigham Young University Press, Utah, 1997.

[121] Augustus De Morgan. *A. Budget of Paradoxes*. Longmans, Green and Co., London, 1872.

[122] Edward Regis. *Who Got Einstein's Office?* Addison-Wesley, Reading, MA, 1987.

[123] Rom Landau. *The Philosophy of Ibn ʿArabī*. Allan and Unwin, New York, 1959.

[124] A. I. Sabra. "The Scientific Enterprise". In *The World of Islam* (B. Lewis, editor), pages 181–200. Thames and Hudson, 1991.

[125] E. G. Browne. *Arabian Medicine*. Cambridge University Press, Cambridge, 1921.

[126] John Walbridge. *God and Logic in Islam: The Caliphate of Reason*. Cambridge University Press, 2010.

[127] Abdulhadi Hairi. *Naṣīr al-Dīn Ṭūsī: His Supposed Role in the Mongol Invasion of Baghdad*. MA thesis, McGill University, 1968. http://digitool.library.mcgill.ca/webclient/StreamGate?folder_id=0&dvs=1420789917871~540.

[128] D. C. Knight. *Copernicus: Titan of Modern Astronomy*. Franklin Watts, New York, 1965.

[129] Anonymous. Christopher Clavius (1537–1612). http://galileo.rice.edu/sci/clavius.html.

[130] Samuel P. Putnam. *Four Hundred Years of Freethought*. The Truth Seeker Company, New York, 1894.

[131] Anonymous. Ibrahim Müteferriqa. https://ottomanhistorians.uchicago.edu/en/historian/ibrahim-muteferriqa.

[132] S. M. Zwemer. Translations of the Koran. *The Muslim World*, 5:244–261, 1915.

[133] D. A. King. Taḳī al-Dīn b. Muḥammad b. Maʿrūf. In Vol. 10 of *Encyclopaedia of Islam* (P. J. Bearman, Th. Bianquis, C. E. Bosworth, E. van Donzel and W. P. Heinrichs, editors), pages 132–133. E. J. Brill, Leiden, 2000.

[134] Svat Soucek. Piri Reis and Ottoman discovery of the great discoveries. *Studia Islamica*, 79?(79):121–142, 1994.

[135] Bariş İlhan. *The Astrology of the Ottoman Empire* (pp. 34–5). https://www.academia.edu/5016755/The_Astrology_of_the_Ottoman_Empire.

[136] Hüseyin Topuz. Takiyuddin, A Great Astronomer and the Demolition of an Observatory in Istanbul in 1580. http://terraspace.wordpress.com/2013/01/10/202/.

[137] Solomon Gandz. The algebra of inheritance: a rehabilitation of Al-Khuwārizmī. *Osiris*, 5:319–391, 1938.

[138] G. M. D. Sufi. *Al-Minhaj: Being the Evolution of Curriculum in the Muslim Educational Institutions of India*. Sh. Muhammad Ashraf, 1941.

[139] Francis Robinson. Ottomans-Safavids-Mughals: shared knowledge and connective systems. *Journal of Islamic Studies*, 8(2):151–184, 1997.

[140] Francis Robinson. *The 'Ulama Of Farangi Mahall and Islamic Culture in South Asia*. Permanent Black, Delhi, 2001.

[141] Daoud S. Kasir. *The Algebra of Omar Khayyam*. Teachers College, Columbia University, New York, 1931.

[142] H. J. J. Winter and W. ʻArafat. The algebra of ʻUmar Khayyam. *Journal of the Royal Asiatic Society of Bengal. Science*, 16(1):27–77, 1950.

[143] A. A. Adivar. Islamic and Western thought in Turkey. *Middle East Journal*, 1(3):270–280, 1947.

[144] G. O. Trevelyan. *The Life and Letters of Lord Macaulay* (Vol. 1). Longmans, Green, and Co., London, 1876.

[145] David Thomas and Alex Mallett (editors). *Christian-Muslim Relations. A Bibliographical History.* Volume 4 (1200-1350). Christian-Muslim Relations. A Bibliographical History. Brill, Leiden, 2012.

[146] Aldous Huxley. *Brave New World*. Penguin, London, 1974.

[147] R. P. Feynman. *What Do You Care What Other People Think? Further Adventures of a Curious Character*. Norton, New York, 1986.

[148] Jacques Sesiano. Quadratus Mirabilis. In *The Enterprise of Science in Islam: New Perspectives*, pages 199–217. M. I. T. Press, Cambridge, MA, 2003.

[149] Jaffur Shureef [Jaʻfar Sharīf]. *Qanoon-e-Islam: Or, the Customs of the Moosulmans of India*. Parbury, Allen, and Co., London, 1832.

[150] Jaʻfar Sharīf (author) and G. A. Herklots (translator). *Islam in India or The Qānūn-i-Islām: Customs of the Musulmāns of India*. Humphrey Milford, London, 1921.

[151] K. R. Popper. *The Open Society and its Enemies*. Routledge, London, 1945.

[152] Yohanan Friedmann. *The History of al-Ṭabarī Vol. 12: The Battle of al-Qādisiyyah and the Conquest of Syria and Palestine A.D. 635-637/A.H. 14-15*. State University of New York Press, Albany, 1992.

[153] S. Khuda Bukhsh. *Essays: Indian and Islamic*. Probsthain & Co., London, 1912.

[154] Ralph Braibanti. *Research on the Bureaucracy of Pakistan*. Duke University Press, Durham, NC, 1966.

[155] The Right Rev Lord Sheppard of Liverpool: England cricket captain who became Bishop of Liverpool. http://www.independent.co.uk/news/obituaries/the-right-rev-lord-sheppard-of-liverpool-6150894.html.

[156] "Mullahs" destroying Islam: Kalbe Sadiq. http://www.hindustantimes.com/News-Feed/NM19/Mullahs-destroying-Islam-Kalbe-Sadiq/Article1-169370.aspx.

[157] A. A. Maududi. *Towards Understanding the Qur'ān* (Vol. 1). Islamic Foundation, Leicester, UK, 1988.

[158] Russell Foster and Leon Kreitzman. *The Rhythms of Life: The Biological Clocks that Control the Daily Lives of Every Living Thing*. Profile Books Ltd., London, 2005.

[159] Lord Dufferin. *Letters from High Latitudes*. John Murray, 1867.

[160] A. J. Wensinck. *The Muslim Creed*. Cambridge University Press, Cambridge, 1932.

[161] F. W. Hasluck. *Christianity and Islam Under the Sultans* (Vol. 1). Clarendon Press, Oxford, 1929.

[162] Alexander Pope and J. B. Seabury. *Pope's Essay on Man, and Essay on Criticism*. The Silver series of English classics. Silver, Burdett and Company, New York, 1900.

[163] R. Ross. A tale of two systems: Beliefs and practices of South African Muslims and Hindus traditional healers regarding cleft lip and palate. *Cleft Palate—Craniofcial Journal*, 44(6):642648, 2007.

[164] Anonymous. *Cleft Deformities*. http://smilebangladesh.org/cleft-deformities.php.

[165] M. A. S. Abdel Haleem. *The Qur'an: A New Translation*. Oxford University Press, Oxford, 2005.

[166] The Noble Quran. http://quran.com/.

[167] H. Melville. *Moby-Dick* (Vol. 1). Constable and Company, London, 1922.

[168] A. J. Arberry. *Revelation and Reason in Islam*. Routledge library editions: Islam. Routledge, New York and Abingdon, 2007.

[169] Niaz Fatehpuri. Man-o-Yazdan (in Urdu). http://niazfatehpuri.com/Writings/Man-o-Yazdan.pdf.

[170] Navid Kermani. From revelation to interpretation: Nasr Hamid Abu Zayd and the literary study of the Qur'ān. In *Modern Muslim Intellectuals and the Qur'ān*, chapter 6, pages 169–192. Oxford University Press, Oxford, 2006.

[171] G. R. Hawting. The significance of the slogan "lā ḥukma illā lillāh" and the references to the "ḥudūd" in the traditions about the fitna and the murder of 'Uthman. *Bulletin of the School of Oriental and African Studies, University of London*, 41(3):453–463, 1978.

[172] A. M. Hagler. *The Echoes of Fitna: Developing Historiographical Interpretations of the Battle of Siffin*. PhD thesis, University of Pennsylvania, (online version available at: http://repository.upenn.edu/edissertations/397), 2011.

[173] Al Ṭabarī. *Tārīkh al-umam wa'l mulūk*. Dār-ul-Ma'ārif, Cairo, Year unknown.

[174] J. N. Dawood. *The Koran*. Penguin, London, 1999.

[175] Laleh Bakhtiar. *The Sublime Quran*. Kazi Publications, Chicago, 2007.

[176] Hans Wehr. *A Dictionary of Modern Written Arabic*. Spoken Languages Services, Inc., Ithaca, NY, 1976.

[177] Mark Davie. Traduttore traditore. http://blog.oup.com/2012/09/traduttore-traditore-translator-traitor-translation/.

[178] Thomas Harriot. *Briefe and True Report of the New Found Land of Virginia*. Dodd, Mead & Company, New York, 1558 (Reprinted 1903).

[179] Ziauddin Sardar. The eternal present tense. http://www.guardian.co.uk/books/2008/jun/21/saturdayreviewsfeatres.guardianreview26.

[180] S. Shaw. *The Works of Revd. Samuel Shaw* (Vol. 1). George Clark, Boston, 1821.

[181] M. Iqbal (Allāma Iqbāl). *The Reconstruction of Religious Thought in Islam*. Javed Iqbal, Lahore, 1944.

[182] Anonymous. Jinn: Born of Fire. http://www.economist.com/node/8401289.

[183] Goat detained over armed robbery. http://www.reuters.com/article/2009/01/24/us-goat-idUSTRE50M4XT20090124.

[184] Nigeria police hold 'robber' goat. http://news.bbc.co.uk/2/hi/africa/7846822.stm.

[185] Voltaire. *Œuvres complètes de Voltaire* (Vol.45). P. Dupont, Paris, 1823.

[186] A. De Morgan. *A. Budget of Paradoxes* (Vol. 2). The Open Court Publishing Co., Chicago, 1915.

[187] R. A. Nicholson. *Studies in Islamic Mysticism*. Cambridge University Press, Cambridge, 1920.

[188] G. B. Shaw. *The Complete Prefaces of Bernard Shaw*. Paul Hamlyn, London, 1965.

[189] G. F. I. Graham. *The Life and Work of Syed Ahmed Khan*. Blackwood, London, 1885.

[190] T. L. Heath. *The Copernicus of Antiquity (Aristarchus of Samos)*. Society for Promoting Christian Knowledge, New York, 1920.

[191] Michael Day. Cardinal Martini. http://www.independent.co.uk/news/world/europe/cardinal-carlo-maria-martini-his-final-interview-and-a-damning-critique-that-has-rocked-the--catholic-church-8101498.html#.

[192] Costanza Barone. Progressive Catholic icon Cardinal Carlo Maria Martini dies after saying Church "200 years" behind. http://www.cbsnews.com/news/progressive-catholic-icon-cardinal-carlo-maria-martini-dies-after-saying-church-200-years-behind/.

[193] Peter Stanford. Cardinal Carlo Maria Martini obituary. http://www.theguardian.com/world/2012/sep/03/cardinal-carlo-maria-martini.

[194] A. H. Strow (Editor). *Emanuel Swedenborg as a Scientist*. Aftonbladets Tryckeri, Stockholm, 1908.

[195] Emanuel Swedenborg: Biography. http://www.swedenborg.org.uk/emanuel_swedenborg.

[196] E. Swedenborg. *The True Christian Religion*. J. B. Lippincott & Co., Philadelphia, 1873.

[197] Swedenborg Foundation. *Who Was Swedenborg and What Are His Writings?* The American Swedenborg Printing and Publishing Society, New York, 1900.

[198] O. B. Frothinghan. Swedenborg. *The North American Review*, 134(307):600–16, 1882.

[199] Oscar Wilde. Lady Windermere's Fan (Act 1).

[200] V. D. Denslow. *Modern Thinkers*. Belford, Clark & Co., Chicago, 1880.

[201] E. A. Hitchcock. *Swedenborg A Hermetic Philosopher*. D. Appleton & Co., New York, 1858.

[202] J. G. Pike. *Swedenborgiansim Depicted in Its True Colors*. Printed for the Publisher, 1834.

[203] Anonymous. Claims of the new church upon unitarians: A fragment. *The Monthly Religious Magazine and the Independent Journal*, 23(5):306–314, 1860.

[204] Octavius Brooks Frothingham. http://en.wikipedia.org/wiki/Octavius_Brooks_Frothingham.

[205] Stephen Hales. Some considerations on the causes of earthquakes. *Phil. Tras, Royal Soc.*, 46:669–681, 1749–1750.

[206] Henry Ward Beecher. http://en.wikipedia.org/wiki/Henry_Ward_Beecher.

[207] Debby Applegate. *The Most Famous Man in America: The Biography of Henry Ward Beecher*. Three Leaves Press, New York, 2006.

[208] Lyman Abbott. *Henry Ward Beecher*. Houghton, Mifflin & Co., Boston, 1903.

[209] H. W. Beecher. Progress of thought in the church. *The North American Review*, 135(309):99–117, 1882.

[210] J. D. Burton. "The awful judgements of God upon the Land": smallpox in colonial Cambridge, Massachusetts. *The New England Quarterly*, 74(3):495–506, 2001.

[211] W. E. H. Lecky. *History of European Morals from Augustus to Charlemagne* (Vol. 2). Longmans, Green and Co., London, 1869.

[212] H. W. Preston (translator). *The Writings of Madame Swetchine*. Roberts, Boston, 1869.

[213] Richard Morin. Fatwa Football. http://www.washingtonpost.com/wp-dyn/content/article/2005/12/17/AR2005121700012.html.

[214] Anonymous. A Fatwa on Football. http://www.theguardian.com/football/2005/oct/31/sport.comment1.

[215] James M. Dorsey. Saudis debate societal merits of football. http://www.hurriyetdailynews.com/saudis-debate-societal-merits-of-football.aspx?pageID=238&nID=62535&NewsCatID=364.

[216] David Hume. *An Enquiry Concerning Human Understanding*. Open Court, Chicago, 1921.

[217] W. H. Draper. *History of the Conflict between Religion and Science*. Appleton, New York, 1875.

[218] A. D. White. *A History of the Warfare of Science with Theology in Christendom, Vol. II (in Two Volumes)*. D. Appleton and Company, New York, 1896.

[219] J. J. Walsh. *Catholic Churchmen in Science*. The Dolphin Press, Philadelphia, 1906.

[220] J. J. Walsh. *The Popes and Science*. Fordham University Press, New York, 1908.

[221] Wolcott Calkins. John Calvin's Calvinism. *Bibliotheca Sacra*, 66(Oct.):671–684, 1909.

[222] R. Wright. *An apology for Dr. Michael Servetus*. F. B. Wright, Wisbech, 1806.

[223] C. T. Odhner. *Michael Servetus, His Life and Teachings*. Lippincott, Philadelphia, 1910.

[224] A. M. T. Dibb. *Servetus, Swedenborg and the Nature of God*. University Press of America, Incorporated, Lanham, Maryland, 2005.

[225] D. D. Whedon. Book Review. *Methodist Quarterly Review*, 67(1):159–163, 1875.

[226] D. D. Whedon. *Statements: Theological and Critical* (pp. 157–63). Phillips & Hunt, New York, 1887.

[227] G. Polya. *Mathematics and Plausible Reasoning: Induction and analogy in mathematics*. Mathematics and Plausible Reasoning. Princeton University Press, Princeton, 1954.

[228] D.C. Lindberg and R.L. Numbers. *God and Nature: Historical Essays on the Encounter Between Christianity and Science*. University of California Press, Berkeley and Los Angeles, 1986.

[229] Alexander Roberts and James Donaldson (editors). *The Ante-Nicene Fathers. Latin Christianity: its Founder, Tertullian*. The Ante-Nicene Fathers: Translations of the Writings of the Fathers Down to A.D. 325 (Vol. 3). The Christian Literature Publishing Company, Buffalo, 1885.

[230] Robert von Helmholtz. Gustav Robert Kirchhoff. *Deutsche Rundschau*, 14(5):232–245, 1887/88.

[231] Alexander Roberts and James Donaldson (editors). *The Ante-Nicene Fathers: Fathers of the Third and Fourth Centuries*. The Ante-Nicene Fathers: Translations of the Writings of the Fathers Down to A.D. 325 (Vol. 7). The Christian Literature Publishing Company, Buffalo, 1886.

[232] Cosmas Indicopleustes (author) and E. O. Winstedt (translator). *The Christian Topography of Cosmas Indicopleustes*. Cambridge University Press, Cambridge, 1909.

[233] Cosmas Indicopleustes (author) and J. W. McCrindle (translator). *The Christian Topography of Cosmas, an Egyptian Monk: Translated from the Greek, and Edited with Notes and Introduction*. Hakluyt Society, London, 1897.

[234] Giorgio Levi Della Vida. ‘Umar (I) b. al-Khaṭṭāb. In Vol. 10 of *Encyclopaedia of Islam* (P. J. Bearman, Th. Bianquis, C. E. Bosworth, E. van Donzel and W. P. Heinrichs, editors), pages 818–821. E. J. Brill, Leiden, 2000.

[235] James I (King of England). *The Workes of the Most High and Mightie Prince Iames, by the Grace of God King of Great Britennie, France and Irelande, Defender of the Faith and C. an Humble Supplication for Tolerance and Libertie by James Great Britain, King I Published by James, Bisho.* James (Bishop of Winton), London, 1616.

[236] T. Scott and S. Miller. *The Articles of the Synod of Dort*. Presbyterian Board of Publication, Philadelphia, 1841.

[237] Christoph Lüthy. *David Gorlæus (1591-1612)*. Amsterdam University Press, Amsterdam, 2012.

[238] Thomas Fuller. *The Church History of Britain, from the Birth of Jesus Christ Until the Year MDCXLVIII* (Vol. 3). Thomas Tegg and Son, 1837.

[239] William Whewell. *The Philosophy of the Inductive Sciences*. John W. Parker, London, 1840 (Third Edition).

[240] J. W. Shirley. An Early Experimental Determination of Snell’s law. *Am. J. Phys.*, 19:507–508, 1951.

[241] J. A. Lohne. Thomas Harriott (1560–1621). The Tycho Brahe of Optics. *Centaurus*, 6(2):113–121, 1979.

[242] Jean Jacquot. Thomas Harriot’s reputation for impiety. *Notes and Records of the Royal Society of London*, 9(2):164–187, 1952.

[243] Stephen Clucas. Thomas Harriot’s Brief and True Report: Knowledge-Making and the Roanoke Voyage. In *European Vision: American Voices*, pages 17–23. The British Museum, Oxford, 2009.

[244] John Ray. *The Wisdom of God*. W. Innys, London, 1843.

[245] William Derham. *Demonstration of the Being and Attributes of God from His Works of Creation*. W. Innys, London, 1720.

[246] B. Nieuwentijdt (author) and J. Chamberlayne (translator). *The Religious Philosopher: Or, The Right Use of Contemplating the Works of the Creator ... Designed for the Conviction of Atheists and Infidels*. J. Senex, London, 1718.

[247] K. E. A. von Hoff. *Geschichte der durch Überlieferung nachgewiesenen natürlichen Veränderungen der Erdoberfläche: ein Versuch* (Vol. 1). Perthes, Gotha, 1822.

[248] John Locke. *The Works of John Locke, Esq: In Three Volumes* (Vol. 3) . S. Birt, D. Browne, T. Longman and others, London, 1751.

[249] W. T. Brande. Outlines of geology, being the substance of a course of lectures .... *The Quarterly Journal of Science, Literature and the Arts*, 19(37):63–92, 1825.

[250] Charles Lyell. *Principles of Geology: Being an Attempt to Explain the Former Changes of the Earth's Surface, by Reference to Causes Now in Operation* (Vol. 1). John Murray, London, 1830.

[251] William Whiston. *The Accomplishment of Scripture Prophecies*. Benj. Tooke, London, 1708.

[252] William Whiston. *Astronomical Principles of Religion, Natural & Reveal'd: In Nine Parts*. J. Senex & W. Taylor, London, 1717.

[253] S. D. Snobelen. William whiston, isaac newton and the crisis of publicity. *Studies in History and Philosophy of Science Part A*, 35(3):573–603, 2004.

[254] J. E. Force. *William Whiston: Honest Newtonian.* Cambridge University Press, Cambridge, 1985.

[255] George Berkeley. *Alciphron: Or, The Minute Philosopher. In Seven Dialogues. Containing an Apology for the Christian Religion, Against Those who are Called Free Thinkers*. G. Risk, G. Ewing and W. Smith, Dublin, 1732.

[256] George Berkeley (author) and A. C. Fraser (editor). *The Works of George Berkeley, D.D., Formerly Bishop of Cloyne.* Vol. III: Philosophical works, 1734–52. Clarendon Press, Oxford, 1901.

[257] George Berkeley (author) and A. C. Fraser (editor). *The Works of George Berkeley, D.D., Formerly Bishop of Cloyne.* Vol. IV. Clarendon Press, Oxford, 1871.

[258] John Aikin, Mr. Nicholson, and Others. *General Biography; or, Lives, Critical and Historical, of the Most Eminent Persons of All Ages, Countries, Conditions and Professions ...* (Vol. 2). J. Johnson, C. J. and J. Robinson, G. Kearsley, London, 1801.

[259] John Aikin, Thomas Morgan, and William Johnston. *General Biography; or, Lives, Critical and Historical, of the Most Eminent Persons of All Ages, Countries, Conditions and Professions ...* (Vol. 4). J. Johnson, C. J. and J. Robinson, G. Kearsley, London, 1803.

[260] Geoffrey Cantor. Berkeley's *The Analyst* Revisited. *Isis*, 75(4):668–683, 1984.

[261] William Cudworth. *Life and Correspondence of Abraham Sharp*. Sampson Low, Marston, Searle & Rivington, Ltd., London, 1889.

[262] S. J. Rigaud. *A Defence of Halley Against the Charge of Religious Infidelity*. Ashmolean Society, Oxford, 1844.

[263] T. S. Kuhn. *The Structure of Scientific Revolutions*. University of Chicago Press, Chicago, 1970.

[264] John Donne (author) and C. E. Norton (editor). *The Love Poems of John Donne*. Houghton, Mifflin and Company, Boston, 1905.

[265] John Aubrey (author) and Andrew Clark (editor). *Aubrey's 'Brief Lives'* (Vol. 1). Clarendon Press, Oxford, 1898.

[266] C. W. Sams. *The Conquest of Virginia: the First Attempt*. Keyser-Doherty Printing Corporation, Norfolk, VA, 1924.

[267] Anonymous. Bangladesh 'Hajj critic' AL Siddique is arrested. http://www.bbc.com/news/world-asia-30195714.

[268] Anonymous. President terminates Latif Siddique. http://www.thedailystar.net/president-terminates-latif-siddique-45311.

[269] AFP in Dacca. Bangladesh ex-minister surrenders after hajj criticism. http://english.alarabiya.net/en/News/asia/2014/11/25/Bangladesh-ex-minister-surrenders-after-hajj-criticism.html.

[270] Asad Hashim. Pakistani Christian couple killed by mob. http://www.aljazeera.com/news/asia/2014/11/pakistani-christian-couple-killed-mob-20141115154959911691.html.

[271] Agence France-Presse in Lahore. Christians beaten to death for allegedly desecrating Quran in Pakistan. http://www.theguardian.com/world/2014/nov/04/pakistan-christian-couple-killed-alleged-blasphemy.

[272] Waqar Gillani. Pakistani Christian Couple Are Tortured and Burned to Death by Angry Mob. http://www.nytimes.com/2014/11/05/world/asia/pakistani-christian-couple-accused-of-blasphemy-is-killed-by-angry-mob.html.

[273] Anonymous. What this—the largest Ebola outbreak in history—tells the world. http://www.who.int/csr/disease/ebola/ebola-6-months/lessons/en/.

[274] UN Security Council. With Spread of Ebola Outpacing Response, Security Council Adopts Resolution 2177 (2014) Urging Immediate Action, End to Isolation of Affected States. http://www.un.org/press/en/2014/sc11566.doc.htm.

[275] Karen Armstrong. *Muhammad: Prophet for Our Time*. Harper Perennial, London, 2006.

[276] F. J. Ziadeh and R. B. Winder. *An Introduction to Modern Arabic*. Princeton University Press, Princeton, 1957.

[277] H. A. R. Gibb and many others (Editors). *The Encyclopaedia of Islam. New Edition* (12 Volumes). Brill, Leiden, 1986–2004.

[278] A. T. Welch. "al-Ḳur'ān". In Vol. 5 of *Encyclopaedia of Islam* (C. E. Bosworth, E. van Donzel, B. Lewis and Ch. Pellat, editors), pages 400–429. E. J. Brill, Leiden, 1986.

[279] Danny Kingsley. The new buzz on antibiotics. http://www.abc.net.au/science/articles/2002/10/01/689400.htm.

[280] A. Stow, D. Briscoe, M. Gillings, M. Holley, S. Smith, R. Leys, T. Silberbauer, C. Turnbull, and A. Beattie. "Antimicrobial defences increase with sociality in bees". *Biol. Lett.*, 3:422–424, 2007.

[281] D. Briscoe, S. Smith, P. Wilson, A. Beattie, C. Turnbull, S. Hoggard, M. Gillings, C. Palmer, A. Stow, and A. Beattie. "Antimicrobial strength increases with group size: implications for social evolution". *Biol. Lett.*, 7:249–252, 2011.

[282] W. Ma, C. Yu, W. Zhang, P. Zhou, and J. Hu. Self-replication: spelling it out in a chemical background. *Theory in Biosciences*, 130:119–125, 2011.

[283] B. Lemaitre and J. Hoffmann. "The host defense of *Drosophila melanogaster*". *Annu. Rev. Immunol.*, 25:697–743, 2007.

[284] S. Natori. "Molecules participating in insect immunity of *Sarcophaga peregrina*". *Proc. Jpn. Acad., Ser. B*, 86:927–938, 2010.

[285] A. Al-Muzain. "Hammas tv cure for AIDS on the basis of a hadith by Prophet Muhammad about the wings of flies". http://www.youtube.com/watch?v=-mdklot7vus.

[286] G. F. Hourani. A revised chrononlogy of Ghazālī's writings. *J. Am. Orient. Soc.*, 104(2):289–302, 1984.

[287] Ghazālī. *Iḥyā'*. http://www.ghazali.org/site/ihya.htm.

[288] Ghazālī. *Iḥyā' ʻUlūm al-Dīn* (Vol. 1). Dar al-Maʻrafah, Beirut (online version available at: http://www.ghazali.org/ihya/arabic/printed/iud-dm-001.pdf), 1982.

[289] Ghazālī. *Iḥyā' ʻUlūm al-Dīn* (Vol. 2). Dar al-Maʻrafah, Beirut (online version available at: http://www.ghazali.org/ihya/arabic/printed/iud-dm-002.pdf), 1982.

[290] Reinhart Dozy and F. G. Stokes (translator). *Spanish Islam: A History of the Muslims in Spain*. Chatto & Windus, London, 1913.

[291] Islam Q&A. "Seek knowledge even if you have to go as far as China" is a false hadeeth. http://islamqa.info/en/13637, 2013.

[292] http://www.usc.edu/org/cmje/religious-texts/hadith/bukhari/.

[293] http://www.sahih-bukhari.com/Pages/Bukhari_1_03.php.

[294] http://www.quranwebsite.com/hadith/bukhari_volume_1.html.

[295] Yoram Erder. The origin of the name Idrīs in the Qur'ān: A study of the influence of Qumran literature on early Islam. *Journal of Near Eastern Studies*, 49(4):339–350, 1990.

[296] W. A. Hammond. The physics and physiology of spiritualism. *The North American Review*, 110(227):233–260, 1870.

[297] D. B. Macdonald. "Budūḥ". In Vol. 12 of *Encyclopaedia of Islam* (P. J. Bearman, Th. Bianquis, C. E. Bosworth, E. van Donzel and W. P. Heinrichs, editors), pages 153–154. E. J. Brill, Leiden, 2004.

[298] Anonymous. Magical Squares. http://www.bedouinsilver.com/jewelry-and/bedouin-jewelry-as-protection/text-and-number-amulets/magical-squares/.

[299] Oliver Heaviside. *Electrical Papers* (Vol. 2). Macmillan, London, 1894.

[300] P. J. Nahin. *Oliver Heaviside: The Life, Work, and Times of an Electrical Genius of the Victorian Age*. Johns Hopkins University Press, 2002.

[301] Stanley Lane-Poole. *The Story of Turkey*. G. P. Putnam's Sons, New York, 1897.

[302] R. C. Martin (Editor). *Encyclopedia of Islam and the Muslim World*. Macmillan Reference USA, New York, 2003.

[303] M. T. Usmani and I. H. Ansari (translator). *Discourses on Islamic Way of Life*. Dārul Ishā'at, Karachi, Year unknown.

Index

www.ingramcontent.com/pod-product-compliance
Lightning Source LLC
Chambersburg PA
CBHW050453110426
42743CB00017B/3344